Loaned

And behold, the Lord passed by, and a great and strong wind rent the mountains, and broke in pieces the rocks before the Lord; but the Lord was not in the wind; and after the wind an earthquake; but the Lord was not in the earthquake; and after the earthquake a fire; but the Lord was not in the fire; and after the fire—

A Still, Small Voice!

I KINGS 19:11-12

THE STILL SMALL VOICE TODAY

Jewish Ethical Living

BOOK TWO

William B. Silverman

BEHRMAN HOUSE, INC. *Publishers, New York*

280.2
Si3
b

To Pearl, Joel, and Eldon

ILLUSTRATIONS BY *Mel Silverman*

Copyright 1957 by William B. Silverman

Published by Behrman House, Inc.
1261 Broadway, New York 1
MANUFACTURED IN THE UNITED STATES OF AMERICA

Library of Congress Catalog Card Number: 57-13252

FOREWORD

This volume is a continuation of *The Still, Small Voice*, which offered youth an introduction to applied Jewish ethics. Its purpose is to afford the student an insight into the ethical teachings of our post-biblical religious literature and the sacred institutions of Judaism.

Provocative questions, realistic problems confronting modern Jewish youth and lessons from Jewish ethical literature are intended to challenge students of Confirmation age to study and apply the requirements of Jewish ethical living today.

It is the prayerful hope of the author that this volume may enhance an appreciation of the ethical literature of our religious faith, demonstrate the application of Judaism as a way of life and strengthen Jewish youth in the search for an answer to a divine mystery—the mystery of the Still, Small Voice.

W. B. S.

ACKNOWLEDGMENTS

Grateful acknowledgment is here made to the following who have contributed to the preparation and publication of this volume:

Rabbi Morrison Bial who devoted many hours to reading and editing the manuscript. His assistance and suggestions were invaluable in preparing this volume for publication.

Rabbi Paul Steinberg who read and evaluated the manuscript.

Joan Pennell who brought the benefit of her skill and sensitivity to the editing of the manuscript.

My students in the Confirmation Classes of The Temple, Congregation Ohabai Sholom, Nashville, Tennessee, who provided much of the motivation material by their frank discussion of the requirements of modern Jewish ethical living.

The post-biblical literature and sacred institutions of Judaism for revealing the moral values and sublime ideals of a God-questing faith.

My devoted wife, Pearl, for her patience, encouragement and love.

W. B. S.

CONTENTS

1

THE VOICE OF THE PRAYERBOOK

The Ethics of Jewish Worship

Are We Fooling Ourselves When We Pray?

"Frankly, I don't believe God hears us when we pray! I don't believe in prayer at all. We should have enough sense to solve our problems without depending on a supernatural power. I think we're just fooling ourselves and wasting time when we pray!"

The members of the class turned quickly in the direction of the student who made this blunt statement. David seemed embarrassed by the attention and slumped quickly into his seat. This happened after the class had assembled for the first session of the religious school.

The class was no different from yours, and you know how the first session begins. Melvin put it this way: "It begins like a boxing match. There are the preliminaries; saying 'hello,' welcoming new students, finding seats, taking attendance, and distributing texts. The teacher and the pupils spar for a while, testing each other for weakness and strength—and then the class session gets under way."

The session that first day started unexcitingly. Rabbi Mayer began by reviewing the work of last year, when the class had searched for the answer to the mystery of the Still, Small Voice. They had discovered that Judaism is a way of life and must be used every day. "This year," he said, "we are going to continue our search through Jewish literature, and study the life of Jews in modern times.

"Since we are going to begin with the prayerbook and consider the ethics of Jewish worship, I'm going to ask you a question about prayer. Don't hesitate to say what you honestly think. Are we fooling ourselves when we pray, or does the Still Small Voice really answer us?"

It was then that David raised his hand and made the explosive statement that "prayer is a waste of time."

The Silent God

Before Rabbi Mayer could comment, Shirley said: "I don't mean to shock you, Rabbi, but, honestly, I don't think that God has ever spoken to me. He may have spoken through the Bible and the Talmud, and to great teachers and prophets, but God never speaks to me. And so I agree with David, and I'm not sure whether I believe in prayer, either. It may be all right for children or those who are old and sick and can't rely on themselves, but maybe we do fool ourselves when we pray."

"These are frank statements," the Rabbi replied. "Is there anyone else who would like to comment?"

Bernice said: "I think prayer is all right if it means talking something over with yourself, but I am not sure that God hears me when I pray. When I was little, I used to say the *Shema* before going to bed. When I grew older, I asked God for all sorts of things, but I never received them. After a while, it seemed sort of childish to keep on asking when I felt that I was just repeating words that nobody ever heard. I wonder if God really hears us, because He hardly ever seems to answer."

Joseph was called upon next. "I'm not sure what I do believe," he said. "I think that the Still Small Voice is really a matter of conscience and that when we pray our conscience tells us what is right and wrong, and what we should do. But, if there is a power outside of ourselves that hears our prayers, I wonder why He doesn't answer. When my aunt was so sick, I prayed with all my heart that she might live. We all did, but our prayers weren't answered, and my aunt died."

Rabbi Mayer thought for a moment, and then he opened the Bible and said: "I asked you to be frank, and I'm glad that you have the courage to express your doubts. Often it is through doubts that we gain the sensitivity to hear even the slightest whisper of the Still Small Voice. Some of you expect me to be shocked by your statements, but there were many before you who also doubted, who also wondered why God never answered. Listen to these selections from the Psalms:

> *How long, O Lord, wilt Thou forget me for ever?*
> *How long wilt Thou hide Thy face from me.*
>
> (*Psalm 13*)

"Other psalmists, too, seemed to think that God had forgotten them and ignored their prayers. The author of the 22nd Psalm prayed:

> *O my God, I call by day, but Thou answerest not;*
> *And at night, and there is no surcease for me.*

" 'Is God able to hear?' wondered the writer of Psalm 28:

> *Unto Thee, O Lord, do I call;*
> *My Rock, be not Thou deaf unto me;*
> *Lest, if Thou be silent unto me,*
> *I become like them that go down into the pit.*
> *Hear the voice of my supplications, when I cry unto Thee.*

"You see, the psalmists, too, yearned for an answer, and they were perplexed when it seemed that God was silent:

> *Hear my prayer, O Lord, and give ear unto my cry;*
> *Keep not silence at my tears...* *(Psalm 39)*

"Now do you see why I'm not shocked because some of you feel that God doesn't seem to answer or give us what we ask? But remember this–God answered the psalmists. The Still, Small Voice responded to their prayers–but not always at once. The answer sometimes came to them in the most unexpected ways. Many times it came in the form of renewed faith and courage. However, when their prayers were to a God of magic asking for a miracle, the answer was 'no.'

"Just as God answered the psalmists, so God answers us, but sometimes we receive our answer in the least expected ways. Yes, we do fool ourselves about prayer–especially when we think of prayer as magic and believe that if we repeat the right words, God will obey us immediately."

"Isn't that what we talked about last year," asked Jonathan, "when we discussed making God a heavenly magician who performs wonders upon request?"

Modern Aladdins and the Lamps of Prayer

"Yes, Jonathan, too many of us think of prayer as magic, just as we think of God as being a heavenly magician. We say we do not believe the story of Aladdin and his lamp, and yet many of us would like to be modern Aladdins and use prayer as a magic lamp. We think that all we have to do is rub the cover of a prayerbook or repeat a few magic words and God will appear, obey our requests, and give us everything we want. When God doesn't answer us immediately, we become disappointed. If our wishes are not granted when we utter the magic words, then many of us say 'God doesn't hear our prayers' and conclude that prayer is a waste of time.

"Just as there is a kindergarten idea of God, so there is a kindergarten idea of prayer. Even though a person may be an adult, he may still have a childish idea of prayer. If you speak to a six-year-old child about his ideas of prayer, you will find that he asks God to give him something: a new toy, a cowboy suit, a bag of candy. Sometimes adults do this too, only they ask for other things.

"Just as we have to grow up and mature physically, so we have to mature religiously. Very often our degree of maturity may be seen by our prayers. For example, the patriarch Jacob had to grow up religiously. When he was forced to flee from the anger of his brother, Esau, and he stopped to sleep, he dreamed of a ladder reaching to heaven, with angels ascending and descending on it. When he awakened he vowed:

> *If God will be with me, and will keep me in this way that I go, and will give me bread to eat, and raiment to put on, so that I come back to my father's house in peace, then shall the Lord be my God, and this stone which I have set up for a pillar, shall be God's house; and of all that Thou shalt give me I will surely give the tenth unto Thee.*
>
> *(Gen. 28.20-22)*

"Notice that Jacob attempts to make a deal with God. It was only later, after he had struggled with his belief in God, that he matured into the Jacob who loved God as a God of holiness, and not as a God who would give him clothing and protection.

"Don't we sometimes make such 'deals' with God in our prayers? If God will do something for us, then we promise to do something for God; give to charity, go to the synagogue more often, or perform some ritual act.

"Sometimes our prayers are childish and selfish. Sometimes what we think of as prayers are really demands—the demands of self-centered children who insist on having their own way. It is as if they tell God: NOT THY WAY, OH GOD, BUT MY WAY! NOT THY WILL, BUT MY WILL BE DONE.

"When we say this, or ask God to help us at the expense of others so that we may have our way, are these petitions to be granted by God? Do we have a right to call them prayers?"

The Answer May Be "No"

"Margaret Blair Johnstone recently wrote a book with the title, *There's No Unanswered Prayer*. She writes that God always answers our prayers, but sometimes the answer is 'no.' Sometimes we are asking Him to break His own laws. Sometimes we have prayed for something selfish or unworthy.

"Mrs. Johnstone is correct. There is no unanswered prayer, but sometimes, just as a father must say 'no' to his children, so our Heavenly Father must say 'no' to us for our own good. Because of this we may pout and rebel and even express antagonism to God, demanding, NOT THY WILL, O GOD, BUT MINE!, and if we don't get our way we may think that we're fooling ourselves when we pray.

"Prayer isn't just asking for something that we want; it's also experiencing something we need. We need to feel the presence of God, and by the holiness of that presence elevate ourselves above pettiness to a mood of reverence. This strengthens us and inspires us to be better and more unselfish than we are and thus to meet our problems with clarity of mind and loftiness of spirit. Prayer is the bridge that enables us to move toward God and communicate with a source of power that can change our lives.

"Now that we have made a distinction between the kindergarten concept of prayer and the mature idea of prayer, I think that we are ready to begin studying our prayerbook. As we continue our search for the Still, Small Voice, we will consider how Jews spoke with God in the past, and perhaps we may learn how to hear God speaking to us today."

WHAT DO YOU THINK?

1 How does the Still, Small Voice answer us when we pray?

2 What is your reaction to David's answer? Do you think that he should have answered as he did?

3 Do you think that it is proper to express your doubts about God, religion, and prayer?

4 How can doubt help to make your faith strong?

5 Do you think that God ever ignores our prayers?

6 What kind of prayers do you consider childish? What kind do you consider grown-up and mature? Give examples.

The Origin of Jewish Prayer

"A long time before there was a prayerbook, the children of Israel worshipped God by offering sacrifices. They expressed their gratitude, they asked for God's forgiveness or help, for victory in battle and for abundance of crops and offspring by giving God fat offerings and the finest animals of the flock. It took many years before they learned the lesson of the prophets that God doesn't want sacrifices, but justice, mercy, and righteous living.

"It was only after the destruction of the first Temple in the year 586 B.C.E. that a regular order of public and private prayer began to develop. The bringing of sacrifices into the Temple had been accompanied by prayers and songs. The prayers, which included some psalms and other parts of our service today, were arranged to correspond with the order of the sacrifices.

"When the Temple was destroyed, however, and the Jewish people were taken captive to Babylon, they gathered together in small groups and instead of offering sacrifices, they offered only their prayers to God. Thus, a regular order of prayer developed, and has continued to the present time.

"Today, there are different Jewish prayerbooks, but the prayerbooks used by Orthodox, Conservative, and Reform Jews are basically the same. Words are changed, the order of prayers may differ, but the hopes and the ideals are alike. Through these prayerbooks we talk with God, and hear God answering through the Still, Small Voice.

The Jew Prays

"Our fathers were not so much concerned about a God who answered all requests. They loved God and expressed their love of God through prayer. In every crisis of life, in joy and in sorrow, in danger and in security, the Jew prayed, and he received an answer. No, God did not hand down platters of food from on high; a man in need didn't always find a treasure chest of precious jewels; and few were rescued miraculously from danger. A Jew never learned how to achieve popularity and acquire a charming personality through prayer. He was never given the formula for success; but through prayer he was granted courage and inner strength to bear the burdens of life. Even more important, he drew near to God to find holiness, beauty and goodness in everything around him.

"Our fathers believed that every act of life required a prayer. As he awakened in the morning to God's presence, the Jew prayed; before he ate and after he ate, he prayed. He prayed three times a day in the synagogue; he prayed at home; he prayed on holidays and festivals and every Sabbath; he prayed when he started a journey and when he returned. He prayed in sickness and in health. He prayed and praised God, even in sorrow.

"So many of us think that the *Kaddish* is a prayer for mourners. However, if you read the English translation you will find that it isn't a prayer of sorrow, but rather a sanctification in praise of God. Even when his heart is torn with grief, the Jew praises God, assured that God's wisdom is greater than his own. He believes that God does not punish His children with death. Death is a part of God's law of nature, and even though we cannot understand why loved ones are taken from us, we repeat the blessing, *Boruch Dayan Ha-Emes (Blessed Be the Judge of Truth)*, in praise of the God of Truth.

"As we read the traditional prayerbook, we find that everything in life calls for a blessing. There are blessings for every occasion: for wine, bread, and other food, for the new moon, holidays and festivals. On smelling fragrant woods or barks, plants, fruits, spices, oils—the Jew prayed. On hearing thunder, seeing lightning, falling stars, lofty mountains, great deserts, the sea, beautiful trees, a rainbow—the Jew prayed. On beholding the blossoming of a tree for the first time, a wise man, a student of Torah, a king, or a dwarf—the Jew prayed. On hearing good tidings and bad tidings—the Jew prayed, and through his prayers he beheld all of life filled with the presence of God.

What Did the Jew Pray For?

"Yes, the Jew did ask God for things, but when his request was not granted he did not say that God was silent. He knew that prayer is more than asking God to perform miracles. Prayer is the means of expressing love of God, gratitude to God, the sense of wonder at the wisdom and glory of God's creation. Prayer was his pathway to the good life, the source of inspiration that enabled him to find holiness, truth, beauty and justice. Prayer was the source of his courage, hope and belief in a better and happier tomorrow.

"In order to understand why he prayed and what he prayed for, let us begin by listing the different types of prayers found in the morning service of the Daily Prayer Book."

Prayer Expressed His Praise of God for the Wonder of the Human Body

> *Blessed art Thou, O Lord our God, King of the universe, Who hast formed man in wisdom, and created in him many passages and vessels. It is well known before Thy glorious throne, that if but one of these be opened, or one of those be closed, it would be impossible to exist and stand before Thee. Blessed art Thou O Lord, who art the wondrous healer of all flesh.*

Prayer Expressed Man's Duty to His Fellowman

> *These are the things, of which a man enjoys the fruits in this world, while the stock remains for him for the world to come: viz., honoring the father and mother, deeds of loving-kindness, timely attendance at the house of study morning and evening, hospitality to wayfarers, visiting the sick, dowering the bride, attending the dead to the grave, devotion in prayer, and making peace between man and his fellow; but the study of the Torah leadeth to them all.*

Prayer Expressed Humility before God

> *Sovereign of all worlds! Not because of our righteous acts do we lay our supplications before Thee, but because of Thine abundant mercies. What are we? What is our life? What is our*

> *piety? What is our righteousness? What our helpfulness? What our strength? What our might? What shall we say before Thee, O Lord our God and God of our fathers? Are not all the mighty men as nought before Thee, the men of renown as though they had not been, the wise as if without knowledge, and the men of understanding as if without discernment?*

Prayer Extolled the Unity of God and the Love of God

> *Hear, O Israel: The Lord our God, the Lord is One.*

"This is the watchword of the Jewish faith. If God is One, it means that no other angel, spirit, power or deity should be worshipped. The oneness of God the Father means the unity of all mankind in one universal brotherhood."

> *And thou shalt love the Lord thy God with all thy heart, and with all thy soul, and with all thy might.*

"The Jew surrendered his mind and heart to God's holy will in love. To love God meant to live and act toward our fellowmen so as to make God and His teaching beloved in their eyes. When we read that we should love God with all our heart, with all our soul, and with all our might, the rabbis interpret this to mean with thy whole life. We show our love of God by our righteous deeds.

The Eighteen Benedictions

"Next to the *Shema*, the Eighteen Benedictions, called *Shemone Esre*, are the most important part of the morning service. This portion is also called the *Amida*, because it is recited standing, or *Tefilla*, "the prayer." These praise the everlasting love, might and holiness of God. They include prayers for the individual and the nation, and express fervent thanksgiving to God for all His blessings.

"They begin: *O Lord open thou my lips, and my mouth shall declare Thy praise*, and then follow benedictions praising God who bestowed loving-kindness upon our fathers, thanking God for His protection and love, and extolling the holiness of God with the familiar words:

> *Holy, holy, holy is the Lord of Hosts,*
> *The whole earth is full of His glory.*

"There are prayers for repentance, forgiveness, deliverance from affliction, sickness and want. The hope is expressed that some day all the exiles will be gathered and united as one holy people.

"There are prayers for protection against slanderers, informers, and traitors; prayers for the rebuilding of Jerusalem, the restoration of the Temple service, and the coming of the Messiah. The Sixteenth Benediction should be of great interest to us because it considers the subject we are discussing: 'Does God Hear Prayer.'

> *Hear our voice, O Lord our God; spare us and have mercy upon us, and accept our prayer in mercy and favour; for Thou art a God who hearkenest unto prayers and supplications: from Thy presence, O our King, turn us not empty away; for Thou hearkenest in mercy to the prayer of Thy people Israel. Blessed art Thou, O Lord, who hearkenest unto prayer.*

"The Eighteen Benedictions conclude with thanksgiving for God's unfailing mercy, and the beautiful *Sim Sholom*, the prayer for peace:

> *Grant peace, welfare, blessing, grace, loving-kindness and mercy unto us and unto all Israel, Thy people. Bless us, O our Father, even all of us together, with the light of Thy countenance; for by the light of Thy countenance Thou hast given us, O Lord our God, the Torah of life, loving kindness and righteousness, blessing, mercy, life and peace; and may it be*

> *good in Thy sight to bless Thy people Israel at all times and in every hour with Thy peace.*

"The concluding meditation is a fervent plea, as the Jew talks to God and makes his petition, not for wealth, or material possessions, but:

> *O my God! guard my tongue from evil and my lips from speaking guile; and to such as curse me let my soul be dumb, yea, let my soul be unto all as the dust. Open my heart to Thy Torah, and let my soul pursue Thy commandments.*

The prayer ends with the familiar:

> *Let the words of my mouth and the meditations of my heart be acceptable before Thee, O Lord, my Rock and my Redeemer.*

Bend My Will to Thine

"There is more to prayer than asking God to give us what we request. There is also the hope that God will guide us in our daily life and strengthen us that we may obey the Still, Small Voice. And so the Jew prays:

> *May it be Thy will, O God, that I walk in Thy law, and cleave to Thy commandments. Lead me not into sin or temptation or contempt. Let not evil desire rule over me. Bend my will to Thine. Keep me from sinful men and worthless companions. Help me to cling to the good and give me grace in Thy sight and in the sight of those about me. Amen.*

"The rabbis designate prayer as the divine service of the heart. One should pray only when there is a longing to do so in one's own heart and the person is attuned to prayer in a spirit of reverence. The

Talmud tells us, 'when you pray, know before whom you stand.' If we stand in the presence of a heavenly magician, then we ask for miracles. If we stand in the presence of a God of justice, mercy and forgiveness, then we ask God to help us practice justice, mercy and forgiveness in our daily life.

The Alenu

"As the morning service comes to an end, the hope is expressed that some day those of every faith and nationality will be united in one brotherhood of man, and that a reign of righteousness will be established and all peoples will worship God in a world of justice and peace. This prayer, the *Alenu,* is one of the oldest and most exalted in the prayerbook. It starts by declaring our duty to praise God who formed the world. God is proclaimed as the supreme King of the Universe, and we bend the knee and bow the head in reverence before the Holy One, Blessed be He, as we express Israel's yearning for a united humanity:

> *We therefore hope in Thee, O Lord our God, that we may speedily behold the glory of Thy might, when Thou wilt remove the abominations from the earth, and heathendom will be utterly destroyed, when the world will be perfected under the kingdom of the Almighty, and all the children of flesh will call upon Thy Name, when Thou wilt turn unto Thyself all the evil-doers upon earth.*
>
> *Let all the inhabitants of the world perceive and know that unto Thee every knee must bow, every tongue must swear allegiance. Before Thee, O Lord our God, let them bow and worship; and unto Thy glorious Name let them give honor; let them all accept the yoke of Thy kingdom, and do Thou reign over them speedily, and forever and ever.*

"This prayer may be worded differently in the Conservative and the Reform prayerbooks, but the ideal of a united humanity under God is the same. The Still, Small Voice speaks to every Jew of his responsibility 'to perfect the world under the kingdom of the Almighty.'

The Worship of the Heart

"Isn't this similar to the teachings of the prophets?" asked Sarah. "The *Alenu* prayer might have been written by Amos or Isaiah. Did one of the prophets write it?"

"It was not written by one of the prophets," Rabbi Mayer replied, "but I can understand why you might think so. It has the ring and spirit of the prophet appealing for a world of justice, brotherhood and peace.

"The prophet, in *Isaiah*, Chapter I, declared in the name of God:

When ye spread forth your hands,
I will hide Mine eyes from you;
Yea, when ye make many prayers,
I will not hear;
Your hands are full of blood.
Wash you, make you clean,
Put away the evil of your doings
From before Mine eyes,
Cease to do evil,
Learn to do well;
Seek justice, relieve the oppressed,
Judge the fatherless, plead for the widow.

"Even to this day, some people offer God 'prayers' just as their ancestors once offered sacrifices. However, a long time ago, Isaiah taught that prayers without justice, and words without righteous deeds are not acceptable to God. The purpose of prayer is to help us to obey God's commandments and practice the moral requirements of the Torah. Prayer is to inspire us to resist evil, to seek justice and to live our faith every day. Isaiah reminds us that if we forget this and make our prayers sacrifices of words alone, without honesty and truth, if we spread forth our hands in false reverence, our prayers will be mockery to God.

"When our prayer has nothing to do with the way we act, and we pray to get favors from God, then it is not 'worship of the heart.' Throughout the ages the prayerbook, filled with the teachings of prophets and psalmists, brought the Jew closer to God—and brought God closer to him. As he drew near to God, he thought of prayer as the torch that lights the way through darkness to justice, mercy, truth and the *kiddush ha-chayim,* the sanctification of life.

"Everyone can approach God through prayer, but the prayer must be sincere and reverent. Sometimes we hear people say, 'I would like to speak with God. I would like to pray, but I don't know how. If I only knew the right words.'

"When we feel that we don't know how to pray, we should think of the story of the ignorant farmer who entered the synagogue for worship. He listened to the worshipers intone their beautiful prayers to God—and he, too, wished to express his love of God. He ascended the pulpit and stood before the Holy Ark. The worshipers were astonished to hear this rustic repeating the letters of the Hebrew alphabet over and over again.

"They nudged each other, commenting on this poor man's ignorance. They laughed because he didn't even know the simplest prayers of the service. Then, as this farmer began to speak, their laughter died and their mockery turned to shame as they heard him say:

> *Lord of the universe, I am an ignorant man. Oh how I wish that I had the words to fashion beautiful prayers to praise Thee—but I cannot find these words. So listen to me, O God,*

> *as I recite the letters of the alphabet. You know what I think and how I feel. Take these letters and form the words that express the yearning, the love for Thee that is in my heart.*

And thus saying, he continued to repeat the letters of the alphabet over and over again.

"We don't have to be masters of language to talk with God, because the real language of prayer is the language of the heart. Just as a parent understands the babbling of a child, so our Heavenly Father understands His children, no matter how they speak, when they call upon Him in sincerity and in truth.

Worship Without Words

"Most of us think that the only way we can worship is by means of words. We speak our praise of God, or express our petition, or voice our aspirations. This is worship, of course, but in Judaism there is also worship without words.

"In the past, the study of Torah was regarded as an equivalent of worship. When a scholar, or even the average person, pondered over the meaning of Bible and Talmud, his study was considered to be the worship of God.

"There is another way to worship without words. The poet, John Greenleaf Whittier, suggested it when he wrote:

> *O brother man! fold to thy heart thy brother;*
> *Where pity dwells, the peace of God is there;*
> *To worship rightly is to love each other,*
> *Each smile a hymn, each kindly deed a prayer.*

"A long time before Whittier, Judaism regarded *ma-aseem toveem*, good deeds, as prayers without words. A man could speak with God and the Still, Small Voice would answer through his deeds.

"The prayer in the *Union Prayer Book* helps us to understand the meaning of worship without words:

> *O Lord, though we are prone to seek favors for ourselves alone, yet when we come into Thy presence, we are lifted above petty thoughts of self. We become ashamed of our littleness and are made to feel that we can worship Thee in holiness only as we serve our brothers in love....*
>
> *Let us then, O Lord, be just and great-hearted in our dealings with our fellowmen, sharing with them the fruit of our common labor, acknowledging before Thee that we are but stewards of whatever we possess. Help us to be among those who are willing to sacrifice that others may not hunger, who dare to be bearers of light in the dark loneliness of stricken lives, who struggle and even bleed for the triumph of righteousness among men. So may we be co-workers with Thee in the building of Thy kingdom which has been our vision and goal through the ages.*

"This idea of worship through deeds is demonstrated in the story of Rabbi Israel Salanter who failed to appear in the synagogue on *Kol Nidre* Eve. His congregation waited, and when the Rabbi did not appear the members became worried and went out to search for him. They found him in a neighbor's barn. What had happened to keep him from leading the congregation in prayer during the holiest service of the year? On the way to the synagogue, Rabbi Salanter had found a neighbor's calf that had strayed and become entangled in the brush. With great difficulty he freed it tenderly and brought it back to the barn. There he was tending to the animal's wounds when the men of his congregation found him. When they protested saying: 'How could you do that? Don't you know that your first duty as a rabbi is prayer?' He answered gently: 'God is called *Rachamona*, The Merciful One. An act of mercy is a prayer, too.'

WHAT DOES PRAYER MEAN TO YOU?

"It seems that I have done most of the talking since we began our study of the ethics of the prayerbook," said Rabbi Mayer, "so I would like to have your reaction to the following statements about prayer."

Is Prayer Begging?

A Christian clergyman, Harry Emerson Fosdick, declared: "Real prayer is always more than begging; it is affirmation.

> *Though I walk through the valley of the shadow of death, I will fear no evil; for Thou art with me—*

that is prayer."

What did he mean?
How would you apply this to the *Shema?*

On The Run

Rabbi Abraham J. Feldman wrote: "There was a little girl who was on her way to school and she was afraid of being late. She turned to her sister and said, 'Let us stop running and pray that we may not be late.' She missed the point in prayer. Her sister was wiser, for she replied, 'Let's pray while we run.' "

What is Rabbi Feldman trying to teach about prayer?

No Easy Answers

Eddie Cantor, the comedian, once said: "Religion is not a soothing syrup. It offers no glib, easy answers to life's problems. You cannot go to church or synagogue and pray and expect to find the road smooth and easy when you come out. Prayer will give you a new outlook, a sense of unity with your fellowmen, the courage to stand up straight on your own two feet and fight a good fight. It gives you the kind of confidence no lesser force can take away."

What are your reactions to this statement?

The President and a Jewish Prayer

Mr. Merriman Smith, United Press White House reporter, writes as follows about President Dwight Eisenhower's participation in the dedication of the temple of the Washington Hebrew Congregation:

"Mr. Eisenhower was deeply moved by a prayer he had heard the other night at the dedication of a new Jewish temple here. The rabbi read:

> *Cause us, O Lord our God, to lie down each night in peace and to awaken each morning to renewed life and strength. Spread over us the tabernacle of Thy peace. Help us to order our lives by Thy counsel and lead us in the paths of righteousness.*
>
> *Be Thou a shield about us, protecting us from hate and war, from pestilence and sorrow. Curb Thou also within us the inclination to do evil, and shelter us beneath the shadow of Thy wings. Guard our going out and our coming in unto life and peace from this time and forevermore.*

Why do you think President Eisenhower was so impressed with this prayer?

What does this prayer mean to you?

WHAT DO THE FOLLOWING EXAMPLES TEACH US ABOUT THE JEWISH CONCEPT OF PRAYER?

If a poor man says anything one pays little regard, but if a rich man speaks, immediately he is heard and listened to. Before God, however, all are equal, women, slaves, poor and rich. How do we know this? Because of Moses, the greatest of the prophets. What is said of Moses is also said of a poor man. Of Moses it is written, 'a prayer of Moses the man of God' (Psalm 90.1). And of a poor man it says 'a prayer of the afflicted, when he fainteth and poureth out his complaint before the Lord.' (Psalm 102.1). In both cases the word 'prayer' is used to teach that before God all are equal in prayer.

MIDRASH EXODUS RABBAH

The Talmud designates prayer as the "divine service of the heart." (Taan 13a.) R. Simeon said: Be careful to read the *Shema* and to say the *Amida*, and when thou prayest, regard not the prayer as a fixed mechanical task, but as an appeal for mercy and grace before the All Present (Aboth 2.18).—The worshipper must feel that he is standing in holy awe before the majesty of God (Sanh. 22a). When you pray know before whom you stand (Ber. 28b.) One should pray only when one has a longing to do so in one's own heart and is attuned to it by reason of a devotional mood (Pesikta Rabbathi 195b, Ber. 3b).

Since everything depends upon devotional fervor, *kavvana*, the prayer should be brief (Mechilta 53a). Prayer should be performed in religious joyousness (Ber. 31a). Since prayer means the raising of the soul upward to God, the prayer of praise is always superior to the prayer of petition. (Ber. 32a)....Prayer must be directed to God alone, and not to the angels or any other intermediary. (Yoma 52a).

When men in prayer declare the Unity of the Holy Name *(Shema Yisroel)* in love and reverence, the walls of earth's darkness are cleft in twain, and the Face of the Heavenly King is revealed, lighting up the universe.

THE ZOHAR

Bless Thou, O Lord our God, this year and all of its harvest for good. And set Thou a blessing upon the face of the earth. May it be Thy will to extend a peace, great and wondrous, in the Universe.

Let all the residents of earth recognize and know the innermost truth: that we are not come into this world for quarrel and division, nor for hate and jealousy, contrariness and bloodshed; but we are come into this world Thee to recognize and know. Be Thou blessed forever!

FROM THE PRAYERS OF RABBI NAHMAN OF BRATZLAV

(18th Century)

WHAT DO YOU THINK?

Dial a Prayer

In many communities there is a service available that enables a person to dial a number and get a recorded prayer, just as they get the weather or the correct time.

This was started by the Rev. Robert W. Youngs, of Scarsdale, New York. His project met with overwhelming success. Thousands called in. The entire telephone system was jammed until the telephone company hastily installed more equipment.

Other communities tried "Dial A Prayer" with equal success. Said Dr. Youngs, "a few people used it for practical joking, but I believe that most of the callers are sincerely seeking comfort and inspiration. This is another evidence that there is a genuine resurgence of religious faith in our country."

What do you think? Would a recorded prayer be of help to you?

Why do you think so many people have reacted favorably to this project? Do you think that Dial A Prayer indicates that there is a genuine rebirth of religious faith in our country?

What Should God Do?

Suppose a man were traveling a dirt road by car to see his dying mother; he would naturally pray for dry weather. Suppose some farmers in a nearby church were praying for rain. What could God do? It would be a chaotic world if man's prayers could change God's immutable laws. Prayer does not move the arm of God; rather it enables the arm of God to move us. Prayer's greatest results are not in the realm of nature, but in the realm of human nature.

GASTON FOOTE

What should this teach us about prayer? Is it proper to ask God to change the laws of nature for us? How do you think prayer achieves its greatest results in the realm of human nature?

What Prayer Can Do for Us

When the class had completed the assignment and answered the questions, David raised his hand and said: "Maybe I spoke too quickly when I said that I didn't believe in prayer. What I should have said is that I don't believe in what you call kindergarten prayers. Now I can see that there is much more to prayer than making God a sort of divine Santa Claus who gives us the things we want. I don't think that Judaism ever wanted me to think of God that way in the first place."

"It's never too late to change your mind or your attitude toward prayer, David," answered the Rabbi. "I don't believe in kindergarten prayers, either. Even though we have caught but a glimpse of the ethics of Jewish worship, we have seen that our people had to grow up from a crude childlike belief in prayer as magic, to prayer as a means of speaking with God and expressing our yearning to sanctify life with holiness.

"Our fathers heard the voice of God as they worshipped Him. We, too, can hear the voice of God if we will only listen. Prayer can help us and strengthen us when we are in trouble. Prayer can show us the right way and give us the courage to do the right thing, when we have to make decisions. Prayer enables us to talk with God, and to hear His response as He answers us through the Still, Small Voice."

QUESTIONS FOR DISCUSSION

1 How can prayer really help us in our daily lives? How can prayer help us to make wise and courageous decisions?

2 Mr. X is grief-stricken. A dear one is dying of what the doctors say is an incurable disease. Should the sick person pray? What kind of a prayer should be uttered? Should Mr. X pray? What kind of a prayer should he offer? Should he ask God to perform a miracle and break His laws of nature?

3 A Jewish scholar said:

> *Too many modern minded men and women reject the practice and the technique of prayer because they profess not to know to whom they can address it. They assert that prayer is a telephone conversation by a mortal with no one at the other end.*

What are your reactions to this statement? Is it possible to pray without believing in God? Explain your answer.

4 The poet, George Meredith, once wrote:

> *He who rises from his worship a better man, his prayer is answered.*

What is your opinion of this statement?

5 Does prayer demand any action on our part, or do we leave everything to God? What can we do to help make our prayers come true? Give examples.

6 The philosopher Yehuda Halevi said that man should look forward to the moments set aside for prayer,

> *because while they last he resembles the truly spiritual being and is elevated, then, above merely animal existence.*

What is your reaction to this statement?

7 A Christian theologian, Reinhold Niebuhr, once wrote this prayer:

> *God grant me the serenity*
> *To accept the things I cannot change;*
> *The courage to change the things I can;*
> *And the wisdom to know the difference.*

Give examples of what you think he meant. How can this prayer help you?

8 Do you think that prayer can change you and make you a better person? Do you think that prayer can change the world and make it better? In what way?

9 Dr. Alexis Carrel, in an article, "Prayer is Power," stated:

As a physician, I have seen men, after all therapy had failed, lifted out of disease and melancholy by the serene effort of prayer. It is the only power in the world that seems to overcome the so-called "laws of nature."

Do you think that prayer can cure diseases and ailments? How can prayer lift us "out of the dumps" when we are sorry for ourselves? How can prayer help us to achieve physical, emotional and mental health?

10 What does the statement in the traditional High Holyday Prayerbook mean when it states:

Penitence, Prayer and Charity avert the evil decree

11 The Talmud warns us not to pray for the impossible. A man whose wife is about to bear a baby shall not pray, "May it be Thy will that the child carried by my wife prove to be a boy (or a girl)." A man who hears a fire alarm sounding in his city shall not pray, "May it be Thy will that the fire be not in my home." Why are these prayers prohibited? Do you agree with the Talmud?

12 Since many scholars, both Jewish and Christian, believe that the Lord's Prayer is derived from Jewish sources, is it proper for Jewish children to repeat this prayer in our public schools?

THINGS TO DO

1 Look up the meaning of the words: *shacharith, minha, musaf, ma-ariv, piyutim, mahzor, amida, tefila, avoda.*

2 Obtain copies of an Orthodox, Conservative and Reform prayerbook. Read *Adoration, Haftarah* blessings, *Amida* in each prayerbook and compare.

3 Together with your class, attend an Orthodox Religious Service. Discuss your impressions of the prayer service following the visit.

4 Find out what the Reconstructionist movement is. Write a theme on how the Reconstructionist prayerbook differs from the Orthodox, Conservative and Reform prayerbooks.

5 Submit a questionnaire to the members of the Board of Trustees on the subject of prayer. They need not sign their names to their answers. Then, analyze your findings.

6 There are many reasons given why "people do not pray." Discuss your opinion in class. Then draw up a plan on how you would go about getting more people to pray.

7 There are some people who say: I don't have to go to a church or a synagogue to pray. I can pray in the privacy of my own room, or I get my religion through music, or I can come closer to God when I am outdoors communing with nature than when I sit with others in a church or a synagogue. Debate in class the proposition: "Public worship is as important as private worship."

8 The first complete *Siddur* (Prayerbook) was drawn up during the Ninth Century of the common era by Rabbi Amram, the head of the Academy of Sura in Babylonia. After doing research, find out when the first prayerbook was printed; the date, and place. List the first Reform prayerbooks, when and where and by whom they were published. Do the same with the Conservative prayerbooks. For reference help, see *Jewish Liturgy* by Abraham Idelsohn.

9 Write an essay on the significance of the *Kaddish* prayer. Trace its origin and its meaning yesterday and today. Explain why in some congregations, only the mourners rise for the *Kaddish*, while in others, all who worship rise.

10 Can you give an example of how prayer has been of help to you at some time when you needed courage, strength, or the character to make a decision?

SELECTED QUOTATIONS

What is Prayer?

Prayer is the bridge between man and God; in prayer, one establishes a face interchange with Him.... Prayer consists of two elements: that a soul shall be oriented toward God, and that whether with words or not, it shall address Him. Since man turns to God in many moods and designs, prayers are equally numerous and diverse as to temper and purpose.... There are prayers of contemplation, adoration, thanksgiving, affirmation, resignation, penitence, protest, quest, petition....

RABBI MILTON STEINBERG

Wireless To God

Prayer is the wireless message between man and God. Religion brings the soul back to God, and prayer is the means which it employs to do this. Every day we send the wireless message of prayer to God, renewing thereby our constant friendship with Him. Those who make prayer a rare practice are only acquaintances but not friends of God.

RABBI HERBERT S. GOLDSTEIN

Are Prayers Repetitious?

You object that prayers are repetitious. So are birth and pain and joy and death. The basic emotions are not many. Every great symphony repeats a limited number of musical ideas. But they set off great surges of feeling in the listener.

It is not what is in the prayerbook that is alone important. What you bring to it is equally important. The more you experience, the more meaning and satisfaction you find in these expressions of universal human sentiments....

Nor need you sacrifice your intelligence, your freedom of inquiry or judgment to gain this faith. You need only sacrifice your smugness, your brittle sensualism, your all-pervasive, all absorbing materialism, your nose to the grindstone absorption in the trivia of life.

Open yourselves to the great organ of our music, to the effulgent radiance of our Sabbath candles, to the joyous sanctification of our *Kiddush*, to the blessed insights of our Torah, to the sacred sublimation into the everlasting stream of life which is the glory of our *Kaddish*—and you will find the faith which made our fathers sing unto the Lord.

RABBI JACOB J. WEINSTEIN

The Siddur

Although the Bible is the basis of the Jewish religion, there is one book which—at least during the past 2,000 years—has been even more familiar to the average Jew than the Holy Scriptures and has more fully reflected his thoughts and feelings throughout the ages. This book is the *Siddur*, or order of daily prayers. It was better known than the Bible because it was the daily companion of the Jewish people, who used it not only at each of the three daily services of the synagogue, but also in the recitation of grace after meals, and on every occasion of joy or sorrow. It mirrors more completely the reactions of the Jewish mind and heart to the vicissitudes which the Jew experienced during his long career, from the time he appeared on the horizon of history until this very day, because the stretch of time covered by its contents extends far beyond the period of roughly one thousand years during which the Hebrew Scriptures were committed to writing.

RABBI SAMUEL ROSENBLATT

Who Searches The Heart

In ancient religions, ritual was virtually the sole form of worship. The performance of certain rites, such as the sacrifice of animals, the burning of incense, the solemn dance and the intoning of potent formulas was the prevalent mode of religious expression. In ancient Israel, however, due chiefly to the creative idealism of the prophets, religion became subjective, turning its attention from the world of outward performance to the inner world of thought and aspiration. With this deepening of the understanding, God was gradually envisaged as the one "who searches the heart" and was therefore to be worshipped not merely by outward ritual (which was never wholly rejected) but also by obeying the behest: "And ye shall seek Me, and find Me, when ye shall search for Me with all your heart." (Jeremiah 29:13).

RABBI SOLOMON B. FREEHOF

SUGGESTED READINGS

Cohon, Samuel S., *Judaism–A Way of Life.*
Cronbach, Abraham, *Prayers of the Jewish Advance.*
Cronbach, Abraham, *Judaism for Today*, pp. 59-70.
Freehof, Solomon, *The Small Sanctuary.*
Glatzer, Nahum, *The Language of Faith.*
Greenberg, Simon, *The Jewish Prayerbook–Its Ideals and Values.*
Gordis, Robert, *The Ladder of Prayer–The Conservative Approach.*
Idelsohn, A., *Jewish Liturgy.*
Union Prayerbook I and II.
Hertz, *Daily Prayerbook.*
Silverman, Morris, *Sabbath and Festival Book.*
Silverman, Morris, *Junior Prayer Book.*
Universal Jewish Encyclopedia, Vol. 8, pp. 617-621.

2

THE VOICE OF THE PEOPLE

The Ethics of the Synagogue

The Students Take Over

"Only three more days," Miriam sighed, opening her textbook.

Helaine turned to Miriam. "Will you stop dreaming long enough to tell me three days until what?"

Miriam smiled and said, "With the important job that you have, it seems to me that you should know."

"Oh, you mean the day students of the civics classes take over the city government! I almost forgot that on Thursday I'll be the new City Attorney, even if it is only for a day."

"Imagine you in City Hall," Miriam giggled.

"It wouldn't seem so funny if I issued an ordinance extending school through the summer. What am I saying!" Helaine clapped her hand over her mouth. "I'll bet Stuart Miller will be the dreamiest City Manager this town has ever seen...."

"And don't forget Gary as the Chief of Police," Miriam added. "What a day that should be! The civics classes will be running the whole city. We'll have our pictures in the paper! I can't wait until—I'll tell you after class. The Rabbi is going to take the attendance."

"If I were the Rabbi," said Helaine, "I wouldn't take attendance. Everything would be voluntary. Say! I'm getting a terrific idea!"

Rabbi Mayer looked up from the desk. "Is there something you want to say, Helaine?"

"It's just an idea, Rabbi, and I don't know whether you will like it, but...."

"Go on, Helaine."

"You see, this Thursday, the civics classes of our High Schools will take over the city. Students have been elected to fill all the important offices. It's only for a day, but we should learn a lot about our city government. My idea is this: why couldn't we do the same thing here at the temple—take over for a day?"

Louis said, "That *is* a terrific idea. One of us could be the rabbi—I don't mean really a rabbi, but the same as next Thursday, be a rabbi for a day."

"Yes," Helaine continued, "and someone could be the Director of the Religious School, and someone else could be the President of the Congregation, and we could have a Board of Trustees and—and maybe the students could even be the teachers! Will you let us try it, and see what we can do?"

"You do have an excellent idea, Helaine," said Rabbi Mayer. "If you are willing to work out the plans with me, I believe we can arrange it. However, if you are going to take over the temple for a day, it seems to me that we should devote some time to a study of the Synagogue: its origin and development, what purpose it serves, the function of the rabbi, and the organization of the congregation, yesterday and today. In that way it won't be just for fun, and you will be prepared to take over the temple for a day with understanding. Do you agree?"

A chorus of assent indicated the enthusiastic response. The date for "T"-Day, Temple Day, was selected, and the class started preparations to take over the running of the temple.

THE PLAN FOR "T"-DAY

A special religious service, conducted by the class, should be held. One student, rabbi for the day, should give the sermon. Students should conduct the services, read from the Torah, provide the choir, and serve as ushers.

A special meeting of the Board of Trustees should be held, with students serving as officers of the congregation and members of the board. An agenda should be drawn up, and an orderly and serious meeting conducted. The real rabbi and officers should be invited to attend this meeting. The matters for consideration should be suggested by the students, with special attention given to the youth program.

On the Sunday closest to "T"-Day (or actually on "T"-Day), a student should take over the class as teacher. The work should be carefully prepared and the session conducted conscientiously, with the real teacher seated in the class. An assembly program should be conducted by the students, with the student director of the Religious School in charge.

For the class study prior to "T"-Day, students should be given special assignments on the following:

A The origin of the Synagogue
B The ceremonial objects *(klay kodesh)* in the Synagogue
C The three-fold function of the Synagogue in the past
D The three-fold function of the Synagogue today
E The differences between the Orthodox, Conservative and Reform Synagogue today
F The role and function of the rabbi, yesterday and today
G How the Synagogue helps the Jewish people to hear the Still, Small Voice

A gripe list of any legitimate student complaints should be drawn up by the student Board of Trustees. A compliment list should also be made by the student Board of Trustees, enumerating all the satisfactory services rendered by the temple.

The student-rabbi, officers, and board should be elected by the class. Those who are not elected will serve as members of the congregation. The size of the board should be determined by the number of students in the class.

The Reports

A. Helaine's Report on "The Origin of the Synagogue"

When the Temple was destroyed in the year 586 B.C.E. (which means Before the Common Era), the Jews were exiled from their native land and taken captive to Babylonia. They wept as they thought of their plundered and desolate land and Temple.

Earlier, Jeremiah had sent his famous letter to the people whom Nebuchadnezzar carried away captive from Jerusalem to Babylonia. In this letter he told them that God wanted them to build houses and dwell in them and plant gardens and eat the fruit that grew in them. He urged them to seek the peace of the city, and assured them that some day they would return to the Land of Israel.

The people adjusted themselves to the new ways and customs of Babylonia, but always hopefully believed that soon they would return to their own land and worship God again. Without the Temple they could not offer sacrifices, and there was no organized priesthood to lead them. However, they asked themselves: "Why can't we worship our God, even here in Babylonia?" Soon they were meeting in small groups. They could never worship *Marduk*, the God of Babylonia, and they lifted their hearts to their own God in prayer. They knew God would hear them, even in Babylonia. They read portions of the Scripture, kept fasts in memory of the fall of the Temple, confessed their sins, and offered prayer. These informal gatherings were the origin of the Synagogue, a Greek word for "assembly" or "community."

When they returned to the Land of Israel in 538 B.C.E., even after the building of the Second Temple in 516, local synagogues continued. The people made pilgrimages to worship in the Temple, but many remained at home to worship in the *mikdash m'at*, which means the "little sanctuary." And so, over 25 centuries ago, the Synagogue came into being. Prayers, particularly psalms, were substituted for sacrifices. Portions of the Torah and the prophets were read, and the people worshipped God in small groups, instructed by teachers who told them of the past, and gave them faith in the promise of the future. The Synagogue became firmly established as a new creation of Judaism.

Many changes have taken place since these first synagogues. Old and new prayers were gathered into a prayerbook. The officials of the Synagogue were given titles. The head was called *Rosh Hakeneseth.* Later he was given the title of *Parnas* or *Gabbai.* His orders were carried out by a *Shammas.* The one who taught and instructed the people was called Rabbi, which means "teacher." The ancient synagogues were far different from our modern synagogues, but their spirit and purpose remain the same. The Synagogue enables the Jew to worship God together with his fellow-Jews, to identify himself with the history and customs of his people and to help him to hear and obey the Still, Small Voice.

QUESTIONS FOR DISCUSSION

1 Imagine a shipwreck. The survivors find their way to an uninhabited island where they are stranded for many years. Those who are Protestants group together for prayer. The Catholics worship together. Those of the Jewish faith decide to meet for services. Tell what you think would happen, giving the order of the service, the types of prayer and the leadership and organization of the island synagogue.

2 Look up these three references in the Bible, and tell which one is the most appropriate for the name of a synagogue: Jeremiah 39:8, Psalm 74:8, and Ezekiel 11:16.

3 What do you think would have happened to Judaism if the Jewish people in Babylonia had not met for worship in small groups?

4 Some of the Jews remained in Babylonia even when they had an opportunity to return to the Land of Israel. Why do you think they remained in a strange land? What do you think happened to their religion? What do you think happened to those who did not attend the synagogues in Babylonia?

5 What is the Hebrew name of your synagogue? What does it mean? Why do you think that name was selected?

B. Louis' Report on "The Ceremonials of the Synagogue"

My report deals with the sacred furnishings of the Synagogue. We are not sure exactly when, but gradually the Synagogue came to have certain holy requirements, the most important being the Holy Ark. The *Aron Hakodesh* was once portable. It was carried by the children of Israel in their travels, and it was thought to bring them victory in their battles. The tablets of the law were kept in the Ark. When the Torah was finally put together and accepted by the Jewish people, the sacred scrolls were kept in an Ark. This is the most sacred part of the Synagogue. Without the Ark, it is not a synagogue, but an auditorium.

Above the Ark is the *Ner Tamid*, the Eternal Light. The Bible commands us: "a light shall be kept burning perpetually. It shall not be extinguished." This light is a symbol—a symbol of the light of God, of learning, of hope and of enlightenment.

In addition to the *Ner Tamid*, most synagogues have the seven-branched candelabrum called the *Menorah*. This, too, is a symbol of God's light.

In order to read the Torah, there must be a reading desk. This was placed in the center of the synagogue and is called an *Almenor*.

The raised platform on which the desk was placed is called the *Bemah.*

In early times, as in the Orthodox synagogues today, there was a partition that separated the men from the women. This special gallery for women was called the *Ezrath Nashim.*

The architecture of synagogues differs. Sometimes a synagogue is a simple structure. Frequently it is elaborate. The real architecture of the synagogue, however, is not the external structure. The Jewishness is in the interior: the sanctuary with the *Ner Tamid*, the *Aron Hakodesh*, the *Menorahs.* The star of David, known as *Magen David*, is often used as a symbol on the altar. The Torahs are decorated with beautiful mantles and breastplates, and a pointer called the *Yad.* Ornaments may be placed on the Torahs. These ornaments, called *Rimonim*, often have little bells that tinkle when the officials walk with the Torahs. A beautiful crown may also be placed on the Torah, or set in the uppermost part of the Ark. Since the Torah is so sacred, it is beautifully adorned. The Ark usually has a *Parocheth*, a curtain. Above the Ark, there may be an inscription such as, "Know Before Whom You Stand," or "I have placed the Lord before me continually." In many synagogues, the Tablets of the Law, the Ten Commandments, are placed above the Ark, guarded by two figures of lions—reminding us to be as strong as lions in pursuing and protecting the law of God.

QUESTIONS FOR DISCUSSION

1 Discuss the different architecture of the synagogues of your community.

2 Discuss the architecture and the interior of a synagogue as compared with a church.

3 What are the advantages and disadvantages of a small and simply-constructed synagogue as compared with a large and costly synagogue?

4 The command to keep a light burning on the altar was made many thousands of years ago. What significance should the *Ner Tamid* have for us today?

5 During World War II, when blackouts were ordered for community defense, no lights were to be kept burning in public institutions. Since the Bible commands us to keep a light burning day and night, what do you think the synagogue did to comply with the order to black out all buildings?

6 What is your opinion about the "separation of sexes" in the synagogue?

7 It has been suggested that we spend less money on synagogue buildings and more money on the program that is conducted within them. What do you think?

8 Look up pictures of ancient and modern synagogues in Europe and America. Discuss some of the changes that have taken place.

9 Until recently, there has been resistance to objects of art in the synagogue. How would you account for this opposition? Do you agree?

10 What do you think is meant by this statement from the Talmud: "A city where the roofs of private houses are higher than the roof of the synagogue is doomed to destruction!"?

C. *Gary's Report on "The Three-fold Function of the Synagogue of the Past"*

In the past, the Synagogue had three primary purposes. These purposes are revealed in the names given to the Synagogue itself.

The Synagogue was known as:

Beth Hatefilah, The House of Prayer. The most important function of the Synagogue was to provide and encourage the opportunity for prayer. Prayers were held three times during the day: *Shacharith,* Morning; *Mincha,* Afternoon (with a *Musaf,* or additional prayers, added); and *Ma-ariv,* Evening.

Beth HaMidrash, The House of Study. Here children were taught the Torah. Adults came to study the *Ethics of the Fathers,* and to linger over the Mishna and Gemara. Since Jewish education is such an important purpose of the Synagogue, the Synagogue itself was called by the German word, *Schule,* which means "school." This story shows how important Jewish education was considered: "Some heathens asked, 'Tell us how we may successfully contend against the people of Israel?' And the answer was, 'Go to their synagogues and schools, and if you hear there the clamor of children repeating their lessons, you cannot prevail against them.' "

Beth Hakeneseth, The House of Assembly. The Jewish people met in the Synagogue not only for prayer and study, but for occasions of joy and sorrow, for weddings, celebrations, and mourning. In times of danger, they met to take counsel with each other. They met to discuss problems that affected them in their own community. They gathered to raise money to redeem their fellow-Jews who were held captive. The Synagogue was their meeting place and they felt at home there. The Synagogue was the meeting-place and the center of all Jewish communal activities.

QUESTIONS FOR DISCUSSION

1 Do you think Jews were more pious in the past than they are now? How would you define piety? What are the reasons for your opinion?

2 With the methods of teaching and the modern audio-visual aids and equipment that we have today, how would you compare Jewish education of the past with the education received by Jewish pupils today? Is there more or less resistance to studying about Judaism today, compared with the past?

3 Is the Synagogue as much a house of assembly today as it was in the past?

4 Which function of the Synagogue was the most important to the Jews of the past: prayer, study, or assembly?

5 To what extent have other Jewish organizations taken away the three-fold purpose of the Synagogue?

6 What is your explanation of this statement: "*Shuls*...we call our houses of worship, and that is what they should be, schools for the grown-up." (S. R. Hirsch)

D. *Miriam's Report on "The Three-fold Function of the Synagogue Today"*

According to the 1956 *Yearbook of the National Council of Churches*, there are 4,079 synagogues in the United States today with a membership of 5,500,000. While this differs from the figures issued by the Synagogue Council of America, which reported that of the 5,500,000 Jews in the United States, some 1,500,000 have no affiliation with religious life, it still shows the phenomenal growth of Jewish congregations, which have almost doubled in the past ten years.

The Synagogue is still a house of prayer, although there are Jews who do not use it as such. They only attend religious services on a *Yahrzeit*, and the High Holydays. But not all Jews were devout and pious in the past either. Some Jews worship three times a day, but there are many more who attend Sabbath services regularly and worship on the festivals and holydays.

Today, we have a more complex organization than in the past, with memberships, dues collections, secretaries, sisterhoods, brotherhoods, and youth groups—but the primary purpose of the modern Synagogue is still the worship of God.

The Synagogue is still a house of study, and Jewish education is becoming more and more important. We don't spend as many hours studying as Jews did in the past, but I believe that the methods of teaching have improved. When we speak of Jewish education we should not think only of children. Many synagogues have adult courses, but unfortunately, most adults do not use the Synagogue to further their Jewish education.

Recently, however, there has been a new emphasis on adult Jewish education, with almost every synagogue offering courses in Bible, Hebrew, Jewish History, Literature and Ethics, as well as forums and discussions.

The Synagogue's third function, as a house of assembly, is even more evident today than in the past. Sisterhoods and brotherhoods have special projects and meetings that are social, cultural and religious. There are youth groups, young married people's groups, and college-age groups. Weddings, funerals, Bar Mitzvahs, and Confirmations and receptions are held in the Synagogue. We still assemble in the Synagogue for occasions of joy and sorrow. The effort to raise funds for our needy brethren still summons Jews to the Synagogue. In addition to this, there is fund raising for hospitals, schools, rabbinical seminaries and other causes.

QUESTIONS FOR DISCUSSION

1 To what extent do you think Jewish centers have changed the three-fold function of the Synagogue?

2 What organizations in modern Jewish life have taken over some of the original functions and purposes of the Synagogue?

3 The Synagogue in the past had fewer members than many of our synagogues. What are the advantages and the disadvantages of the large synagogue?

4 In the year 1887, Rabbi Isaac M. Wise said: "Israel lives in its congregations!" What do you think he meant? Is that statement true today?

5 What are reasons for and against the required attendance of the confirmation class at Sabbath services?

6 Sam Levinson, a television humorist, recently said: "My wife and I and our children like to believe that God still dwells in our house, so we feel that it is only proper that on the Sabbath we should return the courtesy of visiting Him in His house." What is your reaction to this statement?

7 How would you apply Isaiah's pronouncement: "My House shall be called a House of Prayer for all peoples," to the Synagogue today?

8 The rabbis in the *Midrash* asked: "Why did Moses break the tablets of the law?" They answered: "When Moses descended from Mt. Sinai with the tablets of the law in his hands, and saw the children of Israel cavorting wildly around the golden calf, breaking each of the commandments, the letters flew away, leaving only stone so heavy it dropped from Moses' hands and shattered into many pieces." How would you apply this *Midrash* to the Synagogue?

E. *Mark's Report on "The differences between the Orthodox, Conservative and Reform Synagogues"*

THE ORTHODOX SYNAGOGUE

Today, there are three principal interpretations of Judaism, Orthodox, Conservative and Reform. Those who identify themselves with each group have their own synagogue and belong to their own national organization. The Orthodox synagogue today differs little from the Synagogue of the past. The traditional prayerbook is used, and the service is in Hebrew and Aramaic. The children are taught through Talmud Torahs. The seminary that supplies rabbis for Orthodox congregations is called a *Yeshiva.* A prominent *Yeshiva* is the Rabbi Isaac Elchonon Theological Seminary of Yeshiva University. In 1898, the Union of Orthodox Jewish Congregations of America was established. Its principal rabbinic organization is The Rabbinical Council of America. Orthodox Jews wear hats in worship and adorn themselves with the prayer-shawl called the *Talis.* Pious Orthodox Jews put on the *phylacteries,* the *Tefilin,* for morning devotion. Men and women are separated in worship. The Orthodox synagogue attempts to preserve what is called, "Torah-true Judaism."

THE REFORM TEMPLE

In Reform Judaism men and women sit together in worship. Men usually do not wear hats or prayer-shawls. A Reform temple is distinguished from the Orthodox mainly in mode of worship. There is usually no reading desk in the center of the synagogue for the reading of the Torah, which is read from the pulpit. Most of the prayers are in English.

One of the first Reform congregations in America was the *Beth*

Elohim Congregation, in Charleston, S. C. In 1824, members asked the officials to make provision for English prayers in the public service, and introduce reforms in the ritual. Reform Judaism in America was given its major impetus with the arrival of Rabbi Isaac Mayer Wise in 1846.

The first Conference of Reform Rabbis in the United States was convened in Philadelphia in 1869. It was not until 1889, however, that the Central Conference of American Rabbis was organized. Rabbi Wise organized the Union of American Hebrew Congregations in 1873, and the Hebrew Union College, the rabbinical seminary in Cincinnati, in 1875.

In 1922, a second rabbinical seminary identified with the Reform movement was founded in New York City by Rabbi Stephen S. Wise, and called the Jewish Institute of Religion. Today, both organizations have merged and are known as the Hebrew Union College-Jewish Institute of Religion.

While there is no organ or instrumental music used in the Orthodox synagogue, the organ and mixed choir have become a part of the Reform synagogue. Reform Judaism attempts to select the most significant observances of Judaism. It asserts that God revealed the moral laws to Israel, but that the ceremonial laws were made by man and may be changed or eliminated if they are lacking in beauty, meaning or modern significance.

THE CONSERVATIVE SYNAGOGUE

The Conservative movement really originated in America as the reaction to the Pittsburgh Conference of American Rabbis, called by Dr. Kaufmann Kohler in November, 1885. There was antagonism to the platform that rejected dietary laws and abolished all reference to the sacrificial cult, and a return of the Jews to Palestine. Under the leadership of Dr. Sabato Morais, the Jewish Theological Seminary Association was organized in New York City in 1886. New Congregations came into being known as Conservative synagogues.

Men and women sit together in worship, the men wear hats and prayer-shawls, and much of the tradition of Judaism is observed, although certain modifications are made.

By 1913, there were enough graduates of the Jewish Theological Seminary to form a national organization of Conservative congregations. This was founded by Solomon Schechter and called The United Synagogues of America. The organization of Conservative rabbis is known as the Rabbinical Assembly of America. There is no one prayerbook that is identified with the Conservative movement. A prayerbook edited by Rabbi Morris Silverman is widely used, but every Conservative congregation may use any book it wishes.

RECONSTRUCTIONISM

In addition to the three major interpretations of Judaism there is a new movement led by Rabbi Mordecai M. Kaplan, a professor of the Jewish Theological Seminary.

With the publication of his book, *Judaism as a Civilization*, in 1934, a group of men sympathetic with Rabbi Kaplan's views founded a magazine called *The Reconstructionist*. The Jewish Reconstructionist Foundation was founded in 1940 for the purpose of spreading the Reconstructionist philosophy and program. This new group incorporates many of the ideas of Conservative and Reform Judaism. It believes in a maximum of Jewish life, but also believes in change and development. Reconstructionism regards Judaism as a civilization with its own language, land, history, traditions, laws, religion and art.

QUESTIONS FOR DISCUSSION

1 How do you think having several interpretations has strengthened or weakened Judaism?

2 In many of our synagogues we sponsor inter-faith meetings to promote better understanding between Christians and Jews. Do you think we need intra-faith meetings between the three synagogue congregations to promote better understanding? How could this be accomplished?

3 Orthodox Jews are required to observe the *Taryag Mitzvoth,* the 613 commandments of tradition, dietary laws, worship three times a day, and keep the ceremonial laws of Judaism. Do you think that the arguments that "times have changed," or "it is difficult to be observant in this modern age," are used by Orthodox Jews who may not meet the requirements of Orthodoxy? How do you think the Orthodox rabbi would answer?

4 Do you believe that an Orthodox Jew is more Jewish than a Conservative or a Reform Jew? What do you mean by "Jewish"? Is an Orthodox Jew more religious? What do you mean by "religious"?

5 Orthodoxy maintains that all of the Torah was revealed by God and is thus divine. What is the attitude of Conservative Jews about revelation? What is the attitude of the Reform Jew?

6 Reform Judaism maintains that only the moral laws were revealed by God, and that the ceremonial laws of Judaism are man-made. What would an Orthodox and a Conservative Jew say?

7 In the Conservative movement, who determines whether a ceremonial law is to be observed or not?

8 When we use the term "religious," we frequently apply it to those who attend services and observe the rituals. To what extent should honesty, truthfulness and ethics in general be included in the term "religious"? Is a man religious if he attends services, but cheats his neighbor? Is a man religious if he is ethical and moral, but does not attend services?

9 The Reconstructionist movement believes in a maximum of Jewish life, but also believes in change and development. To what extent does this differ from the Conservative and the Reform movements? Read about the Reconstructionist program, and then discuss the question of whether there is a purpose to be served by this group that is not served by any of the other three. Do you think that Rabbi Kaplan's belief that Judaism is a civilization is true? We usually think of Judaism as a religious faith. Rabbi Kaplan calls it a religious culture. What are the differences?

10 Do you think that non-Jews as a rule understand the differences between Orthodox, Conservative and Reform Judaism? Do you think that they regard all Jews as belonging to one group, without different labels? Do you think that most adult Jews understand the differences?

F. *Ellen's Report on "The Role and Function of the Rabbi—Yesterday and Today"*

The function of the rabbi today is far different from that of the rabbi of the past. In the past, his primary purpose was to teach Judaism, to be an expert on Jewish law and to answer questions about ritual, practice and belief. The rabbi was a layman in a sense, and frequently earned his livelihood through another occupation. He did not conduct the prayer service—this was done by a man called a *baal tefilla* or a *hazan*, a cantor. Another organization, called *Bikur Choleem*, visited the sick. Other groups ministered to the dead, and arranged for burial. The rabbi was the scholar, the sage and the judge.

The rabbi's role is very different today. Because of his many tasks, the rabbi may no longer make his livelihood elsewhere. He is a paid professional of the synagogue, administering synagogue affairs, conducting the service, preaching the sermon, superintending the religious school, visiting the sick, officiating at weddings and funerals, and performing many other tasks. He has entered into the field of public relations, and must speak at civic clubs, church groups, and many other community affairs. He leads study groups, and assists in the programs of the brotherhood, sisterhood, and youth group. He may be busy with radio and television activities. Many people come to him for personal counseling and advice, and, therefore, he must prepare himself in the field of psychology and psychiatry. In addition to the work within the synagogue, the rabbi is frequently called upon to lead organizations, both Jewish and non-Jewish, and to give of his time and ability to further many worthy projects. He must be a preacher, pastor, counselor, public relations expert, synagogue administrator, religious school director, and the representative of the Jewish faith to the Christian community.

QUESTIONS FOR DISCUSSION

1 Do you think the rabbi of the past rendered greater service to the Jewish people in his role of teacher and scholar than he does today, performing many roles and services?

2 To what extent do you think Jewish congregations today expect the rabbi to imitate the role and functions of the Christian minister? What are the similarities between the rabbi and minister? What are the differences?

3 Do you think that the rabbi of today is respected as much as the rabbi of the past? Is he regarded with the same degree of awe?

4 Why do you think that Christian ministers are called "reverend" and Jewish spiritual leaders "rabbi"? What do you think is the significance of the terms used?

5 Today there is a shortage of rabbis, and many congregations are without spiritual leadership. Why do you think there is a shortage of rabbis today?

6 Would you like to become a rabbi? If so, give the reasons. If not, tell why you would not care to enter the rabbinate.

7 How do you think we can encourage more young men to enter the rabbinate?

8 Do you think that women should be permitted to serve as rabbis? Why?

9 In your opinion, should the rabbi give up some of his outside activities, such as speaking to civic groups, church groups, etc., and concentrate upon study groups and service to his own congregation?

10 After writing to the Rabbinical Seminary, cite the qualifications necessary to be ordained as a rabbi at Yeshiva University, New York City; The Jewish Theological Seminary, New York City; and The Hebrew Union College-Jewish Institute of Religion, Cincinnati, Ohio.

11 If you were the rabbi of your congregation, what changes would you make in your synagogue? If you were a member of the Board of Trustees of your congregation, what changes would you want to make in your synagogue?

12 There is a story that "when Rabbi Levi Yitzchok was about to be born, Satan complained that if that soul were to descend to earth, it would reform the world and his own power would come to an end. The Holy One comforted Satan and said: 'He will become a rabbi, and he will be too occupied with communal affairs.' " What is the significance of this legend? Do you think it could be applied to the modern rabbi?

13 "Unless you can play baseball, you will never get to be a rabbi in America." This was the statement made by Solomon Shechter, one of the founders of the Conservative movement, to an aspirant. What did he mean?

14 Professor Abraham Heschel said: "We do not celebrate kings and heroes, we celebrate teachers–Moses and Rabbi Akiba. The teacher is the central pillar of Jewish living, past, present, and future." Is he right?

15 Read the article "Rabbi and Rabbinate" in the *Universal Jewish Encyclopedia*, Vol. 9, pp. 48-52, and then write an essay on "The Rabbi as a Teacher" or "The Rabbi as a Layman."

16 Write to the Jewish Statistical Bureau, 320 Broadway, New York, New York, and request the pamphlet *The Rabbis of the United States.* From your study of the pamphlet, do you think there will be more Orthodox, Conservative or Reform rabbis fifty years from now?

G. *Eldon's Report on "The Synagogue and The Still, Small Voice"*

It is largely because of the Synagogue that the Jew was able to hear the Still, Small Voice speaking to him through the prayerbook and through the sermons and teachings of the rabbis.

In his education a Jewish child learned of the word of God and the ethical teachings and exalted ideals that inspired Jews to live lives of generosity, honor, and holiness. Assembling in the synagogues in joy and in sorrow, the Jew found comfort and consolation. He asked God's blessing on a new-born infant and on a bride and groom. He found the inspiration to make a little sanctuary out of his home.

In modern times, the Synagogue still helps us to hear the Still, Small Voice speaking to us. We hear that voice echoing through the prayers, songs and hymns of our faith. From the time that they can first understand, little children are taught the moral requirements and the ethical objectives of Judaism. Through Bar Mitzvah and Confirmation, the Jewish child is identified with the noble heritage of morality bestowed upon us. The observance of the Sabbath and the holydays implies the hope that those who come into the Synagogue will live up to the teachings of Judaism in their relationship with others at home, at school, at work, and at play.

The Synagogue is perhaps foremost among the institutions that have perpetuated the Still, Small Voice in the heart of the Jew. For over 2,000 years, it has served the Jew, and within it the Jew has attempted to serve his God. Synagogue forms, appearances and customs may have changed, but its purpose remains the same—to help us hear God speaking to us and to show us how to answer Him through our deeds and our actions.

QUESTIONS FOR DISCUSSION

1 In what way do you think that regular synagogue attendance strengthens character and the resolve to apply the Jewish teachings of morality to life?

2 Statistics reveal that cases of juvenile delinquency among Jewish youth are relatively infrequent. Do you think that religious school instruction may account for this?

3 Should there be more creative prayer services for youth, emphasizing Judaism as a way of life and stressing truth, justice and kindness in our relationship with others? What changes would you make in your synagogue to give youth greater responsibility, and to encourage greater participation?

4 If you were in charge of the religious school curriculum, would you add more courses on Jewish ethics? For which grades? Would these courses replace or be added to the present courses of Jewish History, Ceremonies, Literature, Hebrew and Modern Jewish Life?

5 Shirley has never attended a religious school. Her parents don't believe that formal religious instruction is essential. They have tried to teach her to be kind, truthful and considerate. Kathy has attended religious school. Her parents have also tried to teach her to be kind, truthful and considerate. Do you think Kathy will be more inclined to apply these teachings than Shirley?

6 We think of the Still, Small Voice as the voice of God speaking to us and within us. To what extent do you think the Synagogue of today helps Jewish youth to be guided by that voice?

7 Jacob Emden, a rabbi who lived two hundred years ago, said everyone should include this prayer in his daily worship: "Blessed is he who has not made me a rabbi." What do you think of this prayer?

8 Do you think Conservative and Reform Judaism will ever merge?

Rabbis and Commissars

After the class discussion, Rabbi Mayer thanked those who had prepared reports on the Synagogue.

"Before we continue with our plans for T-Day," he said, "I want you to think of what would have happened if the Synagogue had never come into existence. Very likely, there would be no Judaism today.

"We have a tragic example of this in our own time when we see what happened to Judaism in Russia under Soviet rule. Once Russia was the scene of flourishing Jewish life and culture, brilliant rabbis and academies of Jewish learning. Today, there are few synagogues, and Judaism is becoming extinct. The few rabbis who remain are controlled by the Russian government. The knowledge of Judaism is disappearing, because the law prohibits a Jewish education for anyone under the age of eighteen.

"Recently, the 'iron curtain' lifted a little, and we caught a glimpse of Jewish life under the communists. In 1956, the Russian government permitted a delegation of American rabbis to visit Russia. Rabbi Morris N. Kertzer described the visit in a series of articles in *The New York Times*. In part, this is what he wrote:

We were ushered politely into a chapel of the Leningrad Synagogue and the door was locked behind us, shutting out the crowd which had been trying to ask questions. We were being officially "protected" from our fellow Jews.

Everywhere, we met anxiety over possible retribution for running afoul of omniscient officialdom. In one small synagogue room, we saw piled against the walls scrolls of the Torah, gathered from synagogues which had been closed permanently. There must be 300 of them, I guessed. "Sssh," cautioned a bystander. "There are spies in this room..."

The word "Jew" is stamped on all the documents of a Jew in the USSR, we learned, but despite being singled out in this manner, Soviet Jews are not permitted to publish their own press or operate their own schools....

Every young person I spoke to during our stay referred to himself casually as an atheist. I attended a dozen services, but did not see a single Russian Jew under thirty-five engaged in prayer.

Religious education is banned in the Soviet Union today.

What Will We Give to the Future?

Lines of sadness creased the brow of Rabbi Mayer. "Without the Synagogue and a Jewish education, what will happen to the Jewish faith in Russia?"

Not a member of the class tried to respond. They knew that their teacher didn't expect them to answer.

Rabi Mayer's expression changed. "How different it is in America," he said. "Here we have the freedom to worship God in our own way. We can build synagogues and temples. We can send our children to Talmud Torahs and religious schools, teaching them the grandeur and the glory of our sacred heritage; imparting to them the ideals of a prophetic and God-seeking faith. America has encouraged the ideals of the Synagogue. The Synagogue has strengthened the ideals of America. The heritage of the past has been given to us. What will we give to the future?"

"But, Rabbi," Helaine asked, "couldn't we make our contribution to the future without the Synagogue—just by being 'good Jews' and living up to the teachings of Judaism?"

"There are some who believe that, Helaine," Rabbi Mayer answered. "However, the purpose of the Synagogue is to help us to be good Jews and live up to the ethical teachings of Judaism. Without the Synagogue it is doubtful whether Judaism can survive. Think of what the Synagogue has meant to the Jewish people. It was the Synagogue that enabled our people to survive the destruction of the Temple. The Synagogue bound Jews together, strengthened them in adversity, comforted them in sorrow, and inspired them to seek God through prayer and worship. It educated children and adults to partake of the spiritual sustenance of the Torah, the tree of life that reached heavenward to God. The joy of Jewish life was intensified through the Synagogue, and there the people celebrated the birth of dear ones, the marriage of their children and the festive seasons and holydays. But, we are most indebted to the Synagogue, past and present, for sensitizing the heart and soul of the Jew to hear and obey the Still, Small Voice which summons him to live by his faith and to apply the moral teachings of the Torah to his home, his work and his relationship with others. Only when we understand this, are we prepared for "T"-Day, and ready to take over the supervision of the synagogue with appreciation and reverence."

THINGS TO DO

1 Organize your own plans for "T"-Day at your synagogue. Ask the rabbi's cooperation and consult with the officials of the synagogue.

2 Rabbi Morris Adler wrote an article called, "If Your Synagogue Could Talk This is What it Would Say." This is a quote from his article:

> Why then, should you not take advantage of the spiritual exhilaration and the mental change of climate the Synagogue offers you not only at the beginning of the Jewish New Year, but also through the entire year? The kind of uplift and liberation you felt on the High Holydays, you can experience every Sabbath, when worship offers you an oasis

in the wasteland of daily duty and burden. To be sure, worship means much more. It is communion with God. It is enlargement of the universe of our feeling and thought which consequently brings about an enlargement of self. It is articulation of high ideals and the re-enforcement of good motives and aspirations. It is union with a noble tradition and cohesion with a community in God-centered dedication....

Write an article from your point of view: "If Your Synagogue Could Talk."

3 Reverend Grant H. Elford had been mulling over the timeworn excuses people give for not going to church, and then wrote "Why I Do Not Attend the Movies." Here are the reasons given:

a The manager of the theater never called on me.

b I did go a few times, but no one spoke to me. Those who go there aren't very friendly.

c Every time I go they ask me for money.

d Not all folks live up to the high moral standards of the films.

e I went so much as a child, I've decided I've had all the entertainment I need.

f The performance lasts too long; I can't sit still for an hour and three quarters.

g I don't care for some of the people I see and meet at the theater.

h I don't always agree with what I hear and see.

i I don't think they have very good music at the theater.

j The shows are held in the evenings, and that's the only time I am able to be at home with the family.

Analyze these reasons and apply them to the reasons people give for not attending synagogue services.

4 A member of a congregation wrote an anonymous statement to his rabbi: "I go to the synagogue because I have need of God–and God has need of me. Divine services help me to keep attuned to my Creator–and when I slip by the way, I am helped back to the road leading to God...." What would you add to this statement?

5 Arrange to visit an Orthodox, Conservative and Reform synagogue. Discuss and compare your reactions in class.

6 Make inquiries about the development of Synagogue art. Bring pictures and photographs to class. Ask some member of the community who is familiar with this subject to speak to the class.

7 Assign the subject of synagogue music to a student who is capable of giving a talk on this theme. The student should consult with the music director or Cantor.

8 Write to The United Synagogue Commission on Jewish Education, 3080 Broadway, New York 27, New York, and ask for the following pamphlets on *Your Child and You:*

a *Bringing Up the Jewish Child*
b *The Mental Hygiene Value of Jewish Education*
c *Jewish Education Begins at Home*

9 There are many secular Jewish organizations. Identify each of the following, and tell which you think will be important in the future.

The Zionist Organization of America
The American Council for Judaism
The American Jewish Congress
The American Jewish Committee
The Anti-Defamation League of B'nai B'rith
The B'nai B'rith
The National Council of Jewish Women
The Jewish Labor Committee
Ort
Hadassah
The Jewish Welfare Board
United Jewish Appeal

SELECTED QUOTATIONS

The Synagogue—Bulwark of Jewish Life

"Wherever ten Jews are found," we read in the Talmud, "they are duty bound to organize a synagogue. Moreover, whoever lives in a place where there is a synagogue, and fails to join it, is not a good neighbor."

In all this, we see how deeply Jewish people realized the value of a synagogue—its worth to society, to the community, as well as its place in the continued history of Israel...the very existence of the Jewish people and its religion have been bound up with the Synagogue.

We know from history what those assemblages meant to Israel! They saved Israel in Babylon. When the Jews came back from exile they brought the Synagogue with them.

But How About the Present?

There are those who would have us believe that the sun of the Synagogue has set. This is an age of many organizations, and often the newest are supposed to be the best. Various foundations of modern stamp—fraternal, philanthropic, cultural, economic and so forth—are pointed out to us, and we are assured that these latter-day creations have supplanted the Synagogue.

One is even supposed to be able to qualify as a good Jew and excellent Jewish leader though standing outside the synagogue and sneering at it.

Yet, a reading of Jewish history will put us on our guard against such disparagement of the Synagogue.

Today, as much as ever, the Synagogue still forms the true center of every Jewish community. The Synagogue is the great unifier, it is eternal, it champions not the object of individual leaders, but the eternal purpose and aim of the Jewish people. It is Israel's ancient anchor in the sea of momentary strifes and rivalries.

The Synagogue is still the center, as well as the symbol, of the spiritual life of every Jewish community; and because it is that, every community needs the Synagogue today as much as ever in the past.

It is here in America that it must proclaim the spiritual purpose of the Jew, signalize the lofty, religious aim of his milennial struggle and endurance, and stand forth as a centre of Israel's organized, collective and active idealism.

America is a country of ideals. Ideals have made America great, and America demands devotion to ideals from its citizens. And from no one more so than the Jew.

What contribution is the Jew making toward the spiritual ideals and the spiritual life of the country? This is the question we are called upon to answer. The answer to this question will be expressed best in the Synagogue.

For the Synagogue represents the spiritual idealism of every Jewish community. It represents it in collective form, in organized form, in active form—in a form best fitted to contribute to the spiritual welfare and progress of the whole community.

RABBI H. G. ENELOW

I Am The Synagogue

I am the Synagogue.

I am the heart of Jewry. I have sheltered you for more than two thousand five hundred years. Through all these cruel ages, swept by wrath of fire and sword, I nursed you with the word of God, healed your wounds with the balm of faith, steadied your minds and hearts with the vision of the Eternal.

When your fathers wept by the waters of Babylon, I came into the world, summoned by their need. In Persia, Greece and in Rome, in the face of the howling crusaders and in the clutches of the Black Inquisition, in the pogroms of Poland and in the Concentration Camps of the Nazis, I have been, and by my presence brought the living waters of the Eternal to the parched lips of your fathers.

When the world derided them, I restored them. When men cursed them, I blessed them.

I bring you peace by teaching you duty. I sanctify your lives with holy seasons. I preserve your heritage. I make the faith of the father, the faith of the children. Behold, a good doctrine do I give unto you; forsake it not.

The Dawning Future

If the Synagogue does its work well, it will enable our generation to move into the future with the scars healed and the spirit unbroken. It will make us learned, sensitive, unashamed Jews, bringing spiritual gifts to the altar of America, aiding America to remain true to its conscience and its destiny, enabling the Jew to march side by side with great Christians toward earth's promised land. To make the synagogue one "of the colonies of the spirit which some day will become empires of the soul" is the task of rabbi and layman alike.

In the spirit of the rabbis of old, by our deeds, our sacrifices and our labors, we Jews in America have the ineffable privilege of becoming not only "Banim," children of the Almighty, but "Bonim," builders for the Almighty—builders out of the ruins of this age of redemptive sanctuaries for the dawning future.

RABBI JOSHUA LOTH LIEBMAN

The Hearth

The Temple was the altar, the Synagogue was the hearth, and the sacred fire burned on each of them. With the fall of the Temple, the fire was quenched on the altar, stamped out under the heel of the conqueror; but it still glowed on the hearth....

In all their long history, the Jewish people have done scarcely anything more wonderful than to create the Synagogue. No human institution has a longer continuous history, and none has done more for the uplifting of the human race.

R. TRAVERS HEREFORD
(Christian Theologian)

A Unique Creation of Judaism

A unique creation of Judaism is the Synagogue, which started it on its world-mission and made the Torah the common property of the entire people. Devised in the Exile as a substitute for the Temple, it soon eclipsed it as a religious force and a rallying point for the whole people, appealing through the prayers and Scriptural lessons to the congregation as a whole. The Synagogue was limited to no one locality, like the Temple, but raised its banner wherever Jews settled throughout the globe. It was thus able to spread the truths of Judaism to the remotest parts of the earth, and to invest the Sabbath and Festivals with deeper meaning by utilizing them for the instruction and elevation of the people. What did it matter, if the Temple fell a prey to the flames for a second time, or if the whole sacrificial cult of the priesthood with all its pomp were to cease forever? The soul of Judaism lived indestructibly in the House of Prayer and Learning.

RABBI KAUFMANN KOHLER

The Synagogue and Jewish Unity

It is one of the most interesting of religious phenomena to observe the essential unity that the Synagogue maintained.... Dispersed among the nations, without a national center, without a synod to formulate its principles, or a secular power to enforce its decrees, the Synagogue found its home and harmony in the heart of a loyal and consecrated Israel.

RABBI SOLOMON SCHECHTER

The Supreme Court Justice and The Synagogue

It has frequently been pointed out that many of our people believe that they are fulfilling their complete Jewish duty when they feed the hungry, clothe the naked and find shelter for those who are homeless.

In other words, they identify Judaism with philanthropy.

Those, however, who are at all cognizant of the true facts realize that while charity has always been a part of Jewish life, it has never been coextensive with Judaism.

The truth is that the Synagogue has been and must remain the inspiring force behind all philanthropic endeavor on the part of the Jew.

There are many institutions that do good work, but it is very questionable whether any of them—the Jewish lodge, the Jewish club, even the Jewish welfare groups would be moved to turn a hand or speak a word in behalf of their stricken co-religionists were it not for the spur given to them by the Synagogue.

They are the echo, of which the Synagogue is the voice. They are the shell, of which the Synagogue is the kernel. They constitute the body, of which the Synagogue is the soul. The Synagogue is the motivating force that drives them all.

Hence, it is very important that the place of the Synagogue in the Jewish community life should be clearly recognized.

We cannot departmentalize our Jewish life overmuch, devoting one portion of our interests to charity, another to education, and another to defense as though they had no relationship whatsoever to our religion and the Synagogue, which is the representative unit of our religious life.

Democracy substitutes self-restraint for external restraint. It demands continuous sacrifice by the individual and more exigent obedience to the moral law than any other form of government.

JUSTICE LOUIS D. BRANDEIS

A Conservative Rabbi Speaks

I come to the synagogue to probe my weakness and my strength, and to fill the gap between my profession and my practice. I come to lift myself by my bootstraps. I come to quiet the turbulence of my heart, restrain its mad impulsiveness. I come for self-renewal and regeneration. I come into the sadness and compassion permeating the synagogue to contemplate and be instructed by the heaving panorama of Jewish martyrdom and human misery. I come to be strengthened in my determination to be free, never to compromise with idolatry, cringe before autocracy or succumb to force. I come to orient myself to the whole of Reality, to the thrusts of power beyond the comprehension of my compounded dust. I come to behold the beauty of the Lord, to find Him who put an upward reach in the heart of man.

RABBI SOLOMON GOLDMAN

The Synagogue and Religions

Its [Judaism's] persistent character, and, it is not too much to say, the very preservation of its existence through all the vicissitudes of its fortunes, it owes more than anything else to the Synagogue. Nor is it for Judaism alone that it had this importance. It determined the type of Christian worship, which in the Greek and Roman world of the day might otherwise easily have taken the form of a mere mystery; and, in part directly, in part through the church, it furnished the model of Mohammed. Thus Judaism gave to the world not only the fundamental ideas of these great monotheistic religions, but the institutional forms in which they have perpetuated and propagated themselves.

GEORGE FOOT MOORE
(Christian Theologian)

The Synagogue and Jewish Life

When the Synagogue was at the height of its strength it was coextensive with Jewish life. No avenue of Jewish thought or interest was closed to it and no concern of Jews was beyond its purview. It was the embodiment of the history, doctrines, ideas, and achievements of the Jewish people. The synagogue and Jewish life were inseparable.

RABBI JACOB SCHWARTZ

A Reform Rabbi Speaks

This is the role of the prophet—and this must be the role of his modern successor, the rabbi. Staunchly, unflinchingly, he must stand for the right, alone if necessary, brave the shout of the mob if necessary. He must champion the cause of the oppressed and distressed—whether it be the cause of his brethren of Israel, or of his brethren of the human family. He must be voice for those who cannot speak. He must be bold and if need be, tactless, as was Nathan the prophet. Not plaudits of the masses nor the favor of the classes should he seek. Not to speak and to preach in generalities that are vapid and meaningless, but to apply these generalities to specific situations. Not merely to preach peace when there is no threat of war, nor to laud justice when there is no injustice. Not career but conviction, not fame but service, not reputation but the love of God and of man, should motivate him. Not narrow denominationalism, but broad universalism, not partisanship but fairness, not malice but mercy, should characterize his work. Not merely sympathetic to everything Jewish, but equally sympathetic to everything human must be he. This is the challenge to the rabbi of today.

RABBI FERDINAND ISSERMAN

Origin of the Synagogue

Originally there were religious services in the synagogues on three days in the week, on the Sabbath, and on Monday and on Thursday, but later there were three services a day, at the third hour (9 a.m.), the sixth hour (noon), and the ninth hour (3 p.m.).

The earliest element of the synagogue service was the Reading of the Law, which was in Hebrew, followed by an explanation in the vernacular Aramaic. The natural development from this was a discourse, since the original function of the synagogue seems to have been that of teaching. Possibly the Reading from the Law was preceded by prayer, and in the prayers was embodied at an early date the *Shema*. This consisted of three passages from the Law, Deut. 6.4-9; 11.13-21; Num. 15.37-41; and it was so called because of its opening word, which means "Hear."

The earliest Readings from the Law seems to have been introduced as early as c. 300 B.C.E. in connection with certain festivals. At first the passages which were read were from Lev. 23, and they consisted of the passages relevant to the particular festival. In course of time these readings were extended to the four special Sabbaths in the month *Adar*, the last month of the civil year, and finally to every Sabbath. Finally, in Palestine, the whole of the Law was arranged in portions to be read Sabbath by Sabbath over a period of three years. The modern custom is to read through the Law once every year, and this was the way in which the Law was read amongst the Babylonian Jews.

There came a time, probably owing to disputes with the Samaritans as to the proper way of observing festivals, when the Law was "concluded" with a verse or two from the Prophets. This Reading from the Prophets was called the *Haftarah* ("Conclusion"), and in time these developed also so that every portion of the Law *(Seder)* had its *Haftarah*. It is not known at what period this full development was in being, but it was probably about the beginning of this era and certainly well before the end of the first century A.D.

NORMAN H. SNAITH
The Jews From Cyrus to Herod

SUGGESTED READINGS

For the Pupil

Edidin, Ben M., *Jewish Community Life in America*, Chapters 5, 6, 7, and 13.

Freehof, Solomon B., *The Small Sanctuary*

Friedman, Theodore and Gordis, Robert, *Jewish Life in America*, pp. 23-74; pp. 75-108; pp. 322-337.

Holisher, Desider, *The Synagogue And Its People*, Chapters 2, 3, and 7.

Schwartz, Jacob, *The Synagogue in Modern Jewish Life* (a pamphlet)

Steinberg, Milton, *Basic Judaism*, Chapter IX, pp. 150-158

Universal Jewish Encyclopedia, Vol. 10, "The Synagogue," pp. 119-130.

Wischnitzer, Rachel, *The American Synagogue*

For the Teacher

Ginzberg, Louis, *Students, Scholars and Saints*

Kaplan, Mordecai M., *Judaism as a Civilization*

Karpf, Maurice J., *Jewish Community Organization in the United States*

Moore, George Foot, *Judaism*, Vol. I, Ch. V, pp. 281-307

Philipson, David, *The Reform Movement in Judaism*

Silver, Abba Hillel, *Where Judaism Differed*

Sklare, Marshall, *Conservative Judaism*

Snaith, Norman H., *The Jews From Cyrus to Herod*, chapter on "Temple and Synagogue"

3

THE VOICE OF THE SHOFAR

The Ethics of Holydays and Festivals

A Banquet on Yom Kippur

"I am going to read you part of a letter that I just received," said Rabbi Mayer. "Please listen to what the writer suggests."

YOM KIPPUR IS THE MOST HUMILIATING DAY IN ALL THE SUPERSTITIOUS ANNALS OF RELIGION. USE THIS DAY FOR RELIGIOUS INDEPENDENCE. LET IT BE AN EMANCIPATION PROCLAMATION TO THE WORLD! ABANDON YOUR TEMPLES. RENOUNCE YOUR ANTIQUATED CREED, AND, BY SO DECISIVE AN ACT, GIVE TO THE WORLD ITS FINEST EXAMPLE OF COURAGE AND INTELLECTUAL HONESTY.

ARISE AND BECOME FREE MEN!

JOSEPH LEWIS, PRESIDENT
Freethinkers of America

Rabbi Mayer put the letter on his desk and turned to the class. "This is one of the annual appeals of the Freethinkers of America. Some of its members were Jews by birth. They have renounced their faith, and have dedicated themselves to ridicule the customs, traditions, and holydays of Judaism and Christianity.

"Several years ago, this organization created a stir in the public press when it sponsored a Yom Kippur banquet. While other Jews were fasting and praying devoutly in their synagogues, these so-called 'freethinkers' were making merry at a banquet table laden with food, to show their contempt for God and their scorn of our holiest day.

The Freedom Not To Be Religious

"Those who respect and cherish Jewish observances will be shocked by this letter ridiculing a holyday. The seal on the stationery shows the Statue of Liberty and the torch of freedom. The freethinkers, however, take advantage of the great American principle that man is free to worship God or not to worship God in accordance with his convictions, by mocking the cherished beliefs and practices of those who are loyal to their religious faith.

"But what about those who do believe? What about those of the Jewish faith who observe Yom Kippur, Rosh Hashanah and the other holydays and festivals of Judaism—how would they answer this letter? How would you answer the charge that 'Yom Kippur is the most humiliating day in all the superstitious annals of religion'? How would you reply to the summons of this organization to 'use this day for religious independence,' 'abandon your temples,' and 'renounce your antiquated creed'?"

What Does It Mean To You?

Bernard could not control his anger any longer. He burst out:

"Who do they think they are to ridicule something that is holy and sacred? Whether these Freethinkers like it or not, Yom Kippur is a holy day to us, and has been to Jews for many, many years. Something ought to be done to stop them from sending out such letters!"

"I don't like the letter any more than you do, Bernard. However, we have the freedom to express ourselves as we wish in America." Rabbi Mayer paused for a moment. "I'm not worried about what the Freethinkers write about Yom Kippur or any other Jewish holiday. Of greater concern to me is what Yom Kippur means to you and others who claim to love and practice Judaism.

"To what extent do we respect Yom Kippur as a holyday? What meaning does it have to us? Is it just a day when you stay out of school and spend some time in the synagogue—or is it a day that enables you to come closer to God, to the highest in yourself?

"Ever since you have been going to religious school, you have studied about the holydays and festivals, and more than that, you have observed them at home and at the synagogue. What I want you to consider now is not the history of our holydays—nor even how we observe them—but *why* we observe them. Not what was the significance of our holydays in the past, but what meaning do they have for us living in America today—and how do they help us to hear and obey the Still, Small Voice?

"Using these questions as a basis for our study, let us begin with Rosh Hashanah and Yom Kippur, and then consider other Jewish festivals in terms of their ethical significance and religious meaning to us in a modern, jet-propelled age.

"Before we do so, it might clarify our thinking if we consider the following questions:

1 How does the secular New Year differ from the Jewish religious New Year?

2 Do you think God will punish you if you don't attend religious services on Yom Kippur?

3 List the reasons why you attend services on the High Holydays.

4 How can High Holyday worship influence you to be more ethical in your daily life?

The Days of Awe

"On Rosh Hashanah there is a sense of awe that sweeps over us as we worship. Unlike the secular New Year, we do not celebrate with drinking, merrymaking, dancing, noisemakers, and paper hats. We do not welcome the Jewish New Year in a nightclub, but in the synagogue. No blaring of horns clashing upon the ear, but the sound of the *Shofar*, penetrating to the heart. No whiskey glasses, but the *Kiddush* cup raised and a sip of sacred wine to thank God, not only for the blessed joys, but also for the solemn responsibilities of life. No popular songs, but hymns of praise welling up to God from choir and congregation.

"Even though some of us forget God during the year, somehow when we enter the synagogue on the High Holydays we yearn to draw close to Him and obey His commandments. On Rosh Hashanah we welcome not only a New Year, but another opportunity, a new chance to begin again, to try again, to be more thoughtful of others, to repent for our sins, and to be a better person in every respect. Through prayer and meditation we talk with God and He answers us.

"The rabbis taught that the High Holydays are an opportunity for *cheshbon hanefesh*, the inventory of the soul. That means that we look inwardly at ourselves, to see ourselves as God sees us—as we really are. We may fool others, but we know that we never deceive God. Therefore, we take stock of ourselves—our bad habits, the weakness of our behavior—and we resolve to try to correct our failings and strengthen our character. Even though at other times we may joke about serious matters, during the High Holydays we think about the real meaning of life, of what is truly important, and what we want to accomplish during our years on earth. We are inspired to turn from our selfish ambitions and petty desires, and lift our thoughts on high to God with the resolve to choose the right and the good, and reject that which is evil and unworthy.

"The blowing of the *Shofar* is more than a traditional observance. The shofar calls to each of us. It is the signal to look within. It is the clarion call to take action against selfishness, ignorance and evil:

May the sound of the Shofar summon us to struggle against the forces of evil within our hearts and in the world. Let it arouse within us the will to righteousness and strengthen our trust in God's justice and love. May it direct our thoughts to the day when the Shofar will sound for the redemption of all mankind.

"Rabbi Joseph Herz, late chief-rabbi of England, summed up the modern meaning of Rosh Hashanah when he said: 'Since days immemorial, the sounding of the ram's horn on the New Year has been interpreted in Israel as the clarion call to repentance and spiritual renewal, saying: Awake, ye sleepers! ... Consider your deeds; purify your hearts. There is an Eye that seeth all things; there is an Ear that heareth all things. There is a heavenly Judge with whom is no unrighteousness, nor forgetfulness, nor respect of persons.

" 'And on the High Festivals the Jew thinks not only of himself, but of peace and blessedness for all mankind. In the most ancient and solemn part of the services, both of the New Year and of the Day of Atonement, he prays God to hasten the time when the mighty shall be just and the just mighty; when all the children of men shall form one band of brotherhood; when national arrogance and oppression shall have passed away, like so much smoke from the earth.'

The Day of Atonement

"The sacred Day of Atonement means different things to different people. To some it means an opportunity to show off new clothes, taking time off from work or school, or it is a form of insurance for a new year of happiness, health and prosperity. To others it means the stirring *Kol Nidre* melody, fasting, asking God to forgive sins, the purification of the heart and mind, repentance for past mistakes, and an opportunity to achieve 'at-onement' with God. What does the Day of Atonement mean to you?

"Fasting is important, of course—but if Yom Kippur is considered solely in terms of eating or not eating, then we miss the real meaning of this most sacred of all Jewish holidays.

"Billy Rose told an intriguing story in his column, *Pitching Horseshoes*. It is called 'Yom Kippur in Korea,' and concerns a corporal named Abraham Geller who refused to eat on the Day of Atonement, even though his regiment was preparing to cross a territory swarming with enemy snipers.

"After the regiment went into action, Corporal Geller, standing only a few feet from his commanding officer, Captain George O'Conner, saw a sniper prepared to shoot. He jerked his bayonet out of his belt and made a dive for the enemy soldier, but was struck by the three bullets which had been intended for O'Conner.

"The captain did the best he could for Abe Geller, but it was almost three hours before the corporal got a shot of penicillin and was carried to a hospital tent.

"The operation lasted over an hour, and when the surgeon finally came out, he announced that Corporal Geller would live despite the fact that the bullets had gone through his abdomen and intestine. Such wounds, he explained, are generally fatal if penicillin isn't administered pretty fast.

" 'I don't get all the words,' said the captain, 'but his pulling through seems like something of a miracle.'

" 'In a manner of speaking it is,' said the surgeon. 'Geller owes his life to the fact that when he was shot there was hardly any food in his stomach.' "

Daniel looked perplexed. He said: "That's too much like the kindergarten God of magic and miracles. What's the story supposed to prove: that God watches over those who fast on Yom Kippur?"

"Some people would interpret it that way," replied Rabbi Mayer. "However, I agree with you Daniel. Yom Kippur means much more to us than such miracles. Most of us are not soldiers, and we would have to think of a better reason than that for fasting.

"We fast on the Day of Atonement in order to devote our thoughts to spiritual ideals rather than our material appetites. Some people fast because it is a religious commandment, or part of our Jewish tradition. Others fast because it is a religious discipline. One man told me that he fasts because he thinks it's a good idea to give his stomach a rest at least one day a year. That certainly is not the religious purpose of fasting on Yom Kippur. There are many reasons why we should fast, but at no time should we make fasting the most important aspect of the Day of Atonement.

"In the *Haftora* for the morning service of Yom Kippur, Isaiah tells us the real reasons why we fast. Speaking in the name of God, he asks:

> *Wherefore have we fasted, and Thou seest not? Wherefore have we afflicted our soul, and Thou takest no knowledge? Behold in the day of your fast ye pursue your business, and exact all your labors. Behold, ye fast for strife and contention, and to smite with the fist of wickedness; ye fast not this day so as to make your voice to be heard on high.*
>
> *Is such the fast that I have chosen? The day for a man to afflict his soul? Is it to bow down his head as a bulrush, and to spread sackcloth and ashes under him? Wilt thou call this a fast, and an acceptable day to the Lord?*
>
> *Is not this the fast that I have chosen? To loose the fetters of wickedness, to undo the bands of the yoke, and to let the oppressed go free, and that ye break every yoke? Is it not to deal*

thy bread to the hungry, and that thou bring the poor that are cast out to thy house? When thou seest the naked, that thou cover him, and that thou hide not thyself from thine own flesh?

Then shall thy light break forth as the morning, and thy healing shall spring forth speedily; and thy righteousness shall go before thee, the glory of the Lord shall be thy rear-guard. Then shalt thou call, and the Lord will answer; thou shalt cry, and He will say: Here I am.

The Ethical Meaning of Atonement

"Isaiah was not opposed to fasting on Yom Kippur," said Rabbi Mayer, "but he did condemn those who ignored the real meaning of atonement, who fasted without reverence, without sincere religious repentance, without any thought of drawing closer to God and living up to the moral teachings of Judaism. To Isaiah, Yom Kippur was a holyday of God-seeking, to inspire the people of his generation to apply their faith by devoting themselves to social justice and eradicating wickedness, oppression and evil.

"So, in modern times, we also need Yom Kippur to help us make atonement, and inspire us to seek social justice. We no longer believe that God sits in heaven with a book containing our sins and shortcomings, but we do believe that when we obey God's moral laws we are rewarded, and when we disobey them we are punished. We not only stand in judgment before God, but we also stand in judgment before our own conscience.

"It is on this day that we think about the wrong we have done, the people we have hurt, and how we have failed to live up to the teachings of our parents, our teachers and our religious faith. Is there any individual so callous that he doesn't feel the need for forgiveness? Is there anyone who cannot join with his fellow-worshippers and confess with them: 'We have sinned; we have transgressed; we have done perversely'?

"Yom Kippur is not limited to fasting and the repetition of prayers alone. It calls us to sincere repentance, and demands that we must first obtain forgiveness from those we have wronged before we can hope that God will forgive us for what we have done. It challenges us to fight ignorance, cruelty and prejudice in our hearts and in our world.

"If we mumble prayers without reverence, then those prayers are meaningless. If we sit in temple for many hours without meditating on the real meaning of life, without determining to be better than we are, then we make a mockery out of atonement. But if we pray sincerely, and examine our souls as we look within, resolving to be clean and pure before God, then do we achieve 'at-onement' with God and the highest in ourselves. Then do we hear the Still, Small Voice answering our prayers for strength, courage, wisdom and holiness."

WHAT DO THE FOLLOWING STATEMENTS TEACH US ABOUT THE DAYS OF AWE?

For transgressions between man and God, the Day of Atonement makes atonement; for transgressions between man and man, the Day of Atonement cannot atone until man appeases his fellowman.

MISHNA YOMA

"Inscribe us in the Book of Life." This must be understood in a spiritual sense. When a man clings to the love of God, and puts his trust in His infinite mercy, he takes upon himself the yoke of the Kingdom of Heaven and therewith inscribes himself in the Book of Life. Whereas the man, a slave to his passions, who so loses his belief in the all-embracing love of God that he fails to repent and return to his Father in Heaven, his despair of the love of God is equivalent to his being inscribed—God forbid—in the Book of Death.

ISRAEL BAAL SHEM, 1760

When there was a cholera epidemic in 1848, Rabbi Israel Salanter posted announcements in all the Houses of Prayer of Vilna on the eve of Yom Kippur, urging the people not to fast on that holy and awesome day, and to cut short the recitation of the liturgical poems of the day, and to go walking in the fresh air. After the Morning Prayer on Yom Kippur he took a roll in his hand and stood on the pulpit and after making the blessing ending "who creates various kinds of foods," ate the roll before the eyes of the entire congregation, that the people might see him and follow his example; for much is permitted where there is mortal danger, and the life of a single person was dearer in his eyes than all the wealth in the world.

S. Y. AGNON
The Days of Awe

A tale is told of one who sat in study before the *zaddik* Rabbi Mordecai of Nadvorna, of blessed memory (19th Century), and before Rosh Hashanah came to obtain permission to be dismissed. That zaddik said to him, "Why are you hurrying?"

Said he to him, "I am a reader, and I must look into the festival prayer book, and put my prayers in order."

Said the zaddik to him, "The prayer book is the same as it was last year. But it would be better for you to look into your deeds, and put yourself in order."

LIKKUTE MAHARIAH

WHAT DO YOU THINK?

1 How can Rosh Hashana strengthen us religiously to meet the problems of life?

2 In what way should Rosh Hashana contribute to Jewish ethical living?

3 Why is the Sabbath of Repentance regarded as one of the most sacred Sabbaths of the Jewish year?

4 What are some of the sins of modern youth? How may we atone for them?

5 What are your reactions to the Billy Rose story? What do you think Isaiah would have said about this story?

6 How would you apply Isaiah's message to the way we observe Yom Kippur today?

7 How can the Day of Atonement contribute to Jewish ethical living?

The Sabbath

"Yom Kippur is the holiest day of the Jewish calendar, but what is the next holiest?" asked Rabbi Mayer. "It is not Rosh Hashana, as so many of us think, but the Sabbath.

"In Exodus, Chapter 20, verses 8-11, we are commanded to remember the Sabbath Day to keep it holy, and refrain from work because God rested on the seventh day, and therefore blessed and hallowed it. In Deuteronomy, Chapter 5, verse 12-15, we are commanded to 'observe' the Sabbath Day to keep it holy, and refrain from work, offering a day of rest not only to the master, but to his family, the servants, and even the beasts of burden. Because our ancestors were servants in the land of Egypt and God delivered them from their bondage, we are to show kindness and consideration to all who labor–even dumb beasts.

"While we consider a day of rest as something quite commonplace today, when the children of Israel ordained the Sabbath, it was the first time in human history that a religious faith set aside one day of every week for rest, for spiritual renewal and for communion with God. The Jews were ridiculed for giving a day of rest to servants, slaves and even the beasts of burden, but through the Sabbath, the Jews insisted upon the dignity of every human being and demonstrated that *gemiluth hasodim*, the doing of kindness, applied even to animals.

"To the Jew, the Sabbath is more than a day of rest and relaxation.

It is more than not working. Both biblical passages command us to make the Sabbath a holy day. The commandment is not 'remember the Sabbath Day,' but 'remember the Sabbath Day to keep it holy.' The Sabbath is a day set aside for holiness, to enable us to think about our ethical relationship to God and our fellowmen.

"But what is holiness? According to the Holiness Code of Leviticus, Chapter 19, holiness is not something vague and abstract. It is religion in action—the very essence of Jewish ethical living. It means respect for parents, assistance to the poor and needy, honesty, kindness, justice and love.

"Recently a modern Jewish youth group wrote a statement to indicate that holiness must be a part of everyday living:

Many are the ways of holiness; varied are its paths.

There is holiness in a lab when a vaccine is discovered to destroy diseases.

There is holiness when nations meet to beat swords into plowshares.

There is holiness when we strive for purity and harmony in family life.

There is holiness when men of different backgrounds work together for a common future.

There is holiness when men seek justice and struggle for righteousness.

There is holiness when men lift up the fallen and free the captives.

There is holiness when men bring consolation to the sorrowing and comfort to the silent sufferers.

There is holiness when men create lasting poetry or song or philosophy.

There is holiness when men gather to seek Thee, O God, through prayer.

Holy, holy, holy is the Lord of Hosts.

National Federation of Temple Youth Service, Oconomowoc, Wisconsin.

The Sabbath of the Past

"In the past," said Rabbi Mayer, "our ancestors welcomed the holy Sabbath as a bride. Throughout the week they struggled to earn enough to provide a meager livelihood, but since the Sabbath was a day set apart, different and special, on that day they managed to have some special delicacy in honor of the Sabbath. They may have been subjected to prejudice during the week, but somehow on the Sabbath, each Jew was a king, his wife was a queen, his children princes and princesses. His self-respect was restored and he remembered that he was part of a people chosen by God.

"The Sabbath was more than a day of rest. It was a day of worship and religious renewal. Through the Sabbath ritual, his home became a sanctuary of God. When he attended the synagogue, through the prayers and the teachings of the Torah, he was taught the moral laws of human conduct. He drew closer to his people, his religion and his God to relive the past, ennoble the present and create hope for the future. Through the Sabbath he heard the Still, Small Voice reassuring him that to be a Jew means to be identified with a kingdom of priests and a holy people, with a sacred mission in the service of God and all mankind."

The Sabbath Today

Billy's face revealed doubt. "That may have been fine for the past," he said, "but what about today? Our fathers earn a good living. We don't need the Sabbath to make us feel important. We're no longer living in ghettos and we're not persecuted by hostile governments. Certainly, I can understand why our forefathers could make the Sabbath a holy day, special and set apart, but times have changed, and the world has changed. They didn't have to punch a timeclock or be at a place of business with employees dependent upon them. Living in ghettos, it was easy to observe the Sabbath. What's more, they didn't have movies, radio, television, baseball games, golf and all the other things a person has today.

"I respect those in the past who observed the Sabbath, but what I want to know is how should we observe the Sabbath today as modern youth living in 20th century America. Can the Sabbath help us to be better Jews and better Americans?"

Rabbi Mayer smiled. "You have asked two significant questions, Bill, but instead of telling you what I think, suppose you and the members of the class do your own thinking about the ethical meaning of the Sabbath to modern Jewish youth. Anticipating our discussion, I have prepared a list of questions, and an account of how a person your age may observe the Sabbath today. After you have given your reactions, I want each of you to write an essay answering Bill's questions."

CHECK WHICH ITEMS ARE PROPER FOR THE SABBATH

1. The recitation of the *Kiddush* and the lighting of Sabbath candles
2. Attendance at the synagogue
3. Going to a show following Sabbath Morning Services
4. Visiting the sick
5. Doing homework for Religious School
6. Doing homework for Public School
7. Staying at home and listening to the radio, television or records
8. Sleeping
9. Playing baseball, basketball, golf or going swimming
10. Doing repairs and helping out at home
11. Going on a picnic with the family

12 Taking a ride in the car
13 Reading a Jewish book
14 Reading a mystery story for relaxation
15 Having a discussion with friends or family
16 Writing letters to relatives or friends
17 Writing letters for the sick or the blind as a deed of loving-kindness

A Modern Youth Observes the Sabbath

"All too often when we discuss the Sabbath, we try to set forth an idealistic picture of one who spends a complete day in Sabbath rest, prayer, meditation and study. There are very few young people today who observe the Sabbath in this way. Therefore, let's take an imaginary boy called Joseph, and follow him from Friday evening through Saturday to see how he observes the Sabbath.

"On Friday evening, Joseph puts on his finest clothes in preparation for the Sabbath meal. Gathered around the table, the family waits for mother to light the candles and recite the blessings. Joseph then lifts the wine cup and makes *Kiddush* with his father. The father blesses his wife and children, and then holding hands to symbolize the unity of the family, all pronounce the *Motzee* thanking God for food and sustenance. At the conclusion of a happy family dinner, they join in singing Sabbath songs. Then the family gets into the car and drives to the synagogue for Sabbath services. Following the services, the family visits friends or spends the remainder of the evening at home in quiet discussion. No quarrels are permitted to bring discord into the Sabbath peace. No other dates or plans ever interfere with the family night—which is Friday night.

"Since Joseph has attended services on Friday evening, he may or may not attend synagogue services Saturday morning. He will probably sleep late, and after a light brunch will play baseball, attend a show or go swimming with the gang. Returning home, he reads a book or looks at television until it is time for dinner. Following this he gets ready for his evening date."

QUESTIONS FOR DISCUSSION

1 How realistic is this imaginary day of Joseph's?

2 Is this a maximal, minimal or average observance of the Sabbath for modern youth?

3 What else should Joseph have done to observe the Sabbath properly?

4 Do you observe the Sabbath more or less than Joseph? Explain.

5 Do you think that modern youth should refrain from attending movies, playing baseball, swimming and looking at television on the Sabbath? What are your reasons?

6 How does the observance of the Sabbath help Joseph to learn more about Jewish ethical living?

7 Is Joseph being a good Jew by observing the Sabbath in the way described?

WHAT DO THE FOLLOWING STATEMENTS TEACH YOU ABOUT THE SABBATH?

The children of Israel shall keep the Sabbath, to observe the Sabbath throughout their generations as a perpetual covenant. It is a sign between Me and the children of Israel forever.

The Prayerbook (Exodus 31.16)

What is a covenant?
What is meant by "a sign"?

The Sabbath is one of the glories of our humanity. For if to labour is noble, of our own free will to pause in that labour which may lead to success, to money, to fame, is nobler still. To dedicate one day a week to rest and to God, this is the prerogative and the privilege of man alone."

C. G. MONTEFIORE

The Kiddush

Half of Judaism's most beautiful and meaningful rites do not take place in the synagogue. Rather, helping to make the home a *mikdash m'at*, a small sanctuary, they are performed within the bosom of the family. So every man is his own priest, every woman a priestess, officiating at the altar of the home.

The *Kiddush* is a prayer recited on the eves of the Sabbath and the holy days. It proclaims the holiness of the day set aside for worship and rest. The Sabbath *Kiddush* expresses gratitude to the Lord for his grace in finding Israel worthy of his favor and for the blessing of the Sabbath as a divine gift, and recalls the deliverance from Egypt. The chanted prayer tells of the double meaning of the Sabbath, historical and religious. As free men, on that day we rest. This is a privilege denied the slave. We also praise our God, for the Sabbath reminds us that the universe is not a product of blind chance, but His creation.

The Havdalah

Havdalah literally means separation or differentiation. Like the *Kiddush,* it is a home ceremony, marking the close of the Sabbath and the return of the week. While the prayer of joyful thanksgiving is chanted, a cup of wine or milk is held, a double-twisted taper is lit and the sweet odor of a fragrant spice-box is sniffed. In this beautiful way farewell is said to the Sabbath and welcome is given to the new workaday week.

The meaning of the *Havdalah* is found in the *Hamavdil* prayer, which expresses the separation the Lord has made between holy and profane, between light and darkness, between Israel and the nations that do not accept Him as their God. This is to impress us that when man remembers to live according to God's moral distinctions he is enacting the true *Havdalah*, for he is truly separating the holy from the profane.

RABBI MORRISON D. BIAL

If I were asked to single out one of the greatest historical institutions more essential for our preservation than all others, I would not hesitate to declare that it is the observance of the Sabbath. Without this, the home and the synagogue, the festivals and the holy days, the language and the history of our people will gradually disappear. If the Sabbath will be maintained by those who have observed it and will be restored to those who have abandoned it, then the permanence of Judaism is assured. CYRUS ADLER

WHAT DO YOU THINK?

1 What is your opinion of the truth of the last quotation?

2 If the Sabbath is "a day of delight," is it proper to have dances and parties in the synagogue on the Sabbath? Why?

3 Is it proper to attend High School parties and dances on the Sabbath?

4 Since most Americans observe Sunday as a day of rest and most stores are closed, do you think we should change the Jewish Sabbath from Saturday to Sunday? Why?

5 Do you think that a Christian living in the State of Israel where Saturday is observed as the Sabbath, has the same difficulties in observing his Sabbath as the American Jew has in observing the Sabbath in this country?

6 How can the observance of the Sabbath enable a person your age to obey the Still, Small Voice?

SOMETHING TO DO

Write an essay giving your answers to the questions:

1 How should modern youth observe the Sabbath?

2 Can the Sabbath help us to be better Jews and better Americans?

Are The High Holy Days Enough?

Sarah raised her hand. "I can understand why we should observe the High Holydays and the Sabbath," she said, "but shouldn't that be enough? Our temples are filled on the High Holydays, but how many attend services on the other festivals? Don't you think that this means that the average Jew doesn't regard the other festivals as important?"

Rabbi Mayer replied: "Before we say whether a Jewish festival is unimportant or not, don't you think we should see what each one teaches us about the Jewish way of life?

"To test yourself, write out the modern ethical meaning of 'The Three Festivals'—Sukos, Passover and Shavuos. After you have done this we will examine them and other festivals briefly.

Sukos—The Feast of Booths

"Don't think for a moment that we would be observing Sukos today if the only reason was to remember that our ancestors constructed temporary booths or huts in the wilderness. Surely there must be something to Sukos other than a reminder of the past. What do you think Sukos should mean to us today?"

Leonard said: "Isn't it the Jewish thanksgiving—when we express our gratitude to God for the bounties of the earth?"

"Yes, it is our Jewish thanksgiving. I'm sure you know that when the pilgrim fathers wished to find some way to express their gratitude to God, they turned to Leviticus, the 23rd Chapter, and after reading about the festival of Sukos, they ordained the American feast of Thanksgiving.

"But Sukos means more to us than thanksgiving. When we look

upon the frail *Suko* that is constructed so quickly and taken down so quickly, we are reminded of the brevity of human life. Life is so short that we must devote ourselves to values and ideals that are meaningful and not waste our years with trivial ambitions.

"There is something else that is taught. The tradition was for the entire family to leave the home and dwell and eat in the simple booth. This was to teach that the real essence of the home is not its size or its cost—but the love and devotion of the members of the family, one to the other. A home may be a mansion, or it may be a hut—but the holiness of the home is the family. If there are quarreling and dissension, the home may be a mansion, but it is a mansion of malice. If there is love, understanding and kindness, the booth becomes a hut of holiness. As the top of the *Suko* is open to permit the starlight of God to shine in, so the light of love and holiness must ever shine into our homes.

"Sukos also speaks to us of something extremely important for the future of mankind. The *Lulav* and the *Esrog* represent different types of people: the proud and the humble, the wise and the simple, those with beautiful appearance but no character, and those with beautiful appearance and good character. When we hold the *Lulav* and the *Esrog* together and wave them in all directions, it is to teach us the magnificent ideal of the unity of man. Even though there are different types of people, wherever men may live, in all parts of the world, all peoples must be bound together in brotherhood. Wherever we wave the *Lulav,* God is there—and as we believe that God is our Heavenly Father, Sukos reminds us that all men are God's children.

"So you see that Sukos means more than just constructing a booth, or remembering that our ancestors built temporary shelters in the wilderness. When we look upon the *Suko,* we are reminded of the Jewish thanksgiving and express our gratitude to God not only with words, but by giving to those in need. We remember how brief is the span of human life, and we try to live by the teachings of God. We think of the sanctity of the family and the holiness of the home, and try to act so that the light of God may shine into our lives. On Sukos, we hear the Still, Small Voice speaking to our hearts of Judaism's great ideal, the unity of all people, children of the one God.

"As Sukos comes to a close, we observe Simchas Torah, the rejoicing in the Law. It is at this time that we express our joy that God has given us the Torah. We march in a circle called *Hakafa*, to show that Judaism never ends, that the study of Torah is never completed. This joyous conclusion of Sukos is proof that Judaism is not to remind us of sadness alone, but of the joy of being a Jew, and the happiness that comes to us through the Torah.

"We need this festival of joy, especially today, when we are inclined to think of Judaism in terms of persecution, sadness or prejudice. 'The Torah is a tree of life to those who take hold of it—and those who support it are happy. Its ways are ways of pleasantness and all its paths are peace.'

"Throughout the entire festival, we are reminded by the Torah and the prayerbook, by the ritual and the symbols, that Sukos is to inspire us to Jewish ethical living. This is summarized in the story of a *Hasid* who asked the Dzikover Rabbi before Sukos to grant him a blessing so that he might have an exceptionally fine palm branch, *Esrog*, myrtle twigs and willows for the festival. The Rabbi replied: 'What you need for Sukos is a kind heart, a humble spirit, a truthful mind, and the will to perfect yourself. After you have attained these, it will be time to concern yourself regarding an exceptionally fine set of the symbols for Sukos.'

Passover—The Feast of Freedom

"All of us have attended a Seder and observed the Passover. We have been taught the history of Passover, the redemption of the children of Israel from slavery, and the crossing of the Red Sea. We have learned this by reading the Bible and the Hagaddah. But what does Passover mean to us today?

"To some people, Passover means good eating. To others, Passover is the festival when we don't eat bread. Passover should mean much more. On Passover, we join ourselves with the past, and participate in the stirring drama of freedom. We relive the time when we were slaves to Pharaoh, when we drank of bitter tears and ate the bread of affliction as we groaned under the sting of the taskmaster's lash. We were there when the children of Israel crossed the Red Sea to a new life and a new religious destiny. In the words of the Hagaddah, 'Each Jew must regard himself as though he had been redeemed from slavery in Egypt.'

"On Passover, we emphasize the sanctity of the home as the family is united at the Seder table. When we recite the story of the deliverance from Egypt, we not only identify ourselves with Jewish history, but we experience a renewal of family love and joy.

"Each Passover, the Jew hears the Still, Small Voice reminding him that there are millions of people shackled by oppression and enslaved by tyrants. In many parts of the world, men still cry and pray for freedom. Knowing that as long as men are enslaved by hatred, greed and tyranny, God's kingdom on earth cannot be established, the Jew prays in the words of the Hagaddah:

> *May He who broke Pharaoh's yoke forever shatter all fetters of oppression, and hasten the day when swords shall, at last, be broken and wars ended. Soon may He cause the glad tidings of redemption to be heard in all lands, so that mankind—freed from violence and from wrong, and united in an eternal covenant of brotherhood—may celebrate the universal Passover in the name of our God of freedom.*

"This is Passover's message to all mankind: The God of Freedom demands that we work in behalf of human rights and liberties in all lands. When any man is enslaved, we are enslaved. When God's children suffer the degradation of tyranny, we suffer with them.

Our mission as Jews is to bring God's commandments to all peoples so that there may be the universal Passover that will witness the liberation of all mankind.

"The real significance of Passover to us today must not be lost in the festivities of the Seder. We need Passover to remind us that the Jew must ever combat tyranny, resist oppression, and proclaim to the world that no society can endure if men are denied freedom.

"Do we need Passover today? As long as men are deprived of their rights because of their race or religious faith, we need Passover. As long as peoples are made slaves of dictator governments, we need the story of our liberation from slavery. As long as strangers are regarded with suspicion and hostility, we must remember to love the stranger, 'for ye were strangers in the land of Egypt.' As long as men despair of building a better world, we need Passover to direct our thoughts and our deeds to that glorious future when 'the earth shall be full of the knowledge of the Lord, as the waters cover the sea.' Through the inspiration of Passover, we renew our faith in the future and believe that the God who brought the children of Israel out of the house of bondage speaks to us today, as He did to our fathers, and commands us to dedicate ourselves to the building of His Kingdom of justice, brotherhood, and liberty for all."

WHAT DO THESE QUOTATIONS TELL US ABOUT THE FESTIVAL OF FREEDOM?

Passover affirms the great truth that liberty is the inalienable right of every human being.... Passover has a message also for the conscience and the heart of all mankind. For what does it commemorate? It commemorates the deliverance of a people from degrading slavery, from most foul and cruel tyranny. And so it is Israel's, nay, God's protest against unrighteousness, whether individual or national....

The world is thousands of years older than it was when the first Passover was celebrated, but the lessons taught by the ancient deliverance retain their original force. Injustice and cruelty have by no means vanished from the world. But Passover brands all such crimes as an abomination in the sight of God....

MORRIS JOSEPH
Judaism as Creed and Life

The Seder, too, has exerted great influence upon Christianity. In his book on Jewish contributions to civilization, Joseph Jacobs writes: "The central function of the church service, the Mass (or in Protestant churches, the Communion), derives its "elements" in the last resort, from the wine and unleavened bread used at the home service of the Passover; and Bickel (in *The Lord's Supper and the Passover Ritual)* has shown that the original ritual of the Mass is derived from that of the Seder service.

The Union Hagaddah

The disciples of an eminent Hasidic Rabbi were on their way to supervise the baking of Matzos. "What shall we look for, to make certain that these Matzos meet the dietary requirements?" they asked. The Rabbi replied: "Be certain that the women who bake the Matzos receive sufficient pay."

From Hasidic Literature

We recall at Passover that men can be enslaved to themselves. When men let vanity or emotion sway them to their discredit, when they permit harmful habits to tyrannize them, they are slaves. When indolence or fear keeps them from doing what they know in their hearts to be just—they are slaves. When ignorance, jealousy and bitterness blind their eyes, they are slaves to themselves. Men can be enslaved by the chains of their own forging as well as by poverty, inequality and intolerance....

Passover calls upon us to free ourselves from the injustices of our fellow men, and from the injustices we do to ourselves. It cries out for harmonious understanding among mankind, and for the end to the shackles of ignorance, jealousy, vanity and false ambition. It fervently denounces these bonds, which keep us from enjoying to the fullest our privilege and responsibility for continuing to grow in character, intellect and talent to the maximum of our capacity.

ROBERT MILLS

Shavuos—The Season of the Giving of the Law

When Rabbi Mayer came to the discussion of Shavuos, Paula said: "It seems to me that if it hadn't been for Confirmation, Shavuos might have died out as a Jewish festival. I've talked with others, and the only reason they can give for observing Shavuos is that Confirmation is held at that time. How much would Shavuos be observed today without Confirmation?"

"It is true, Paula, that without Confirmation our temples would not be filled on Shavuos, but should we judge the worth of a Jewish festival by the number of people who attend the services? This idea of numbers being a proof of success is a dangerous way of thinking. We are inclined to think in terms of large numbers; the size of a crowd, the thousands of people who jam into a stadium for a football game.

"How many great musicians, artists and poets do you think there are? How many scientists are there in comparison with the total population of a country? Progress is not always determined by the many, but more often by the few. God said to Israel: 'The Lord did not set His love upon you, nor choose you, because ye were more in number than any people—for ye were the fewest of all peoples—but because the Lord loved you.'

"Even though the people of Israel have been small in number, their contributions to the moral thinking of mankind are beyond our ability to estimate. So let's not look down upon the few—or think that because people neglect something, what they neglect may not be important.

"Shavuos is important to us because, according to tradition, it was at this time that Moses received the Ten Commandments and Israel accepted God's Torah, saying: 'We will do and we will obey!' The Decalogue, which has exerted a profound religious influence upon countless millions, came from a people few in number.

"Notice that Shavuos comes after Passover, the feast of liberation. It is through freedom that the children of Israel were able to advance to Sinai and receive God's law. Shavuos is known as the *zman matan Torah*, the season of the giving of the Law. Blessed with the freedom that America grants to its citizens, we pledge ourselves to live up to the teachings of the Torah. That is why we observe Confirmation at this season, as our boys and girls confirm their identity with the Jewish faith and promise to obey God's moral laws.

"According to Rabbi Meir, when God asked Israel for a pledge to guarantee loyalty to the Torah the children of Israel offered their possessions, their wise men and their elders, but God did not find these acceptable. Finally, when our people offered their children, God accepted the pledge and offered the Torah to Israel. Each year, as our confirmands consecrate themselves to the Torah, this promise made at Sinai is fulfilled.

"There is another reason why Shavuos is important to us today. The Talmud teaches that the Ten Commandments were given in the seventy languages of the seventy nations of the world, to teach us that the revelation of God belongs to all peoples. The Torah was given through Israel to all the nations and peoples of the world. Shavuos reminds us not only of the unity of God, but the sacred ideal of the unity of all mankind, and the hope that a day will come when all the earth will be obedient to the voice of God.

Purim—The Feast of Lots

"After Germany was defeated in World War II and the Nazi leaders were placed on trial for crimes against helpless civilians, many were found guilty, and some of them were sentenced to be hanged for the monstrous extermination of millions of innocent people. Among these leaders was the notorious Julius Streicher, Hitler's henchman, a man who directed the effort to defame the Jews and goad the people to destroy them. When the executioner placed a noose around his neck, just before the trap was sprung, he cried out wildly: 'Purim, 1946!'

"This is not a pleasant story," said Rabbi Mayer, "but neither is the tragic destruction of almost all the Jews of Europe, together with non-Jews who spoke for freedom and resisted the Nazi evil. It is a story we would like to forget, but just as our tradition insists that we must 'remember Amalek,' Pharaoh, Torquemada, and Haman who sought to destroy the people of Israel, so we must remember Hitler, Streicher, Stalin and all the mad dictators of history. We remember them not for reasons of vengeance, but rather to renew our faith that those who violate the moral laws of God will be vanquished, and that goodness, decency and truth must prevail.

"It is on Purim that we remember that 'not in one country alone nor in one age have violent men risen up against us, but in every generation and in every land, tyrants have sought to destroy us.' Tyrants have boasted that they would exterminate the people of God, but *am Yisroel chai*, 'the people of Israel lives,' and will continue to survive the dictators and tyrants of the present and the future."

"But I always thought that Purim was a time of fun and carnival," said Eldon. "This story of Hitler is sad and terrible. There's not much reason to celebrate the Hitler Purim, is there?"

"What you say is true, Eldon," Rabbi Mayer replied. "The Jews of Europe were not as fortunate as the Jews of Persia. Many of them defended themselves, and the heroism of the defenders of the Warsaw and Vilna ghettos will live forever. A handful of people defied the power of the Nazi military machine. Most of them were destroyed, but they showed the world that the human spirit cannot be conquered by force. But we continue to observe Purim to remind ourselves that Hitler did not prevail, that the evil was destroyed, and that the Jews have survived to continue their efforts to fulfill the destiny of a holy people.

"The other day I picked up a newspaper clipping. This is what I read:

> Berchtesgaden, Germany (WNS)—The former hunting lodge of Nazi leader Herman Goering was the scene of two four-day Torah Convocations held this week for American Jewish military men in this favorite town of Hitler's. The convocations, devoted to a better understanding of Judaism, were attended by more than 400 Jewish GI's and officers from U. S. Army and Air Force units throughout Europe.

"Can you imagine how the 400 Jewish men in the armed forces felt when they gathered together at Berchtesgaden where Hitler vowed that he would destroy the Jews? After placing a mezuzah on the doorposts of their barracks, they assembled for Sabbath worship. On the very spot where thousands of Nazis screamed their 'Sieg Heils,' hundreds of voices were lifted to God affirming the eternal watchword of the Jewish faith, *Shema Yisroel.* That night under the stars, do you know what song they sang during the *Oneg Shabbat?* It was '*Am Yisroel Chai,*' 'The People of Israel lives!'

"When Hitler was at the height of his power, who would have thought that he could ever be conquered? And yet, at the very time when it seemed that his triumph was inevitable, Jews read the Megillah during Purim and remembered what happened to Haman, and they were strengthened in their conviction that dictators must perish—even Hitler. Their belief in the utimate triumph of the moral law gave hope and courage to all peoples to resist the evil of Nazism.

"Even when Hitler was no more, and there were people who spoke with admiration about Stalin in Russia and believed that a Communist dictatorship would prevail, those who knew Jewish history could and did insist that his dictatorship, or any dictatorship, is a menace not only to Jews, but to human rights and human freedom everywhere. Stalin died, but other Russian dictators have sprung up to replace him.

"The story of Purim, repeated year after year, inspires us with the conviction that all dictators will be destroyed. No matter what kind of a dictatorship it may be, the tyranny of one man or a group of men over people is dangerous, and leads to slavery of body and mind. We have learned through our history that the kingdom of God can never be established by dictators, but only by people who are free–free to live up to the moral commandments of God.

"That is why Purim is important to us. It does more than commemorate what happened thousands of years ago in Persia. It is more than eating *hamantaschen* and celebrating with parties and carnivals. Purim warns against the dangers of idolatry, and teaches us that Jews should bow in reverence to no one but God. Purim is the Jewish message that tells the world to beware of dictators, and proclaims the belief in the final triumph of goodness over evil."

Hanuka–The Feast of Lights

"The Holydays and festivals enable Jews to relive historic and sacred experiences of the past," said Rabbi Mayer, "but they also speak to us of our ethical obligations and moral responsibilities for the present and the future.

"A good example of this is Hanuka. If we think that the sole purpose of Hanuka is to light candles, then we forget the real meaning of the Feast of Lights.

"It really isn't important whether the story of the cruse of oil is a legend or not. We know that the Maccabees did fight for religious freedom. They refused to yield to idolatry and give up their worship of the God of holiness. They refused to bow down to pagan images and participate in heathen worship. Other nations surrendered politically and religiously, but the Jews were determined to fight for and win their religious freedom. By resisting the Syrians, removing the pagan idols from the Temple and rededicating it to the worship of the God of justice and holiness, they taught future generations that Jews must resist idolatry in every age, and rededicate themselves to their holy faith in every generation. The lighting of the cruse of oil was a symbol of the fight against darkness, and Israel's dedication to light, justice and truth.

"And so on the Feast of Lights, we see the gleaming Hanuka candles as symbols reminding us that each Jew must be identified with light—the light of freedom, of decency, of justice. God's first command was 'Let there be light,' and that command has been sacred to the Jew. Throughout the ages, we have declared with the Psalmist 'The Lord is my light and my salvation.' In every period of history, we have sought direction from God praying: 'Oh send forth Thy light and Thy truth, and let them lead me.' The prophet summoned Jews in every generation, 'O House of Jacob, come ye, and let us walk in the light of the Lord.' Every Jew must remember the mission of Israel: 'to be a covenant of the peoples and a light unto the nations.'

"On Hanuka we relive the struggle of the Maccabees for religious freedom, and remember the light they kindled by their devotion to God. We are inspired to rededicate ourselves to the moral law, to identify ourselves with light, and to resist the darkness of ignorance, evil, prejudice, and hatred.

"We conclude our discussion of Hanuka with this story from *Hasidic* tradition. It concerns the pupils of an eminent rabbi who approached him with a complaint about the existence of so much evil in the world. When they asked their rabbi to advise them how to drive out the forces of darkness, he suggested that they take brooms and attempt to sweep the darkness from the cellar. The bewildered pupils went down to the cellar and attempted to sweep out the darkness. When this failed, they again approached their teacher, and he advised them to take sticks and beat vigorously at the darkness. They did so, but to no avail. The rabbi then suggested that they descend into the cellar and shout at the darkness, and curse it, and protest loudly against it. When this likewise failed, he said: 'My children, let each of you meet the challenge of darkness by lighting a candle.' The students descended to the cellar and kindled their lights. They looked, and behold! The darkness had been driven out! Each year, it is through the Feast of Lights that we renew our devotion to light, and revitalize ourselves for the battle against darkness."

QUESTIONS FOR DISCUSSION

1 What is meant by this statement in the High Holyday Prayerbook: "The great shofar is sounded and a still, small voice is heard"?

2 What does this tell us about the Jewish idea of repentance: "Thou desirest not the death of the sinner but that he return from his evil way and live"?

3 Jewish tradition teaches that a sinner who repents is more pleasing to God than one who has never sinned. What is your opinion?

4 Why do you think the story of Jonah is read as the Haftora on Yom Kippur?

5 Should we forgive Nazis and Communists who say they have repented of their sins and beliefs?

6 A 19th Century Jewish Leader, Judah Leib Gordon, advised: "Be a Jew at home and be a man abroad." What did he mean? Do you agree or disagree?

7 A modern Jewish poet told of his home life and stated: "There was no mark of Judaism in my childhood home except for a silver ceremonial goblet.... There was not a trace of Jewish culture that I could feel—no stories, no songs, no special food—but then there was no cultural background that could make itself felt. I grew up among a group of Jews who wished more than anything else, I think, to be invisible...." To what extent do we have invisible Jews today? Give examples.

8 What are your reasons for or against joint holyday observances in the public schools, such as Christmas-Hanuka programs, and Easter-Passover programs?

9 A rabbi adorned himself with a beard and flowing robes and called himself Uncle Judah as he distributed gifts to children on Hanuka. He thinks that this is a Jewish answer to the Christian Santa Claus. What do you think?

10 There are some people who say that we don't need symbols and ceremonies to remind us of Jewish ideals. What would be your answer to them?

11 Suppose a man takes the American flag, throws it to the ground, and presses it into the mud. When a crowd gathers and expresses anger, he says: "Why get so agitated? This is only cloth with color and design." How would the crowd react? What would you say to him if you were present?

Suppose a man takes the Torah Scroll and throws it to the floor in your presence. When you become angry he says: "Why become angry? This is only parchment on rollers with words." What would you say to him?

How would you apply this to the symbols and observances of Jewish holydays and festivals?

THINGS TO DO

1 Write an essay on the history and significance of the Kol Nidre.

2 Read through the Afternoon Service for the Day of Atonement and record the ideas that show the ethical requirements of Judaism.

3 Read the *Avinu Malkenu*, 'Our Father, our King,' prayers in the High Holyday Prayerbook and then tell why you think these prayers have meant so much to the Jews throughout the ages. What do they mean to us today?

4 Give an example of sincere repentance in the life of a prominent person.

5 State the meaning and significance of:

a The extra soul given to us on the Sabbath

b *Mitzvah*

c *Oneg Shabbat*

d Ten Days of Penitence

e The Sambatyon River

6 Write to the American Jewish Congress, 15 E. 84th Street, New York, and the Anti-Defamation League of B'nai B'rith, 515 Madison Avenue, New York 22, New York, to find out their reactions to joint holyday programs in the public schools.

7 Write an essay on the heroism of the Warsaw ghetto.

8 Write an essay describing the relationship of the Jewish holydays and festivals to the home.

9 List the differences in the Orthodox, Conservative and Reform observance of the holydays and festivals. Are the ethical ideals different or the same?

SELECTED QUOTATIONS

The Influence of the Sabbath

The Sabbath is a genuinely Jewish institution. It arose in the dim and hazy past; it came down through the centuries. It engraved itself upon the hearts of our people generation after generation. It sustained and supported the souls in Israel more than any other Jewish observance. It was the sanctified rest day for generations that knew only bitter travail and toil for the remainder of the week. It healed hearts that were broken, it banished despair, it brought hope when all sign of hope seemed completely gone. It stimulated singing in the midst of sorrow. It engendered joy while life was in grave jeopardy.

RABBI SAMUEL H. MARKOWITZ

Goodbye, God

The story is told of the little girl who spent a week with her grandparents. She came from a "modern," unobservant home and she delighted in the beauty of the Jewish ways revealed to her for the first time in the home of the older folks. They recited the traditional blessing over the bread at each meal; they blessed the candles on Sabbath eve, and they chanted the old words of the *Kiddush* before drinking the heavy, sweet wine. What child could fail to be impressed by such piety?

When the time came to leave, the child took a tearstained leave of her mother's parents. "Goodbye, Grandma, goodbye Grandpa," she said. "Goodbye, religion, goodbye, God."

Many of our children grow up in homes where the amenities of the Jewish faith have been abandoned. While their physical and cultural needs are catered to, their spiritual yearnings go unrecognized. Some parents have yet to learn this fact of life: Man does not live by bread alone.

RABBI ABRAM VOSSEN GOODMAN

Thanksgiving and Sucos

The Thanksgiving Day that Americans celebrate was first observed as a harvest holiday in 1621 by the Pilgrim men and women who had survived their first terrible winter on the Massachusetts coast at Plymouth. The Pilgrims were deeply religious people and they were familiar with the Bible's description of the harvest festival of Sucos. When their pastor, John Robinson, spoke to them of the Jewish holiday, they compared their hardships with the struggles of the Jews in ancient Palestine, and as the Jews do on Sucos, offered thanks for their bountiful harvest.

Today we have even more to be thankful for than did the early Pilgrims. We have the freedom they sought, and none of their hardships. Our harvest is bountiful, our country united. For this we offer thanks to God on Thanksgiving Day.

World Over

The Real Miracle of Chanukah

How could they (the nations) know the miracle of Israel's history? How could they understand that the light of the rededicated Temple was a promise and a declaration that Hanuka never ends; that Israel never dies; that the *Ner Tamid*...burning in the hearts of however few, is brighter than all artificial glittering enthusiasm; that though the tempests may do their worst, they cannot quench this fire.

RABBI LEO JUNG

Aiding the Needy

Purim comes as a ray of light and salvation.... The timely deliverance of the Jews from the Persian enemies, and their vindication, are celebrated as a "feasting and gladness, and sending portions to one another, and gifts to the poor." The Jew gives expression to his joyful gratitude by aiding the needy....

RABBI PHILIP GOODMAN

Passover and Freedom

Passover is the Festival of Spring....But it is an historical festival—Israel's birthday—as the annual commemoration of an event which has changed the destiny of mankind, and it proclaims the man-redeeming truth that God is the God of freedom. Even as in Egypt He espoused the cause of brick-making helots against the mighty royal oppressor. He forever judgeth the world in righteousness and the peoples with equity. There is an overruling Providence that exalts righteousness and freedom and humbles the dominion of iniquity and oppression. This teaching has been as a light unto the nations of the western world in their weary, age-long warfare for liberty.

RABBI JOSEPH H. HERTZ

The Protest of the Angels

When God was about to give Israel the Torah, according to rabbinic lore, the angels protested. "Man is impure, unreliable; he will not fulfill the commandments. But we are holy and ever-faithful. Pray, give us the Torah; we will always obey it." "For that reason," replied the Almighty, "I will not give it to you. You do not need My law. But man cannot live without it." "Not perfection," said the rabbis, "but the right way; not sure knowledge of the final rewards, but enough light to see God's way, is what man needs."

RABBI PHILIP BERNSTEIN

The Class Room and the Living Room

It would be well nigh a miracle if the Jewish school could make loyal Jews out of children whose parents never go to services, never observe a single Jewish ceremony, never participate in Jewish affairs. The Jewish school's greatest success is with the children of parents who themselves are committed to Judaism. Its most frequent failures are among those whose homes are sealed off from all Jewish interest and observances....

The answers to some of the Jewish school's problems lie not in the class rooms, but in many a living room....

RABBI DAVID POLISH

The Voice of Mitzvoth

A definition or paraphrase of the word "mitzvah" is difficult to frame. In other languages there are separate words for the different meanings which in Hebrew are conveyed by the single word mitzvah. It denotes not only commandment, but also the law, man's obligation or the deed, particularly as an act of benevolence or charity.

Its meanings range from the acts performed by the high priest in the Temple to the most humble gesture of kindness to one's fellow man, from acts of external performance to inner attitudes, in relation to others as well as in relation to oneself. It is often used in the wide sense of "religion" or "religious." It combines all levels of human and spiritual living. Every act done in agreement with the will of God is a mitzvah.

RABBI ABRAHAM HESCHEL

SUGGESTED READINGS

For The Student

Edidin, Ben M., *Jewish Customs and Ceremonies*
Golden, H., *Treasury of Jewish Holydays*
Goodman, Philip, *The Purim Anthology, pp. 125-141*
Joseph, Morris, *Judaism As Creed and Life*
Millgram, Abraham, *Sabbath*
Segal, Samuel M., *The Sabbath Book*
Solis-Cohen, Emily, *Hanukkah*
Universal Jewish Encyclopedia, Vol. 5, pp. 410-416

For The Teacher

Agnon, S. Y., *Days of Awe*
Bettan, Israel, *The Five Scrolls*
Gaster, Theodor H., *Festivals of the Jewish Year*
Gaster, Theodor H., *New Year: Its History, Customs and Superstitions*
Goodman, Philip, *Rejoice In Thy Festival*

Heschel, Abraham J., *The Sabbath—Its Meaning for Modern Man*
Idelsohn, A. Z., *The Ceremonies of Judaism*
Markovitz, Samuel, *Leading a Jewish Life in the Modern World*, pp. 83-295
Schauss, Hayyim, *The Jewish Festivals*

4

THE VOICE OF JEWISH LAW

The Ethics of the Codes

The Problem

Rabbi Mayer's secretary came into his office to tell him that Alan Gordon would like to see him. "By the way," she said, "there is a young lady with him."

"Ask Alan and the young lady to come in," said the Rabbi. "I haven't seen Alan since he was Confirmed about eight years ago."

Alan Gordon and a young woman he introduced as Betty Fox came into the study. After the usual greetings Alan said, "Rabbi, I have come to see you about getting married, but I want you to know that Betty is not of the Jewish faith. She is a very ardent church member. We had talked about getting married by a Justice of the

Peace, but Betty and I agree that we want a religious ceremony. Frankly, Betty wanted her minister to officiate, but I feel that a rabbi should marry us—and she has consented to a Jewish ceremony."

Rabbi Mayer paused a moment, and said, "Alan, I think you know my opinion that for the sake of a united home, both of you should be of the same faith."

"I know your views, Rabbi," said Alan, "and Betty and I have discussed them. It doesn't seem fair to ask Betty to give up her faith, and I certainly don't want to give up mine. Since we love each other so much, we feel that we will be able to work out any difficulties and have a happy home. We are in love, and we are going to get married. Her parents object, and my parents object. We are sorry about this, but our love is bigger than parental objection, religious differences, or anything else. Everything would be so much easier if you would officiate at our marriage and give us your blessing. Will you do it?"

WHAT DO YOU THINK?

1 If you were the Rabbi, what would you have said to Alan? What would you have said to Betty?

2 Do you think that rabbis should officiate at the marriage of a Jew and a Christian? What are your reasons?

3 What would Rabbi Mayer have done if Betty had been willing to accept the Jewish faith?

4 How is a Christian converted to Judaism?

5 Is it easier and more practical for a Christian to become a Jew, than for a Jew to become a Christian?

6 If your community didn't have a rabbi, and someone asked you whether Judaism permits the marriage of Christians and Jews, how would you go about finding the answer to the question?

Was the Rabbi Right?

Several weeks after the young couple had visited the Rabbi, Gilbert said in class: "May I ask you a question?"

"Certainly, Gilbert," the Rabbi replied. "What is it?"

"Well, maybe it's none of my business, but I have heard a lot of discussion about mixed marriage lately. Do you remember when Alan Gordon came to see you and wanted you to officiate at his marriage?"

"I remember very well, Gilbert," said the Rabbi.

"The other night, I heard a discussion about your decision. My parents had some friends visiting and there was quite a debate. Some thought you were right in refusing to marry the couple. Others said that since the young lady was willing to be married by a rabbi, you should have officiated. By saying 'no' and refusing, you may have turned both away from Judaism. What I want to know is..." Gilbert hesitated.

"Go on, Gil. It's perfectly all right for you to ask."

"What I want to know," continued Gilbert, "is on what basis you made your decision. Is it your own opinion, or is there a Jewish law that tells you what to do?"

"I'm glad you asked that question, because it is important. Most rabbis will not officiate at mixed marriages, that is, the marriage of people of different faiths, because of their belief that there must be a united home in order to achieve happiness. Frequently, there are problems in determining what religious faith the children shall follow. When there is a conversion to the Jewish faith, however, then it is no longer a mixed marriage. The Christian has accepted Judaism and the Rabbi is officiating at the marriage of two Jews."

"Jewish law and tradition are opposed to rabbis officiating at mixed marriages. That is the law, and therefore I could not officiate."

The Jewish Codes

"But what does a rabbi do when he doesn't know the answer to a question of Jewish law?" Gilbert asked.

"If it is a question he can't answer with certainty," said Rabbi

Mayer, "he searches through the codes of Jewish law to find out what authorities have stated in the past."

"Codes?" Gilbert frowned questioningly. "Is that a secret way of writing, like the codes used by Army Intelligence?"

"Not that kind of a code, Gilbert, although it does sound mysterious. A Jewish code is a book or a collection of books dealing with Jewish law. It determines the correct way of practicing Judaism. Let me describe the various types of Jewish codes.

"The earliest of the Jewish codes are the legal portions of the Torah, such as the Book of the Covenant (Ex. 21 to 23), the Deuteronomic Code (Deut. 12 to 26), the Holiness Code (Lev. 17 to 26) and the Priestly Code (Ex. 25 to Numbers 10). In the year 135 C.E., Rabbi Akiba classified the laws of the Torah as well as the additional laws established by the scholars. This code was known as the Mishna and was completed by Judah Hanasi about 200 C.E.

"The Talmud is also a code of Jewish Law, but the laws were not always clearly or specifically explained in the Talmud. That is why there are many commentaries offering explanations. Frequently, laws that really should have been placed together were widely separated in the Talmud. Scholars grouped the laws together and attempted to explain how they should be interpreted and applied. These groupings and explanations were known as codes.

"There were other codes, but it wasn't until the time of Maimonides in the 12th century that a new system of codification was offered. Maimonides' *Mishneh Torah* organized the whole of Jewish law. The next important code to challenge the *Mishneh Torah* was compiled by Jacob ben Asher (1269-1343), and was called the *Tur*, which means "row." It was divided into four sections.

"In the 16th century, Joseph Caro attempted to popularize this scholarly work, and make it available and understandable to the average person. His code was called the *Shulhan Aruch* (Prepared Table). Later Moses Isserles added his commentary called *Mappah*, or "tablecloth." The *Shulhan Aruch* and the *Mappah* together became the code of Orthodox Judaism, and it is regarded as the authoritative code of Jewish law to this day.

"I'm sure that some of you are wondering what Jewish codes have to do with the Still, Small Voice, or with modern Jewish life," said Rabbi Mayer. "Perhaps you are even more perplexed as to why I should discuss this in connection with my refusal to officiate at a mixed marriage.

"The decisions that a rabbi makes should depend upon the spirit of Jewish law. In order for modern rabbis to determine what is right or wrong, and in order for us to know the Jewish way, we must look back to the teachings revealed in the Jewish codes.

The Mishna

"These are the six orders of the Mishna:

1 *Zera'im (Seeds).* This deals with prayer, the rights of the poor, and regulations concerning offerings and tithes.

2 *Mo'ed (Festivals).* Here we find laws dealing with the Sabbath, festivals and holydays.

3 *Nashim (Women).* Jewish law specifies the rights of women, marriage, divorce, property settlements and the holiness of the Jewish home.

4 *Nezikim (Injuries).* Every aspect of life is regarded as part of Judaism. Rules and regulations concerning injuries, compensation for damages, sales, leases, civil and criminal law and oaths are given in detail as religious teaching. The most famous section of the Mishna, *Pirke Avoth,* The Ethics of the Fathers, is found here.

5 *Kadoshim (Holy Things).* This deals with laws related to sacrifices, punishment and excommunication. Holiness is to be achieved through the daily practice of Jewish observances and Jewish ethics.

6 *Tohorot (Purifications)*. Even such matters as purifying utensils were considered to be part of Jewish law. Other matters included were: purification of dead bodies, leprosy, ritual bath, and personal cleanliness. . . .

Law and Ethics

"You look puzzled, Miriam. Do you have a question?" asked Rabbi Mayer.

"I was wondering," Miriam said, "what all of this has to do with ethics and the Jewish way of life. It sounds so legal."

"It is legal, Miriam. It is important to understand that Judaism never considered religion as something separate from life and the every-day problems of the people. Every act of life brings us closer or takes us farther away from God. Jewish law was related to ethics, because the purpose of the law was to help the people understand and obey the Still, Small Voice.

"Here are examples of how a legal code such as the Mishna deals with Judaism as an ethical way of life. Instead of explaining them to you, I want you to analyze these statements and apply them to Jewish life today."

FROM THE MISHNA

These are things for which no measure is prescribed: *Peah*, First-fruits, the Festival Offering, deeds of loving-kindness and the study of the law. These are things whose fruits a man enjoys in this world while the capital is laid up for him in the world to come: honoring father and mother, deeds of loving-kindness, making peace between a man and his fellow; and the study of the Law is equal to them all. (Berakoth)

Rabbi Eliezer says: He that makes his prayer a fixed task, his prayer is no supplication. Rabbi Joshua says: He that journeys in a place of danger should pray a short prayer, saying, "Save, O Lord, the remnant of Israel; at their every cross-road let their needs come before thee. Blessed art thou, O Lord, that hearest prayer!" (Berakoth)

If a man wounded his fellow he thereby becomes liable on five counts: for injury, for pain, for healing, for loss of time, and for indignity inflicted. "For injury"—thus, if he blinded his fellow's eye, cut off his hand, or broke his foot, [his fellow] is looked upon as if he was a slave to be sold in the market: they assess how much he was worth and how much he is worth now. "For pain"—thus, if he burnt his fellow with a spit or a nail, even though it was on his finger-nail where it leaves no wound, they estimate how much money such a man would be willing to take to suffer so. (Baba Kamma)

The Mishneh Torah

"In other words," said Lee, "Jewish law considers how to apply justice and righteousness to the ordinary deeds of every-day life."

"Exactly, Lee." Rabbi Mayer opened a large volume. "This is part of the *Mishneh Torah*, compiled by Maimonides. It proves Lee's point. Completed in 1180, it took Maimonides ten years to write. In over one thousand chapters the Rambam, as Maimonides was called, attempts to show the people how they may apply the teachings of the Still, Small Voice to life. The *Mishneh Torah* includes:

I. *Book of Knowledge*
Fundamental Principles of Judaism

II. *Book of Love*
Prayer and other Personal Observances

III. *Book of Seasons*
The Sabbath, Fasts and Feasts

IV. *Book of Women*
Marriage, Divorce, etc.

V. *Book of Holiness*
Forbidden Foods and Illicit Unions

VI. *Book of Distinct Utterances*
Vows and Oaths

VII. *Book of Seeds*
The Land and its Produce; Tithes, Jubilee, etc.

VIII. *Book of Service*
The Temple of Service

IX. *Book of Offerings*
Private Sacrifices at the Temple

X. *Book of Uncleanness*
Ritual Defilement

XI. *Book of Harms*
Harm to Person and Property

XII. *Book of Property*
Purchase and Acquisition of Title

XIII. *Book of Civil Laws*
Bailments; Debt; Claims; Inheritance

XIV. *Book of Judges*
The Sanhedrin; Evidence; the Monarch;
Mourning and other topics.

"Maimonides' code begins with these words: 'The foundation of foundations and the pillar of all Wisdom is the recognition that an original Being exists, who called all creatures into existence; for the recognition of this thing is a positive command, and is the great principle on which all things stand.' Beginning with God, the *Mishneh Torah* proceeds on its way, codifying the 'philosophical, the ethical, and ceremonial sides, and also the emotional side of Judaism as expressed in its Messianic ideals,' until it closes with the fervent hope for the time when 'the earth will be filled with the knowledge of God as the waters cover the sea.'

Eight Degrees of Charity

"During the last assembly, we discussed our charity collections, and I wonder if you remember the name for charity in the Jewish tradition. Burton, do you remember?"

"You said that the real meaning is *Tzedakah*, justice. It isn't just handing out money to the poor as charity—but rather doing what is just and right for our fellow human-beings."

"The reason I wanted to know whether or not you understood this is because Maimonides sums up eight degrees of charity—the Jewish attitude in giving to the poor and needy. He says:

> There are eight degrees of alms-giving, one higher than the other: Supreme above all is to give assistance to a fellow Jew who has fallen on evil times by presenting him with a gift or loan, or entering into partnership with him, or procuring him work, thereby helping him to become self-supporting.
>
> Inferior to this is giving charity to the poor in such a way that the giver and the recipient are unknown to each other. This is, indeed, the performance of a commandment from disinterested motives and it is exemplified by the Institution of the Chamber of the Silent which existed in the Temple, where the righteous secretly deposited their alms and the respectable poor were secretly assisted.
>
> Below this degree is the instance where the donor is aware to whom he is giving the alms but the recipient is unaware from whom he received them; as, the great Sages who used to go about secretly throwing money through the doors of the poor. This is quite a proper course to adopt and a great virtue where the administrators of a charitable fund are not acting fairly.
>
> Inferior to this degree is the case where the recipient knows the identity of the donor, but not vice versa; as, the great sages who used to tie

sums of money in linen bundles and throw them behind their backs for poor men to pick up, so that they should not feel shame.

The next four degrees in their order are: the man who gives money to the poor before he is asked; the man who gives money to the poor after he is asked; the man who gives less than he should, but does it with good grace; and lastly, he who gives grudgingly.

From the *Yad Hachazakah.*

The Shulhan Aruch

"There were many codes of Jewish Law, but few exerted such a powerful influence upon the Jewish people as Joseph Caro's *Shulhan Aruch.* It was supposed to be a popularization of his earlier code of law called the *Beth Yosef.* Only the scholars studied the *Beth Yosef,* but the people looked to the *Shulhan Aruch* as the guide to Jewish living. It told them how and when to pray, and the proper way to observe the Sabbath, festivals and holydays. Whenever there was any question of Jewish practice, the Prepared Table was consulted. Strangely enough, Caro wrote it for those who were too ignorant to understand the *Beth Yosef,* and for 'young students.'

"Modeled after the *Tur* of Jacob ben Ashur, the *Shulhan Aruch* is divided into four parts: *Orah Hayim* (Way of Life) containing the regulations about the fringes *(tzitzith),* phylacteries *(tefillin),* prayers, synagogue, benedictions, Sabbath and festivals; *Yoreh Deah* (Teaching Knowledge), dealing with ritual slaughtering, dietary laws, idolatry, interest, purity vows, respect for parents and teachers, circumcision, the sick, the dying and mourning observances; *Eben Haezer* (the Stone of Help) laws relating to marriage and divorce; and, *Hoshen Hamishpat* (Breastplate of Judgment) covering civil and criminal law.

"In the Prepared Table, as in other codes of Jewish Law, we see the practical application of Judaism to assist the poor, pursue justice and righteousness, and learn to obey the moral and ethical commandments of God revealed in the Torah."

THINGS TO DO

Apply the following statements from the Shulhan Aruch to present day Jewish life:

Charity

It is forbidden to turn away the poor, who begs empty handed, even if you give only one dried fig, for it is said: "Oh let not the oppressed return confounded" (Ps. lxxiv, 21). If you have naught in your possession to give him, then appease him with words. It is forbidden to rebuke a poor man or to raise an angry voice against him for his heart is broken and humble; and lo it is said: "A broken and a contrite heart, O God, wilt Thou not despise" (Ps. li, 19). Woe unto him who has put the poor to shame. One should be as a father unto him, both in tender mercy and in words for it is said: "I was a father to the needy." (Job. xxix, 16)

Generosity

He who desires to make himself worthy must suppress his evil passions and open wide his hand, and see that everything he does for the glory of God, shall be of the best. If he build a synagogue, it must be more beautiful than his own home; when he feeds the hungry, he must feed them with the best food from his table; when he clothes the naked, he must clothe them with his best garments, and when he consecrates a thing, he should consecrate his best possession.

Eating

Therefore the man who is desirous of preserving his physical health must take care to adopt the golden mean in eating, depending upon the nature of his body, neither too little nor too excessive. Most maladies which befall men arise either from unwholesome food or from excessive eating even of wholesome food.

Anger

Anger is likewise an extremely bad vice, and it is proper that one should keep away from it, and he should accustom himself not to get angry even at things that he needs become angry. But when necessary to exercise his authority over his children and his household, he may pretend to be angry in their presence in order to chastise them, while inwardly he should retain his composure. Said Elijah to Rabbi Judah, "Do not become angry and you will not sin; do not become intoxicated and you will not sin." Again said our rabbis, of blessed memory, "he who becomes angry it is accounted to him as if he had worshipped idols."

Theft and Robbery

It is forbidden to buy from a thief or a robber the article which has been robbed, and it is immaterial whether he be a Jew or a non-Jew, for the latter is bound by the commandment prohibiting theft and robbery. It is a serious transgression to buy from the thief or robber for this only encourages the wrong-doer, and with reference thereto it is said: "Whoso is partner with a thief hateth his own soul" (Prov. xxix, 24), causing the thief to steal again, for he will desist if he find no purchaser. Although the thief could take the stolen article to a place where he would not be known, still this course is not a likely one.

It is forbidden to derive even the slightest benefit from the property that was stolen or robbed as long as it remains in the hands of the thief or the robber. Even if the theft be insignificant so that the owner would not be concerned at his loss, e.g., to change currency for the money that was stolen or robbed, it is forbidden to do this. It is also forbidden to enter a house that was robbed, on account of the heat or rain, or to pass through a field which was acquired by robbery.

Consideration for One's Neighbor

One must take care not to throw pieces of broken glass or the like in any place where they can cause harm to anybody.

If one's neighbor have a headache which would be aggravated by the noise of hammering, then it is forbidden even in one's own house to pound grains of corn or anything like it whereby the noise of hammering will reach his neighbor's house and annoy him.

There are many other things relating to damages to one's neighbor or to the general public, but the general rule is this. It is forbidden to do anything, even on one's own premises and especially on a public thoroughfare, that may cause any damage to one's neighbor or to the wayfarer on the public highway.

When one sees his neighbor in distress and it is in his power to save him, or he can employ others to save him, it is his own duty to make strenuous efforts or to employ others in order to save him.

Marriage

A man ought always to strive to win in marriage the daughter of a Torah scholar, and to give his daughter in marriage to a Torah scholar. If he cannot find the daughter of a Torah scholar, let him seek to marry the daughter of renowned communal leaders; if he cannot find one of these, let his choice be the daughter of a congregational leader; if not one of these, then the trustee of a charitable fund; if not one of these, let him select the daughter of an elementary Hebrew teacher, but let him not marry off his daughter to an ignorant man. This means one who is so ignorant that he is indifferent in obedience to the commandments of our faith....

Be Strong to Obey the Will of God

It is therefore incumbent upon every man to strengthen himself like a lion. Immediately upon awakening from his sleep he must rise quickly, and be ready to serve his Creator, blessed be He, before the evil inclination is given an opportunity to prevail over him with the claims and designs not to rise. In the winter, for instance, the evil inclination attempts to persuade him with the subtle argument: "How can you rise now so early in the morning when the cold is so intense?" In the summer he uses this argument: "How can you rise now when you have not had sufficient sleep?" or with other pretensions. For the evil inclination well knows how to catch man in his net so that he shall neglect to rise. Therefore every man who fears and trembles at the word of God, must overcome him and disobey him. Even when it is burdensome for him to rise because of heaviness of body or because of habitual laziness, he shall make it as his aim to fulfill the will of the supreme King of kings.

The Significance of the Shulhan Aruch Today

When the class had completed the discussion of the statements from the *Shulhan Aruch*, Rabbi Mayer said: "I wonder if you realize that this code of Jewish law written in the 16th century is authoritative for Orthodox Judaism to this day?"

Eleanor didn't seem convinced. "It's hard for me to believe," she said, "that the ritual commandments and practices that applied so long ago could still be today's authority. I can understand how moral laws might apply in any age, but that all Jews still regard the Prepared Table as the authority, I just can't see."

"I didn't say *all* Jews, Eleanor," answered Rabbi Mayer. "I said *Orthodox* Judaism still regards the *Shulhan Aruch* as binding."

"Does that mean Conservative and Reform Judaism don't abide by it?" Eleanor asked.

"Conservative Judaism still looks upon the *Shulhan Aruch* as the guide for Jewish practice," said the Rabbi. "But not all of the laws and practices are strictly observed. There have been modifications, but Conservative Judaism still regards the *Shulhan Aruch* as an extremely important code of Jewish law."

"Well, then, what about Reform Judaism? Does it accept the Prepared Table as authoritative?" asked Gilbert.

"No, Gilbert," said Rabbi Mayer. "That is why Reform Judaism has modified and changed some of the practices. Reform Judaism insists that the moral laws of God are authoritative, but that the laws of the *Shulhan Aruch* are man-made, and may be changed or eliminated altogether."

"In that case," Gilbert said, "I don't see how the Conservative or the Reform rabbi can decide on questions of Jewish practice. Suppose there are new problems that come up in modern times. How does he decide?"

Rabbi Mayer smiled. "That is a good question. Conservative and Reform rabbis meet at their Rabbinical Conferences to discuss and decide on matters of Jewish law and practice. They try to make their decisions consistent with the spirit of Judaism, past and present.

Responsa Literature

"Earlier in our discussion, Gilbert asked me what I would do in case I didn't know the answer to a question of Jewish law. I said that I would look it up in the codes. But suppose a rabbi can't find the answer in the codes? Suppose a situation arises that had never been considered by his Rabbinical Conference, what should the rabbi do?"

Esther raised her hand. "It would seem to me," she said, "that the rabbi would consult with some outstanding scholars on Jewish law."

"You are right, Esther," said Rabbi Mayer.

"That's exactly what happened in the past, and that is still being done to this day. The rabbi writes to scholars who are experts in Jewish law. The experts give him their answers. This question and answer *(sheelot u-teshuvot)* correspondence was and is still known as a *Responsum.*

"In the Talmud there are references to letters from scholars in Palestine who wrote to the authorities in Babylonia for answers to questions of Jewish law. In Babylonia, there were the academies of learning of Sura and Pumpeditha. The chief teachers had the title of *Gaon* which means Eminence. From every country where Jews lived questions came to the *geonim.* In time, the answers, the *responsa,* of the *geonim,* were accepted as the correct interpretations of the law. It is difficult for us to imagine how much it meant to the scattered Jews to know that there was an authoritative decision that could be made about the problems that confronted them. The correspondence continued through the centuries. Even when the schools of Sura and Pumpeditha were no more, and the *geonim* had ceased to be, the Jews continued to write to the leading rabbinic authorities wherever they might be for decisions on Jewish laws.

"Rabbi Solomon Freehof in his book, *The Responsa Literature*, tells us that as Jewish life developed in the various countries, historical, political and economic changes raised new questions. As the number of talmudic scholars, teachers of *yeshivot*, communal rabbis, increased, so did the number of *responsa* writers. There are by now about fifteen hundred books dealing with *responsa* alone and perhaps five hundred more which deal primarily with other branches of rabbinic literature but also contain a number of *responsa*.

"This *responsa* literature has continued to the present and whenever a rabbi has a question he cannot answer, he writes to the Responsa Committee of his Rabbinical Conference. The answer he receives, a *responsum*, will help him make his decision in the spirit of Jewish tradition.

"In order that you may understand the practical use of this literature, let us consider some of the responsa:

The Responsa of the Past

Removing Hatred

A reader who has enemies in the congregation may not be appointed to officiate at a synagogue service. Rabbi Meir ben Isaac Katzenellenbogen (15th-16th Cent.) wrote in his *Responsa* (No. 64), "And if the congregation desire him for their Reader, he is obligated to remove the hatred from his heart, and to say explicitly that he will include his enemy in his prayer, the same as every other man." Now the same was the custom of the ancients; when a man could sense a feeling of ill will against him in the heart of the Reader, he would compel the Reader to say that he would include him in his prayer.

Must Prayers Be In Hebrew?

On the question of prayer in any language other than Hebrew,

Rabbi Aaron Chorin begins as follows: Our great teacher (Yehuda ha-Nasi) laid down a great rule in the Mishna—that prayer may be uttered in any language. To which the Talmud adds: Prayer is a plea for mercy; therefore one may voice it in any way he wishes.... The author of *Magen Abraham*, quotes the words of the *Sefer Hasidim* (Book of the Pious): it is better for a man to read the *Shema* and the (accompanying) blessings in the language which he understands than to pray in Hebrew if he does not understand it...for he who does not understand should not pray, since prayer depends upon the heart (that is, upon the understanding and not merely upon the recitation of the words).

Rabbi Akiga Eger disagreed saying: Even though it is, indeed, the law that one may pray in any language, that law refers only to occasional or incidental prayers. But to fix the regular congregational worship in any other language but Hebrew, God forbid!

Instrumental Music

In response to a question about the use of an organ in the synagogue, Rabbi Moses Kunitz states: The use of the organ is for the glory of God, for it will serve to bring back to the synagogue those who for a long time have kept themselves away from the "Courts of God." Thus they will be sanctifying the name of God among the multitudes. There can be no greater *mitzvah* than this....

Covering the Head

Question: For the one whose head is heavy (that is, subject to headaches), is it permitted to sit and to eat with uncovered head?

Answer: I do not know of any prohibition against pronouncing blessings without covering the head. It is true that to Israel Isserlein it was an evident fact that it was forbidden to mention God's name with uncovered head. But I do not know whence he derived this. For, behold, I have found in the tractate *Soferim* that there is a disagreement on the matter.

The Matzo Machine

Abraham of Sarchov, the author of *Abnei Nezer*, wrote in 1902: Your letter about the matzot-machine has reached me, and although I have never seen the machine, still the words of the Gaon of Kutna are valid, namely, that, since the great ones who preceded us have prohibited it and stormed against those who permitted it, for whatever reason it may be, they must have had good reasons for doing so.

In spite of all the strong opposition to the innovation, the use of the machine spread, chiefly in Western Europe and in other lands, especially in America.

Quoted in *The Responsa Literature*
by Solomon B. Freehof

Converting a Church into a Synagogue

About a question from America to Joseph Saul Nathanson (1808-1875), rabbi of Lemberg:

In the year 5618 (1858) a letter came to me from New York in the land of America, from Rabbi Judah Mittelman, who asks as follows: "There is (in New York) a house of prayer, a Lutheran church. At first it was a private house, and afterwards the private owner turned the house over to the church. Over the lintel of the gate of the house, they wrote in English, 'Welsh-Scotch Methodist Church,' and the interpretation of these words is, 'Lutheran Church of the descendants of the land of Wales and the descendants of Scotland.' They utter songs and prayers referring to 'that man,' and they dance. Then one man arises and preaches to them about the greatness of 'that man,' and they stand and listen. When he finishes, they sing and dance. These worshippers are Protestants, without any images or likenesses (in their church)." And now his honor...is in doubt as to...whether worship was regular in that house, but the house was not specifically set aside for that purpose; also whether it is permitted for us to pray in it only occasionally but not regularly; and, above all, whether we may make of it a house of study for the community. Now it is clear that the intention of the *Keneset hagedolah* is that it is permitted to pray in it even regularly, provided the house was not specifically set aside for the purpose of idolatry.

Nathanson ends the first *responsum* by saying: The law seems to me to be that here, since the building does not contain any likeness or image, it is permitted to turn this into a house of study (and prayer) and it is, in fact, a virtue (a *mitzvah*) thus to sanctify God's name.

What is your opinion?

Responsa for Modern Times

"Some people think that these *Responsa* apply only to the past," Rabbi Mayer said. "This is not so. The Central Conference of American Rabbis has had a Responsa Committee since approximately 1890. The Rabbinical Assembly has a Responsa Committee, and questions of law are referred to experts for opinion.

"Gilbert asked me why I refused to officiate at a mixed marriage. In 1918, a rabbi wasn't quite sure what to do—although a resolution of the Central Conference of American Rabbis passed in 1909 states specifically that Reform rabbis are discouraged from officiating at mixed marriages—and he wrote to Rabbi Kaufman Kohler, the Chairman of the Committee on Responsa, on October 30th:

" 'I have been asked by a Jewish gentleman of my congregation to unite him in wedlock with a Gentile. Is it compatible with Judaism for a rabbi to perform such a marriage when the Gentile does not accept the Jewish religion? And is it in keeping with his position and dignity as rabbi to perform such a marriage when the Gentile does not accept the Jewish faith?

"The answer: 'Unless the person whom a Jew or a Jewess is to marry adopts in some form the Jewish religion, after having learned its tenets to know what the steps taken by such a one means, no rabbi who wants to be true to the tradition of Judaism can perform the marriage ceremony.

"If you were Chairman of the Responsa Committee, what would you have answered?

Children of Mixed Marriages

"In January 1919, Rabbi Kaufman Kohler gave this answer to a question about the religious status of the children of mixed marriages:

The Talmud and the *Shulhan Aruch* you correctly refer to are certainly in force, and consequently the child of a non-Jew has its character determined by the mother. The Christian wife of your member should, therefore, be persuaded, as far as possible, especially for the sake of the husband who wants to have a Jewish home, to become a Jewess in order to have her expected child born as a Jew. The mode of her conversion and adoption into Judaism might in this case be facilitated. Of course, when raised as a Jew, the child could afterwards through Confirmation be adopted into the Jewish fold like any proselyte. On the other hand, it must be stated that the rabbi who solemnized the marriage of a Jew to a non-Jewess did not act in conformity with the Jewish law, no matter whether she promised to raise her children as Jews or not. Mixed marriages belong before the civil magistrate who is to give them legal sanction. The Jewish religion cannot consecrate a home divided by two different creeds, as you well state.

What is your opinion?

Here are two more present-day responsa:

Burial of a Non-Jew in a Jewish Cemetery

On January 2nd, 1919, I was asked for my opinion on the following case: About a year ago a brother of a member of the congregation died in a distant town and was buried on the latter's lot. Afterwards his wife died, and her wish was to be buried next to her husband. She being a Christian, the board of trustees want to do nothing contrary to Jewish Law and custom, and therefore, waits for a decision, as the brother-in-law is willing to have her buried on his lot.

I answered as follows: There is no law forbidding a non-Jew to be buried in a Jewish cemetery. While there are congregations whose constitution expressly prohibits non-Jews, respectively non-Jewish wives or husbands, to be buried in their cemeteries, such restrictions were undoubtedly made with the view of preventing mixed marriages in the congregation. At the same time, it cannot be denied that in case a Jew, whether a member of the congregation or not, has married a non-Jewess, though contrary to the Jewish law, his legally married wife, though a non-Jewess, has a just claim to being buried alongside of her husband on the plot owned by him or given him for burial by his brother.

Another point for consideration is that we have no consecrated ground which would exclude non-Jews. Each plot is consecrated—by the body buried there. Hence the owner of the plot ought to have full disposal of the same. It is his family plot.

K. KOHLER

Do you agree or disagree with Rabbi Kohler's opinion?

Ordination of Women as Rabbis

Question: Is it proper to ordain women as rabbis?

Answer: The ordination of a woman as rabbi is a modern issue due to the evolution of her status in our day. The Central Conference of American Rabbis has repeatedly made pronouncements urging the fullest measure of self-expression for woman as well as the fullest utilization of her gifts in the service of the Most High and gratefully acknowledges the enrichment and enlargement of congregational life which has resulted therefrom.

Whatever may have been the specific legal status of the Jewish woman regarding certain religious functions, her general position in Jewish religious life has ever been an exalted one. She has been the priestess in the home, and our sages have always recognized her as the preserver of Israel. In view of these Jewish teachings and in keeping with the spirit of our age, and the traditions of our Conference, we declare that woman cannot justly be denied the privilege of ordination.

RABBI HENRY COHEN AND COMMITTEE, 1922

1 What is your opinion about the ordination of women as rabbis?

2 What would be the advantages and the disadvantages of a woman rabbi?

Law and Ethics

"Many questions continue to come before the Responsa Committees," said Rabbi Mayer. "The questions deal with every aspect of ethics, law and life. This religious correspondence has been carried on for the past two thousand years, and these questions and answers have created a body of rabbinic opinion that has made for unity and understanding wherever Jews have lived. Thus, continuity of the Jewish codes has been unbroken from the early codes in the Bible, through the Mishna and Talmud, the *Mishneh Torah* of Maimonides, the *Shulhan Aruch* of Joseph Caro, and the *responsa* literature that started two thousand years ago and is still being added to by new interpretations of the law offered by our present-day rabbinical authorities.

"Some of you may be of the opinion that these codes are dull and legalistic, but to those who wanted an orderly system of law to guide them in their observance of Judaism, they were extremely important.

"The Jew never separated law from ethics. The law was to help him apply the moral teachings of Judaism to life. That is why he listened to the Still, Small Voice speaking through the practical wisdom of the Jewish codes."

QUESTIONS FOR DISCUSSION

1 Why was it necessary to compile the Mishna? Why weren't the Biblical laws sufficient for the people in post-biblical days?

2 Review Maimonides' eight degrees of charity. Do you agree with the order in which he lists them? If you were to list eight degrees of giving to charity today, how would they differ?

3 Do you think that the people would have been just as ethical and just as moral without the Mishna and the *Mishneh Torah?*

4 Some scholars maintain that the *Shulhan Aruch* is one of the reasons why Reform Judaism, and ultimately Conservative Judaism, came into being. How would you explain this?

5 Do you think that Conservative and Reform Judaism should have a modern, up-to-date *Shulhan Aruch* for our generation?

6 How would you answer the following questions asked of rabbinical responsa committees:

- *a* What is the attitude of Jewish law towards the practice of autopsy?
- *b* Does Judaism favor or oppose cremation?
- *c* What is the attitude of Judaism toward euthanasia (mercy killing)?
- *d* Must a Jewish soldier during war-time observe dietary laws and keep the Sabbath?

7 Is there ever a situation where a rabbi–Orthodox, Conservative or Reform–should officiate at a mixed marriage? Discuss such a situation.

8 If a person of the Jewish faith plans to marry a Christian, do you think that the rabbi should officiate if the Christian refuses to become converted to Judaism, but promises to practice the Jewish faith and bring up the children as good Jews?

9 Do you think that we need a Guide of Jewish Ethics more than we need a Guide of Jewish Practice? What would such a Guide include?

THINGS TO DO

1 Write a paragraph on the following Bible codes: The Book of the Covenant (Ex. 21-23); The Deuteronomic Code (Deuteronomy 12-16); The Priestly Code (Ex. 25–Numbers 10).

2 What does the Holiness Code (Lev. 17-26) teach us about Ethical Monotheism?

3 As a class project, write a *Shulhan Aruch* for youth today. Assign different students in the class sections such as: Sabbath observance, synagogue attendance, festival and holyday regulations, etc.

4 Find out what a Christian has to do to become converted to Judaism.

5 Write to the Division of Religious Activities of the Jewish Welfare Board and ask how you may obtain a copy of *Responsa in War Time* for your class. When you receive the copy, discuss the problems of the religious Jew in the armed forces.

6 Write a brief biography of Akiba, Maimonides, Jacob ben Asher, Joseph Caro, Yomtov Lipman Heller, Ezekiel Landau, Meir Ben Baruch of Rothenberg.

WHAT DO YOU THINK?

1 The Talmud debated this problem:

"....what should be done if, of two wayfarers in the desert, one had little water while the other had none? If one of them should drink all the water, he would be able to get out. If they should divide it both of them would die. Ben Paturi said they should both drink and die for it is written 'and thy brother shall live *with* thee' (Lev. 25.36). Rabbi Akiba replied: 'Thy brother shall live with *thee;* thy life take precedence of his life. You must be alive if he is to *live with you.*'"

2 The following article appeared in a Jewish newspaper:

PARENTS WARNED HOW NOT TO CHOOSE COLLEGES

PENALTY OF BAD CHOICE MAY BE INTERMARRIAGE

Richmond, Va. (NJP)—Parents who send their children off to colleges where there is little Jewish life might have to pay the penalty in the form of intermarriage, Rabbi Jacob Milgrom asserted.

Reporting on his recent visit to a college campus where he found the Jewish boys outnumbering the Jewish girls 10 to 1, with the result that the Jewish boys were dating non-Jewish girls, Rabbi Milgrom said that both the students and their parents had to share the blame.

"One intermarriage had already taken place, three others were contemplated," the rabbi wrote.

He added that he need "not elaborate on the broken hearts, distraught minds and guilt-ridden emotions besetting the parents, families and students involved."

"As much as the students themselves are to blame," he continued, "for theirs was the choice of the college, their parents must share the spotlight of accusation—for theirs was the responsibility of guiding the choice."

He then listed five questions which should be on every Jewish fact sheet for college inquiry:

Is the Jewish student population large enough?

Is the number of boys and girls about equal?

Is there a Hillel Foundation or any other Jewish religious organization on the campus?

Is the organization effective? (By that, I mean the number and variety of activities: services, interest groups, classes, dances, socials.)

Is there a rabbi or some other religious functionary giving his full time to the organization?

Rabbi Milgrom concluded that "If any of these questions have to be answered in the negative, then the happiness of your son or daughter hangs in serious jeopardy."

SELECTED QUOTATIONS

Ethics Through Law

The Torah was not for the Jewish Doctors of the Law merely...a volume of statutes on all kinds of subjects, ritual and ceremonial, criminal and civil; it was—to give it modern expression—a revelation of God's ideal for men's conduct and character.

GEORGE FOOT MOORE
Judaism, Vol. II

Mishneh Torah

This "Second-to-the-Torah" is a complete systematic code of the rules of the Torah "written" and "unwritten," logically arranged under fourteen grand divisions or Books which total one thousand chapters. Completed in 1180, it took ten years in the writing and is one of the greatest works of scholarship in any language. In plain concise Hebrew, a style akin to the Mishna, Maimonides digests and restates the conclusions of the Mishna, of both Talmuds and their kindred works, and of the writings of the *Geonim.* It is a marvel of logical structure and arrangement. General principles and fundamental propositions precede the exposition of details. The structure of the whole work is like a great piece of architecture. First the broad basic principles are laid down, then the pillars of traditional lore are set up and finally details and particulars are placed each in their proper place.

GEORGE HOROWITZ

Is Mercy Killing Ever Justified?

The Jewish ideal of the sanctity of human life and the supreme value of the individual soul would suffer incalculable harm if, contrary to the moral law, men were at liberty to determine the conditions under which they might put an end to their own lives and the lives of other men.

RESPONSA OF THE CENTRAL CONFERENCE
OF AMERICAN RABBIS

A Guide of Conduct

Do we desire a guide for Reform Judaism? Indeed we do. Not for ritual and rites alone but for righteous conduct and decent behavior between man and man; not merely for the forms of services but for the service of God in the affairs of men; not merely as a minimum code for liturgical worship but as a minimal code of moral conduct incumbent upon anyone who calls himself a Reform Jew presuming to be the heir of Hebrew prophet and sage. Even the prophet prefaced his command to "walk humbly" with the demand to "do justly and to love mercy." The resemblance between the noble name we bear and our bearing toward our neighbor must be more than coincidental. It must be fundamental. It must translate our preachment into practice, our dogmas and doctrines into deed, our creed into conduct, our prayers into programs of moral righteousness and social justice, our invoking of God's name—too frequently in vain—into the establishment of His Kingdom on earth.

RABBI MAURICE EISENDRATH

SUGGESTED READINGS

For the Pupil

Bokser, Ben Zion, *The Legacy of Maimonides*

Brav, Stanley, *Marriage and the Jewish Tradition*

Caplan and Ribalow, Great Jewish Books, *Shulhan Aruch*, pp. 215-225

Freehof, Solomon B., *The Responsa Literature*

Gittelsohn, Roland B., *Modern Jewish Problems*, Chapter IV

Universal Jewish Encyclopedia, Codes, Vol. 3, pp. 230-232; Responsa Literature, Vol. 9, pp. 137-139; Mishna, Vol. 7, pp. 581-582; Maimonides, Vol. 7, pp. 288-295; Shulhan Aruch, Vol. 9, pp. 521-522

Yellon and Abrahams, *Maimonides*

For the Teacher

Danby, Herbert, *The Mishna*

Ginzberg, Louis, *On Jewish Life and Lore*, pp. 169-184

Goldin, Hyman E., *Code of Jewish Law*

Horowitz, George, *The Spirit of Jewish Law*

Strack, Hermann, *Introduction to the Talmud and Midrash*, Ch. III, pp. 26-28; Ch. IV, pp. 29-59

5

THE VOICE OF THE GENERATIONS

Hebrew Ethical Wills

It's Unfair to Youth

The first thing the students noticed as they entered was a mimeographed paper on each desk.

"What is this," Stuart asked indignantly, "a surprise examination? I think it's unfair!"

"Before you get so burned-up, why don't you see what it is?" said Nancy.

Stuart picked up the paper and read the following:

1 "Our earth is degenerate in these latter days. There are signs that the world is coming to an end. Children no longer obey their parents. Everybody wants to write a book. The end of the world is near."

2 "The children now love luxury, they have no manners. They show contempt for authority, are disrespectful to their elders and love to chatter instead of exercise.... They contradict their parents, misbehave before company, gobble up dainties at the table, cross their legs and tyrannize their teachers."

"Hey, just look at this!" Stuart shouted. Somebody's always condemning modern youth. We're always being typed as juvenile delinquents. I wonder who wrote this nonsense? I'd like to tell him a thing or two!"

"You would have to go back about 6,000 years to do that, Stuart," said Rabbi Mayer.

Stuart looked up in surprise. "Six thousand years? Is that what you said?"

"Yes, that's exactly what I said," answered Rabbi Mayer. "The first statement was made by an Egyptian priest nearly 6,000 years ago, and the second was made by Socrates 2,000 years ago."

Daniel exclaimed: "Go beat that! Six thousand years ago they were condemning youth, and they are still doing it today."

"The reason I put these papers on your desks," said Rabbi Mayer, "is to show that the same ethical problems that disturbed people thousands of years ago still concern us—even the complaints against the wildness and disobedience of youth.

"I happen to believe that modern youth is certainly no worse than the youth of the past. In fact, modern youth is even better and more responsible than the youth of past ages. But it is natural for parents and teachers to worry about children and youth. That is the reason why so many parents and teachers attempted to instruct their children and pupils by means of ethical wills.

"I'm sure that you have never heard of a Hebrew ethical will before. Think about these three words—Hebrew ethical wills—and see if you can analyze what they mean."

WHAT DO YOU THINK?

1 What do you think is meant by a Hebrew ethical will?

2 How does an ethical will differ from any other kind of a will?

3 Do you think that modern youth is better, worse, or the same as the youth of past ages?

4 Do you think that grown-ups just forget what happened in their youth when they accuse modern youth of being rebellious, wild and irresponsible?

5 How do you think modern Jewish youth compares with the Jewish youth of past ages in terms of obedience to parents, Jewish learning, synagogue attendance and ethical behavior?

6 How do you think that modern Jewish youth compares with modern Christian youth in terms of obedience to parents, church and synagogue attendance, devotion to religious holidays and ethical behavior?

A Class Will

"I imagine you now have some idea of the distinction between an ethical will and other wills," said Rabbi Mayer. "Can you think of any other types of wills?"

Daniel said: "I know of one—a class will. I mean the kind of will that a Senior Class writes for the Junior Class: We hereby will and bequeath to the Junior Class the misery of Latin verbs, our crowded classrooms, the wheezing radiators and the privilege of taking college entrance examinations."

When the members of the class laughed, Rabbi Mayer said: "Daniel may be joking, but suppose a Senior Class did make a serious will to advise the Juniors?"

"Then it would be an ethical will," said Susan.

"That is right. An ethical will attempts to give practical advice about duties and obligations. It offers the experience of those who have gone before and learned from their mistakes.

Ethical Wills in the Bible and Talmud

"We find ethical wills first revealed in the Bible. Jacob, you remember, gave advice to his sons on his death bed. According to the Midrash, when the patriarch felt that death was near, he cried out to God, 'Ruler of the World, take not my soul until I have instructed my children.' God granted his wish, and Jacob was able to give his children ethical advice before he died.

"Moses gave his advice to the children of Israel before he was taken from this earth. His charge to the Hebrew people is found in the 32nd chapter of Deuteronomy.

"David offered practical wisdom to his son, Solomon, saying: 'I go the way of all the earth; be thou strong therefore, and show thyself a man; and keep the charge of the Lord thy God, to walk in His way, according to all that is written in the law of Moses, that thou mayest prosper in all that thou doest.'

"In this spirit, rabbis and pious laymen of the Middle Ages set forth rules for the guidance of their descendants. They were seldom able to bequeath much property, and so there developed the tradition of writing ethical wills, leaving to their children an inheritance of morality, a wealth of idealism, treasures of wisdom, and riches of the spirit.

"We are now going to consider some of these Hebrew ethical wills, from Medieval Times to the present day."

The "Paths of Life" by R. Eleazar the Great (1544)

My son! In the house of learning, speak no idle words; but incline thine ear to the discourse of the wise. Consider nothing negligible; despise no man. For many pearls are found in the poor man's tunic. Nor may any man invade his neighbor's bounds, nor expect to discover doctrine which his fellow is appointed to reveal, seeing that all was ordained before the Lord from the day on which the Law was created.

My son! Be zealous in visiting the sick, for sympathy lightens pain. Urge the patient to return, a penitent, to his Maker. Pray for him, and depart! Do not fatigue him by staying too long, for his malady is heavy enough already. Enter cheerfully, for his heart and eyes are on those who come in.

My son! Comfort the mourners, and speak to their heart. The companions of Job were held punishable merely because they reproached when they should have consoled him. Thus it is written: "Ye have not spoken of Me the thing that is right, as My servant Job hath."

My son! Show honor to the poor, and draw out thy soul unto him. Be punctilious to offer thy gift, in secret, not in the public gaze.

My son! Crush not the poor with harsh words, for the Lord will plead his cause. Such conduct rouses on high many accusers, to whom there is no defense. But he who treats the poor with good-will and generosity acquires intercessors to plead his cause.

My son! Keep far from a wicked neighbor, and from him whose reputation is evil, for what they say of him below accords with what they say of him on high.

My son! "Rejoice not when thine enemy falleth, and let not thy heart be glad when he stumbleth, lest the Lord see it and it displeases Him, and He turn away His wrath from him (to thee)." But "if thine enemy be hungry give him bread to eat."

Which aspects of this ethical will no longer apply today? What advice do you regard as the most important for modern Jewish youth?

Books and Writing

My son! Make thy books thy companions, let thy cases and shelves be thy pleasure-grounds and gardens. Bask in their paradise, gather their fruit, pluck their roses, take their spices and their myrrh. If thy soul be satiate and weary, change from garden to garden, from furrow to furrow, from prospect to prospect. Then will thy desire renew itself, and thy soul be filled with delight!

My son! If thou writest aught, read it through a second time, for no man can avoid slips. Let not any consideration of hurry prevent thee from revising a short epistle. Be punctilious as to grammatical accuracy, in conjugations and genders, for the constant use of the vernacular sometimes leads to error in this regard. A man's mistakes in writing bring him into disrepute; they are membered against him all his days.

JUDAH IBN TIBBON *(1120-1190)*
"A Father's Admonition"

Mohammed called the Jews the people of the Book. Do you think that applies to modern Jews?

Pride

And now, my son! Understand clearly that he who prides himself in his heart over other men is a rebel against the Kingship of Heaven. Such a one presumes to adorn himself in the robe of the Omnipresent. For it is God, enthroned, who wears the mantle of majesty. And wherefore shall the heart of man be puffed up? Is it because of wealth? It is God who maketh poor and maketh rich. Or is it because of honor? But honor is of God. And how shall a man boast in an honor which is his Maker's? Does he glorify himself because of his wisdom? Lo, God "removeth the speech of men of trust and taketh away the sense of the elders." In a word, all are equal before the Lord. For in His anger He bringeth down the high and in His good pleasure He elevates the low. Therefore debase thyself and let the Omnipresent raise thee up!

NAHMANIDES *(1194-1270)*
"The Virtue of Humility"

How do we show "pride" in our daily life?

A Jewish Letter

We should, I say, put ourselves to great pains for our children, for on this the world is built, yet we must bear in mind that if children did as much for their parents, the children would quickly tire of it.

A bird once set out to cross a windy sea with its three fledglings. The sea was so wide and the wind so strong that the father bird was forced to carry his young, one by one, in his claws. When he was half-way across with the first fledgling the wind turned to a gale, and he said: "My child, look how I am struggling and risking my life in your behalf. When you are grown up, will you do as much for me and provide for my old age?" The fledgling replied: "Only bring me to safety, and when you are old I shall do everything you ask of me." Whereat the father bird dropped his child into the sea, and it drowned, and he said: "So shall it be done to such a liar as you." Then the father bird returned to the shore, set forth with his second fledgling, asked the same question, and receiving the same answer, drowned the second child with the cry, "You, too, are a liar!" Finally he set out with the third fledgling, and when he asked the same question, the third and last fledgling replied: "My dear father, it is true you are struggling mightily and risking your life in my behalf, and I shall be wrong not to repay you when you are old, but I cannot bind myself. This though I can promise: when I am grown up and have children of my own, I shall do as much for them as you have done for me." Whereupon the father bird said: "Well spoken, my child, and wisely; your life I spare and I will carry you to shore in safety."

Autobiography of Gluckel of Hamlen
(17th Century)

Interpret this story and apply it to yourself. Do you think that parents today are over protective and try to do too much for their children? Are we getting soft because our parents indulge us too much?

More Important than Money

Say not: I will bequeath to my children money and means for their support. Know that the sons of man are like the grasses of the field, some flourish and others wither, each being born under his star, and under the Providence of the Most High God. The heirs of a wealthy man rejoice at his death, to inherit his estate, while he descends to the grave and leaves his wealth to others. So it was said of R. Simeon ben Lachish, who left behind him nothing more than a measure of saffron, that he applied to himself the text: "and leave their wealth to others." Woe and alas for the sins of men who toil and moil to leave their children money and goods and full houses! All this is vanity, for the only profit in sons and daughters is their Torah and their virtue. He who created them, creates also their means of support. A man's main concern should be to acquire the future world by the charitable and benevolent use of his money, honoring the Lord with his substance.

Letter of Elijah (Gaon) of Wilna
(1720-1797)

1 What is your opinion of the advice given by Elijah Gaon?

2 Do you think that parents should spend their money during their lifetime, without providing for their grown children?

3 Are children better off if they are forced to earn their own livelihood and make their own success?

4 What does this statement tell us about the Jewish idea of wealth? The writers of ethical wills suggest that there are possessions more valuable than money. What are these religious possessions?

The Inheritance of Torah

Think not in your heart that the Torah is an inheritance from your fathers, and needs no personal effort to win it. The matter is not so.

If ye toil not therein, ye shall not acquire, and more than ordinary will be your punishment, in that ye forsake your family tradition.

The Testament of Judah Asheri (1250-1329)

"For the commandment is a lamp and the Law is light," but "the reproofs of instruction are the way of life." This transcends all conceivable fasts and penances; and he who succeeds in muzzling his mouth, will merit in measureless abundance of the Light treasured up in the future world. And the Scripture saith: "Who is the man that desireth life, and loveth days that he may see good therein? Keep thy tongue from evil, and thy lips from speaking guile."

Furthermore, bring up your sons in the right way and with gentleness. Their teacher must be constantly in your house, and you must pay him generously. All a man's expenditure is appointed from the New Year, but (as the Talmud adds) this does not apply to expenditure on education. I have left the necessary books for tuition. Pay careful heed to the children's health and diet, so that they never lack anything. They should first study all the Pentateuch, learning it practically by heart. Let not the teacher impose his yoke heavily on them, for instruction is only efficient when it is conveyed easily and agreeably.

Letter of Elijah (Gaon) of Wilna

And this is the text of the Testament which I, the aforesaid Solomon, have drawn up for my children, may God preserve them! That each of them shall pray thrice daily, and strive to utter his prayers with devotion. Again, that prayers shall be said in the *Bet Hamidrash* or in the synagogue together with the congregation. Again, that each shall apply all his power to maintain the synagogues and houses of study and the endowments which our fathers, and I also, have built and established. Let each endeavor to imitate them to the end that good word shall never cease from among them.

Again, that each shall always have in his house a chair on which a volume or two of the Talmud, or any other talmudical work, shall rest; so that he can always open a book when he comes home. Let him read what he can, making it a duty to read in any book he likes at least four lines before taking his meal. Again that he shall not omit to read every week the Pentateuchal lesson twice in the Hebrew text and once in the Aramaic version.

Testament of Solomon Son of Isaac
(14th or 15th Century)

What is the practical value of this advice?

The Ideals of an Average Jew

On holidays and festivals and Sabbaths seek to make happy the poor, the unfortunate, widows and orphans, who should always be guests at your tables; their joyous entertainment is a religious duty. Let me repeat my warning against gossip and scandal. And as ye speak no scandal, so listen to none, for if there were no receivers there would be no bearers of slanderous tales; therefore the reception and credit of slander is as serious an offence as the originating of it. The less you say, the less cause you give for animosity, while "in the multitude of words there wanteth not transgression."

I earnestly beg my children to be tolerant and humble to all, as I was throughout my life. Should cause for dissension present itself, be slow to accept the quarrel; seek peace and pursue it with all the vigor at your command. Even if you suffer loss thereby, forbear and forgive, for God has many ways of feeding and sustaining His creatures. To the slanderer do not retaliate with counterattack; and though it be proper to rebut false accusations, yet is it most desirable to set an example of reticence. You yourselves must avoid uttering any slander, for so will you win affection. In trade be true, never grasping at what belongs to another. For by avoiding these wrongs—scandal, falsehood, money-grubbing—men will surely find tranquility and affection. And against all evils, silence is the best safeguard.

Testament of Eleazar the Levite of Mayence
(14th Century)

Eleazar of Mayence set this forth as the ideals of an average Jew. Write out your own opinion of "the ideals of an average modern Jew."

Anger

Never allow anger to master thee. A father must guard himself against hasty temper in his treatment of his children and household. On the Sabbath, particularly, he must be very patient in his home, lest he destroy the Sabbath rest which should pervade his heart. It is a wise habit not to reprove a child immediately on the offense. Better wait till irritation has been replaced by serenity. Let melancholy and passion, born of spleen and bile, be banished from all hearts on the Sabbath day. Happy the lot of those who succeed! For, while irreverence obstructs the reception of the Face of the *Shekinah*, anger is a yet greater obstructive.

Counsels of a Mystic (From the
Testament of Moses Hasid)
(18th Century)

Hear, my son, the instruction of thy father, and forsake not the law of thy mother. My son, my beloved, accustom thyself always to speak gently to every man, at all times and seasons; thereby thou shalt avoid anger which is a very bad and blameworthy disposition, for it leads to sin, as our teachers of blessed memory said, "If one gets angry, it is regarded as if he worshipped idols."

NAHMANIDES

Kindness

If ye render a kindness to any man, do not recurrently remind him of it. This is a despicable habit. It is comparable to the son who feeds his father on dainties, yet inherits *Gehinnom*. So was Nehemiah punished—his Book not being named after him—because of his boast: "Remember unto me, O God, for good, all that I have done for this people." But fix ye this maxim in your hearts: Do what you say, but say not what you do!

Elijah De Veali to His Children
(18th Century)

Judge every man charitably, and use your best efforts to find a kindly explanation of conduct, however suspicious. Give in charity an exact tithe of your property. Never turn a poor man away empty-handed. Talk no more than is necessary, and thus avoid slander. Be not as dumb cattle that utter no word of gratitude, but thank God for his bounties at the time at which they occur, and in your prayers let the memory of these personal favors warm your hearts, and prompt you to special fervor during the utterance of the communal thanks for communal well-being. When words of thanks occur in the liturgy, pause and silently reflect on the goodness of God to you that day.

The Will of Eleazar the Levite
of Mayence (1357)

Seek To Know Thy Maker

My son! Give glory to God and offer unto Him thanks. Remember that He created thee out of clay, and brought thee into the world, fashioning thy body and its parts without help from thee. For thou hast need of Him, He has no need of thee....My son! Love the wise, and attach thyself to them. Seek to know thy Maker, for "that the soul be without knowledge is not good." Salute all men and speak the truth.

RABBI ELEAZAR THE GREAT *(1544)*
Paths of Life

Peace

To be at peace with all the world, with Jew and Gentile, must be your foremost aim in this terrestrial life. Contend with no man. In the first instance, your home must be the abode of quietude and happiness; no harsh words must be heard there, but over all must reign love, amity, modesty, and a spirit of gentleness and reverence. This spirit must not end with the home, however. In your dealings with the world you must allow neither money nor ambition to disturb you. Forego your rights, envy no man. For the main thing is peace, peace with the whole world. Show all men every possible respect, deal with them in the finest integrity and faithfulness. For Habbakuk summed up the whole law in one sentence: "The Righteous Shall Live by His Faith."

JOEL, *Son of Abraham Shemariah*
(18th Century)

Modern Ethical Wills

"It seems to me that most of these were written in the Middle Ages. Do people write ethical wills today?" Stuart asked.

"I'm sure that modern Jews still write ethical wills," said Rabbi Mayer. "However, many of us are so concerned with leaving financial security to our children, that we unfortunately do not give the proper attention to leaving our children a legacy of faith and a religious inheritance."

Shirley raised her hand and said: "I don't want this to sound smart-alecky, but I think it's more important for parents to leave their children financial security than to leave them ethical wills. After all, if they have the money, then they won't have to be concerned about the material things of life and they will have more time to devote themselves to moral and religious values."

"Rather than comment on this, Shirley, I'm going to let the class decide. Which do you think is more important: for your parents to leave their children a financial inheritance, or by their moral example, and the lessons of character they have taught, leave their children religious security and a treasure of morality? Which has the greater value?

A Rabbi's Bequest

Rabbi Samuel Wolk of Albany, N. Y., left the following modern Ethical will:

"These worldly goods are of small material value. I am in possession of a far richer store. It is a way of life transmitted to me, through thousands of years, by prophet, sage and martyr of my people. It embodies a counsel for life which if taken diligently to heart and practiced by all men, would lead to larger understanding, less bloodshed, and more brotherhood. It is a counsel which thinks of man as 'a little lower than the angels' rather than as kin to beasts. That counsel I gladly bequeath to all mankind, without regard to family ties or color or creed. It is a rich heritage which, without distinction, I will to friend and foe alike.

"IN WITNESS WHEREOF, I have hereunto set my hand and seal this 14th day of March, in the year One thousand nine hundred and fifty-six."

SAMUEL WOLK

Value or Price?

"We have learned that the Hebrew ethical will was another link in the chain of Jewish literature that bound the Jew to his faith and enabled him to hear the Still, Small Voice summoning him to justice, truth, kindness and virtue.

"The concern of the Jew has ever been the value of Jewish living and not the price. Each Jew assumes a sacred trust from past generations. It is his duty to transmit this legacy to his children and his children's children as a precious inheritance of faith."

QUESTIONS FOR DISCUSSION

1 What is your reaction to the following advice taken from an ethical will: "Every night before thou retirest to rest, forgive whoever has offended thee. If men curse or revile thee, answer not a word. Be of the insulted, not of the insulters."?

2 A Medieval sage urged his children "to accustom yourselves to nice, clean clothes, so that God and men may love and honor you." What did he mean?

3 Elijah Gaon of Wilna advised his disciples: "When you lead your sons and daughters in the good way, let your words be tender and caressing, in terms of discipline that win the heart's assent." Do you think that children are more obedient to parents who are strict and stern, than to parents who are easy-going and less demanding?

4 In the ethical wills there are references made to "the fear of God." What is the real meaning of the Hebrew word that is usually translated as fear? Do you think it is more important to fear God, or to love God? Will the fear of God incline people to be more ethical than the love of God?

5 Alexander Suesskind refers to "unintentional offenses against the will of God." What are some unintentional offenses against God? What is the Jewish way of atoning for those offenses?

6 Israel Baal Shem tells his children to concentrate on thoughts of the *Shehinah*. What is meant by the *Shehinah?* Why does he refer to it as feminine?

7 Do you agree with Joel, Son of Abraham Shemariah, that "peace with all the world, with Jew and Gentile, must be your foremost aim"? Is it proper to surrender ideals and principles to avoid conflict and achieve harmony and peace?

THINGS TO DO

1 Write an ethical will giving moral and ethical instruction to a younger brother, sister or friend.

2 Write a book report on the story called "Four Generations and Four Wills," by Isaac Leib Peretz.

3 Work on the project of a class will. The result should be a serious, ethical will to be given to the class that is to follow yours.

4 In the selected quotation that follows, there is a paragraph dealing with a different type of ethical will left by Chaim Weizmann. List other ways for a person to leave an ethical will that is a concrete project rather than a written statement.

5 There are examples of statements to children in the *Apocrypha*. Look up the command of Hannah to her sons. What was the spoken ethical will of Mattathias to his sons?

SELECTED QUOTATIONS

The Art of the Good Life

In Judaism, the life process is one of continuous education for character and, therefore, requires not only practice of good deeds but constant preparation through study for situations which cannot be anticipated. The discovery of what is right under complicated conditions is not easy and does not come from intuition.

We are fortunate in having in the literature bequeathed us by our fathers a vast storehouse of religious and ethical experience. The more we study the cases with which our ancestors dealt, the better we will be able to handle the complications of our time, as individuals and as a group. But an even greater step will be taken when each of us, following in the footsteps of our great teachers, sets aside time each day for the contemplation of man's moral dilemmas and tries to prepare himself to achieve greatness in the art which alone is common to all people—the art of the good life.

RABBI LOUIS FINKELSTEIN

Ways of Life

Asher, the son of Yechiel (fourteenth Century), called his will "Ways of Life," and it includes 132 maxims, which are often printed in the prayer-book. Here are some of them: "Do not obey the Law for reward, nor avoid sin from fear of punishment, but serve God from love. Sleep not over-much, but rise with the birds. Be not over-hasty to reply to offensive remarks; raise not thy hand against another, even if he curse thy father or mother in thy presence."

A Moral Balance

Keep careful accounts, and strike an annual balance. Apply the same rule to your moral conduct, and look to it that ye strengthen the house where necessary. Search with strong lights, make search on search—use light on light to pry into all the crevices of your soul, and make haste to ascend to your Father in Heaven with prayer, repentance, and charity....

From the Testament of ELIJAH SON OF RAPHAEL DE VEALI *(18th century)*

On Making a Will

A member of the Temple came to see me not long ago about making his will. Since I am not an attorney, I asked him, "Why did you come to consult a Rabbi?" "Oh," was his reply, "I know what to do about the property; one third to my wife, one third to each of the two children. But, a will ought to be more than that. I want you to help me set forth the purposes of my existence on earth which ought to be expressed in my last will and testament."

A good question. Besides your property, what will you be leaving your children? What is their real heritage?

I hope to leave my children an appreciation of little things, the enjoyment of music, the thrill of a new tone, the joy of saying, "I have it, I played it." I leave them the dandelions of the fields, and the privilege to play with them freely, warning them against the thistles. And I will leave them the long merry days to be joyful in, and the trails of the milky way. I hope to give them a star that shall be theirs. I leave them—a faith that says, "This I believe"—a heritage which speaks of history and music and ideas of Jews through the ages....I leave them God who watches over them—who slumbers not—who will be with them in their downsitting and their uprising....

I leave them not much in worldly goods. I hope to put God in my will.

RABBI BURTON E. LEVINSON

Heavenly Treasures

King Monobaz, who in the days of the Second Temple became a proselyte to Judaism, unlocked his ancestral treasures at a time of famine, and distributed them among the poor. His ministers rebuked him, saying, "Thy fathers amassed, thou dost squander." "Nay," said the benevolent king, "they preserved earthly, but I heavenly, treasures; theirs could be stolen, mine are beyond mortal reach; theirs were barren, mine will bear fruit time without end; they preserved money, I preserved lives. The treasures which my fathers laid by are for this world, mine are for eternity."

The Talmud

Torah

During the Middle Ages, a traveler came upon a band of people who kept a *Sefer Torah* in a cave, and on occasion came to the cave to prostrate themselves before the Torah. They hardly knew what it was. They could not read it. All they knew was that their ancestors who had been Jews had bequeathed the scroll to them. What a deterioration they and their Torah had undergone. It had become a superstition-riddled talisman, and nothing else. Such is not the heritage we want to leave our children. We want to transmit to them a Judaism that lives and inspires, and makes life desirable. Such a Judaism is "not in the heavens above nor in the earth beneath." It is to be found in the pages of the Jewish book, near at hand to all who will reach out to it. It will be well for us to apply these thoughts to our own lives.

RABBI DAVID POLISH

Tsava'ah

In Hebrew, the word is *Tsava'ah,* and it means a testament or a will.

Perhaps the most remarkable *Tsava'ah* in modern Jewish history is one left to his people by Chaim Weizmann. It exists not as a document, although part of it was written; nor is it speech, although part of it was also spoken. His *Tsava'ah* is rather an institution. It bears his name—The Weizmann Institute of Science—and it stands by his grave at Rehovot, in the heart of Israel.

EDITH BRODSKY

SUGGESTED READINGS

Abrahams, Israel, *Hebrew Ethical Wills*, Part I and Part II
Abrahams, Israel, *Chapters on Jewish Literature*, Chapter 19
Universal Jewish Encyclopaedia, Vol. 10, pp. 523-524
Runes, D., *Letters To My Daughter*

6

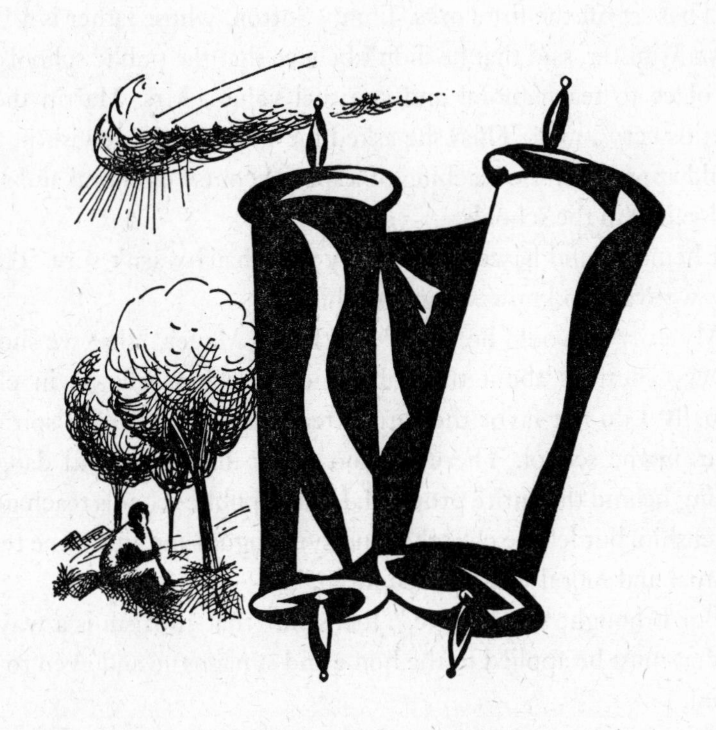

THE VOICE OF MUSAR

The Ethics of Jewish Moralists, Mystics and Philosophers

The Problem

"Before we begin the class session, Rabbi, I wish that you would help us with a problem that we have been discussing in school. We're all mixed up," said Joel, "and we don't know the right answer."

"What is the problem?" Rabbi Mayer asked.

"It's not easy to put into words, but the other day in class Mrs. Martin, our teacher, said that she would like the schools to teach moral and spiritual values in a special course.

"That set off the fireworks. Jimmy Sutton, whose father is a Unitarian Minister, said that he didn't believe that the public school was the place to teach moral and spiritual values. Mrs. Martin didn't like this very much. Then she asked me whether the Jewish people would approve of the teaching of a special course on moral and spiritual values in the schools.

"I hemmed and hawed and finally said that I wasn't sure. That's why we want to know what you think."

"My answer would be, Joel," said Rabbi Mayer, "that we should be very cautious about this subject of teaching religion in class. Actually I do not favor the formal teaching of moral and spiritual values in the school. There are too many difficulties and dangers lurking behind the entire proposal. Let the public schools teach good citizenship, but let the churches and synagogues and the home teach spiritual and moral values to children."

"But I thought you believe," Joel said, "that Judaism is a way of life that must be applied to the home and synagogue and even to the school."

"That is right, Joel. Judaism must be applied by those of the Jewish faith in school, in the schoolyard, in athletics and everything else, but Judaism should be *taught* in the home and synagogue and religious school.

"Everything we have studied thus far in our effort to understand the mystery of the Still, Small Voice has been Jewish ethics. We are taught moral and spiritual values through the Bible, Talmud, the prayerbook, our festivals and holydays, the inspiration of the Synagogue, Jewish codes and Hebrew ethical wills. All of Judaism teaches spiritual and moral values, but these values are taught in the home, the synagogue and the religious school. Christians, too, teach their children through their sacred literature and observances, and in the home and church. When we try to find a 'common ground' for teaching both faiths, I'm afraid there will be difficulties and a great deal of misunderstanding. The American school system has always been based on the separation of Church and State, and when we bring formal religion into the schools we are asking for trouble.

"Let me give you some further examples of how Judaism has taught spiritual and moral values, through the ethics of Jewish moralists, mystics and philosophers.

The Moralists

"The moralists were Jewish sages who wrote practical, ethical wisdom to guide the people. Ethical instruction was called *Musar*, which means moral admonition, or ethical advice. That is why they are called moralists.

"Among these moralists, the greatest were Bachya Ibn Pakuda, Maimonides, Solomon Ibn Gabirol, Judah of Regensburg and Moses Hayim Luzzato. As we consider their teachings, we are impressed with how modern and meaningful they are.

"Bachya Ibn Pakuda lived in Saragossa, Spain, at the end of the 11th Century. His greatest work was called *Hovoth Halevavoth, The Duties of the Heart*. Its purpose is to show that Judaism requires much more than the outward observance of the Law. Only when we have right attitudes in our mind and heart can Judaism properly be practiced, and the individual find his way to God. Here are some quotations from Bachya's wisdom:

Humility

The man who does good works is more likely to be overtaken by pride in them than by any other moral mischance, and its effect on conduct is injurious in the extreme. Therefore, among the most necessary of virtues is that one which banishes pride; and this is humility.

First among the signs by which the meek are known is that when misfortunes come to them their endurance triumphs over their fear and grief, and they willingly submit to the decree of God, and own that His judgments are righteous.

In matters of justice, however, the meek will be high-spirited and fearless, punishing the wicked without fear or favor. They will help the oppressed and rescue him from the power of the oppressor.

Do Thy Task Every Day

O my soul, prepare provision in abundance, prepare not little, while thou art yet alive, and while thy hand has yet strength, because the journey is too great for thee. And say not: "I shall prepare provision to-morrow;" for the day has declined, and thou knowest not what the next day may bring forth. Know likewise that yesterday shall never come back, and that whatever thou hast done therein is weighed, numbered, and counted. Nor shouldst thou say: "I shall do it tomorrow;" for the day of death is hidden from all the living. Hasten to do thy task every day, for death may at any time send forth its arrow and lightning. Delay not to do thy daily task, for as a bird wanders from its nest, so does a man wander from his place.

The Evil Urge

Every man's enemy is within himself.

A pious man said to victorious veterans returning from battle, "Now equip yourselves for the great war!" "And what is that?" they asked. He replied: "The war on the evil urge."

How would you interpret this?

The Choice is Ours

Trust in God does not signify that one should neglect one's work, be careless of one's life, health and well-being, or abandon one's effort to provide for one's family and dependents. No, one must do all these things conscientiously, at the same time feeling that if not for the help of God, all effort would be in vain. In the matter of doing one's duty and observing the commandments, whether of the limbs or the heart, trust in God can apply only to the last step in the process, namely, the realization in practice. He must trust that God will put out of the way all obstacles and hindrances which may prevent him from carrying out his resolutions. The choice and consent must come from a man's own will, which is free. The most he may do is to trust that God may remove temptations.

1 Bachya taught the importance of humility. How do we distinguish between pride and self-respect? We constantly speak of being "a Jew and proud of it." How do you think Bachya would interpret this? The greater the person, the more humble the person. Why do you think this is true?

2 We all have the temptation to put things off until tomorrow. If a person does this in little things, will he do the same with his obligations to his God, to his religion, and to his community? What is your opinion?

3 A Rabbi once said: "It is not that I am not tempted to eat forbidden food or yield to improper sexual desire. I am tempted to eat forbidden food. I am tempted to yield to improper sexual desire—but I must control myself because the Lord has forbidden me." How does this apply to modern youth?

4 What would Bachya have said to one who declared—"I don't go to the synagogue. I don't pray, or give enough to charity, but I am a Jew at heart."

5 What in your opinion are the modern "Duties of the Heart"?

"Maimonides was born in Cordova, Spain, in 1135. Later he and his family were forced by persecution to leave Spain, and they settled in Fez, Morocco. Arab intolerance drove them out and they found refuge in Cairo. Maimonides was a physician, philosopher, codifier, writer and moralist. His main work, finished in 1190, was called *Moreh Nevuhim* (Guide for the Perplexed). This was to guide those who were uncertain and perplexed about their faith. In his writing, Maimonides gave practical advice about ethical living. We can understand then why it was said: 'from Moses to Moses, there arose none like unto Moses.' These are quotations from the wisdom of Maimonides."

God Does Not Decree Good or Evil

Since all the wicked deeds which we have committed have been committed with our full consciousness, it befits us to turn in penitence and to forsake our evil deeds; the power of doing so being still in our hands. Now this matter is a very important principle; nay, it is the pillar of the Law and of the commandments.

God does not decree that a man should be good or evil. It is only fools and ignoramuses among Gentiles and Jews who maintain that God decrees at a man's birth whether he shall be righteous or wicked. Any man born is free to become as righteous as Moses, as wicked as Jeroboam, a student or an ignoramus, kind or cruel, generous or niggardly. The subject of man's freedom and God's fore-knowledge is profoundly difficult for man to grasp, as difficult as it is for man to understand God. We believe that the actions of man are in God's hands, and yet God does not coerce man or direct him to act one way or another.

The Merciful Heart

There is a large class of laws in our Torah, the sole purpose of which is to fill our hearts with pity for the poor and infirm, to teach us never to hurt their feelings, nor wantonly to vex the helpless. Mercy, likewise, is the object of the ordinance, "Thou shalt not deliver unto his master the slave that is fled from his scourge." But in a wider sense we derive from this example the duty to defend those who seek our protection; nay, more, we must look after their interests, be kind to them and never hurt their feelings by harsh and cruel words.

The Pure Lips

You know we condemn lowness of speech, and justly so, for the gift of speech is peculiar to man and a boon which God granted to him, that he may be distinguished from the rest of living creatures. This gift, therefore, which God gave us in order to enable us to perfect ourselves, to learn and to teach, must not be employed in doing that which is for us most degrading and disgraceful. We must not imitate the songs and tales of ignorant and lascivious people. It may be suitable to them, but it is not fit for those who are told, "And ye shall be unto Me a kingdom of priests and a holy nation." (Exod. 19:6).

Reward

The sole object of seeking wisdom is to know more. The sole object of seeking truth is to know truth. Torah is truth; the sole object of studying the Torah is to do what is prescribed therein.... It is forbidden to a man of mature mind to ask: what reward will I receive for doing good or refraining from doing evil? This is the way of a child who needs to be enticed to do what he should do, by the promise of sweets, nuts or figs. There is nothing wrong about these beliefs which the Sages "permitted" the masses, in their spiritual immaturity, to entertain; for from performing the commandments not for their own sake, they might ultimately come to perform them for their own sake.

1 What is the relationship of freedom of will to morality? If man's actions are determined, why should he be blamed for doing wrong or praised for doing right?

2 How does the Jewish belief in freedom of will relate to your deeds, your acts and your character?

3 It is easy to accept the idea of mercy in principle. How may we accept it in practice?

4 Why does Judaism regard slander as moral leprosy? Indicate how the evil tongue can do more damage than a sword.

5 According to Maimonides, what is the reward of goodness?

"Moses Hayim Luzzatto was born in Padua, Italy, in 1707. He studied the *Kabbala* day and night and tried to find hidden meaning in the Torah. His best known work was called *Mesillat Yesharim* (Path of the Upright). It shows the various stages that lead to the goal of holiness, and is one of the classics of Jewish moralistic literature.

"The following are excerpts from *Mesillat Yesharim:*

The Eternal Presence

When a man is convinced that, wherever he is, he always stands in the presence of God, blessed be He, he is spontaneously imbued with fear lest he do anything wrong, and so detract from the exalted glory of God. "Know what is above thee," said our Sages, "a seeing eye and a hearing ear, and all thy deeds written in a book" (Abot 2.1). Since the Holy One, blessed be He, exercises His providence over everything, and sees and hears all things, everything that man does is noted and recorded as merit or demerit.

Loving-kindness

Loving-kindness requires that we shall not inflict pain upon any living being, even an animal. We should be merciful and compassionate toward animals, as it is said, "A righteous man regardeth the life of his beast" (Prov. 12.10). Some are of the opinion that cruelty to animals is prohibited even by the Torah. In any case, it is certainly prohibited by the Rabbis (Shab. 128b). The sum of the matter is that in the saint's heart compassion and benevolence must be firmly rooted. His striving must be always to increase the happiness of the world's creatures, and never to cause them any pain.

Lust for Honor

Even worse than greed is the lust for honor. A man may control his craving for wealth and for pleasure, but the craving for honor is irresistible because it is almost impossible to endure being inferior to one's fellows. This is why so many people stumble and perish.

Protest Against Wrong

Our Sages denounced the man who had it within his power to protest against wrong, but failed to do so. They held him responsible for the sin of the wrongdoers (Shab. 54b).... And this matter is self-evident, that as he who loves his neighbor cannot bear to see him maltreated or insulted, so he who loves the Holy One, blessed be He, cannot bear to see His name profaned, and His commandments transgressed.

Anger

We shall now speak of anger. There is, first, the irascible person. Concerning him our Sages declared, "He who gives vent to anger commits as grave a sin as though he worshipped strange gods" (Shab. 105b). Such a man usually flares up whenever anyone crosses him. He becomes so enraged that he is distraught, and loses all control of himself. He would destroy the entire world, if he had the power. His mind can no longer restrain him. For the moment, he is actually deprived of his reason, so that he acts like a wild beast. To him may be applied the words, "Thou that tearest thyself in thine anger, shall the earth be forsaken for thee?" (Job 18.4). Being at the mercy of his anger and following it blindly, he is liable to commit any conceivable transgression.

Ridicule

If a man happens to be in the company of someone who ridicules him, let him ignore the ridicule. Let him rather scorn those who laugh at him. Suppose he were engaged in some transaction through which he might earn a large sum of money, would he give it up for fear that his neighbors might ridicule him? All the more reluctant should he be to allow his soul to be destroyed simply because he is afraid of ridicule.

Of Watchfulness

A man should be watchful of his conduct. He should scrutinize and pass in review all his actions and habits to determine whether they are right or not, so that he may save his soul from the peril of destruction, and not grope about like a blind man. It is to this conclusion that reason impels us. Since man has the knowledge and understanding to save his soul from destruction, how is it that he deliberately shuts his eyes to his salvation? Can there be any greater brutishness? He who acts thus is lower than the beasts, whose nature it is to obey the law of self-preservation and to avoid everything from which they apprehend danger.

A man who goes through life without regard to whether or not he follows a virtuous way is like a blind man who walks along the edge of a river. He is in constant danger and more likely to suffer harm than to escape it.

1 Moses Hayim Luzzatto's "Path for the Upright" leads to a greater sensitivity to The Still, Small Voice. How can moral and spiritual values help us to feel "The Eternal Presence" in our lives?

2 An over-eagerness for honor may corrupt character. Do you think this applies to youth?

3 List the situations where somebody your own age may stand by without protesting against injustice and wrong.

4 A newspaperman recently asked a group of people: "Do you know how to get a line on a man's character in a hurry? Ask him what ten things in the last year made him maddest." Try it out on yourself! What ten things irritate you the most? How does this give you an estimate of your character?

5 How is fear helpful in following the path for the upright?

6 A person is frequently judged by his companions. To what extent is this fair and unfair?

7 Luzzatto advises us to ignore those who ridicule us. Do you agree or disagree? What are your reasons?

8 We go to the Doctor for a physical check-up. How important is it to have a religious check-up, to examine our conduct? Who is best qualified to make this type of examination?

Mysticism

"Moral and spiritual values were also taught through Jewish mysticism," said Rabbi Mayer. "The mystic is one who attempts to look beneath and beyond the obvious to find hidden meanings. He tries to enter into a communion with God to explore the secrets of the universe."

Billy said: "That sounds sort of spooky, doesn't it?"

"In a way it is, Bill, but a mystery isn't always spooky." Rabbi Mayer referred to a volume on his desk. "This book is a part of *The Cabala. Cabala* means 'tradition,' the teachings that tell of the Jewish speculation on the mysteries of God and the universe. It is based on the conviction that God is near, and that individuals may enter into a relationship with God that will enable them to understand hidden meanings and solve the mysteries of life.

"Such an attempt to probe these mysteries is not without danger. The Talmud tells us that four sages entered the 'garden'—a term used by mystics to describe secret teachings. The four were Akiba, Ben Zoma, Ben Azzai and Elisha ben Abuyah."

"What happened to them?" asked Linda. "Did they ever return to earth?"

"According to the Talmudic legend, they all returned, but only one was not affected by the experience. Ben Zoma became insane; Ben Azzai died young; Elisha ben Abuyah became a heritic. Only Akiba entered in peace and departed in peace. This story is a warning against the danger of undue speculation about religious mysteries.

"There were many cabalistic writings. An important work was called *Sefer Yetzirah*. This was written in the 8th century and attempts to offer secret meanings by the use of numbers. It is a sort of mystical arithmetic. The most important mystical book, however, appeared later. This was the *Sefer Hazohar*, The Book of Splendor, commonly known as the *Zohar*. Modern scholars believe that it was a collection of mystical writings put together by Moses de Leon, a Jewish mystic, who lived in Cordova in the 13th Century. As soon as it appeared, it became the most popular book of Jewish mystics in all lands. When the Jews were threatened in Spain at the time of Ferdinand and Isabella, there was a yearning for supernatural deliverance. This made the *Zohar* ever more popular. Later, Isaac Luria organized mysticism into a system. He invented what was thought to be a practical use of the *Cabala* and *Zohar* by charms, mystic words and numbers, in order to overcome evil and hardship.

"What interests us is not the charms and the juggling of words and numbers, but rather the moral and spiritual values taught through the *Cabala* and *Zohar*. The following are examples taken from the *Zohar:*

The Hidden Meaning of the Torah

Thus the tales related in the Torah are simply her outer garments, and woe to the man who regards that outer garb as the Torah itself, for such a man will be deprived of portion in the next world. Thus David said: "Open Thou mine eyes, that I may behold wondrous things out of Thy law" (Ps. 119:18), that is to say, the things that are underneath. See now. The most visible part of a man are the clothes that he has on, and they who lack understanding, when they look at the man, are apt not to see more in him than these clothes. In reality, however, it is the body of the man that constitutes the pride of his clothes, and his soul constitutes the pride of his body.

So it is with the Torah. Its narrations, which relate to things of the world, constitute the garments which clothe the body of the

Torah; and that body is composed of the Torah's precepts, *gufey Torah* (bodies, major principles). People without understanding see only the narrations, the garment; those somewhat more penetrating see also the body. But the truly wise, those who serve the most high King and stood on mount Sinai, pierce all the way through to the soul, to the true Torah which is the root principle of all. These same will in the future be vouchsafed to penetrate to the very soul of the soul of the Torah.

The Power of Forgiveness

Sitting one day at the gate of Lydda, Rabbi Abba saw a man approach and seat himself on a ledge which jutted out over the hollow ground far beneath. The man was weary with travel, and fell asleep. Rabbi Abba beheld a serpent crawling toward the man, and it had almost reached him when a branch hurtled from a tree and killed it. Now the man awakened, and, seeing the serpent before him, he jumped up; at this instant the ledge collapsed and crashed into the hollow below.

Rabbi Abba approached the man and said: "Tell me, why has God seen fit to perform two miracles for you? What have you done?"

To which the man answered: "Whosoever wronged me, at any time, always I made peace with him and forgave him. And if I failed to effect peace with him, then I refrained from going to take my rest before I forgave him, and along with him, forgave any others who had vexed me; at no time did I brood on the injury the man had done to me; rather, I made special efforts of kindness from then on to such a man."

"Thou art greater than Joseph," said Rabbi Abba. "He forgives his brethren, but thou forgivest strangers as well."

The Gates of Tears

One may ask, "If a man be deeply troubled and sunk into sorrow, and his heart is heavy, yet because of tribulation he feels the urge to go to the heavenly King to seek solace; is he then to desist from praying because of his sorrowfulness? What shall he do, since he cannot help it that his heart is heavy?"

The answer is that "from the day of the destruction of the Temple, all gates to heaven have been closed, but the gates of tears have not been closed," and suffering and sadness are expressed in tears. Standing over the gates of tears are certain heavenly beings, and they break down the bars and locks of iron, and allow the tears to enter, so that the entreaties of the grieving supplicants go through and reach the holy King, and the place of the Divine Presence grieved by the sorrow of him who prays, as it stands written: "In all their afflictions He is afflicted" (Isa. 63:9)....

And when the King, entering the place of the Presence, finds her grieving, then all her desires are granted to her. Hence the supplication of him who sorrows does not revert empty to him, but the Holy One, be blessed, has pity on him. Blessed is the man who sheds tears as he prays before the Holy One, be blessed.

The Zohar declares: "When the High Priest was to appear before God in the Sanctuary, he was to enter that holy place with joy, and all things about him were to express joy—for in God's service there is no room for sadness."

The Temple of the Heart

"Create in me a clean heart, O God, and renew a right spirit within me" (Ps. 51.12). Know thou that the heart is the source of life, and is placed in the center of the body as the Holy of Holies, as stated in the Book *Zohar*, is the central part of the world. Therefore one must have his heart cleansed from evil and all evil thoughts, otherwise he introduces an idol into the innermost part of the Temple, which ought to be a dwelling-place for the *Shehinah.*

1 The Jewish mystic was not concerned with numbers, words and mystery as a game. He was ever searching to find God. That is why he persistently looked for hidden meanings in the Torah. Reread the Ten Commandments and see if you can find hidden meanings that enable us to practice a more ethical way of life.

2 You have heard a great deal about the importance of forgiveness in Judaism. It is easy to talk about forgiveness, but extremely difficult to practice it. What do we gain by carrying a grudge? What do we gain through forgiveness?

3 In the quotations you have read, there is a statement about "the gate of tears," saying that one should enter the Divine Presence with tears. The next statement tells us that one should enter the sanctuary with joy, for in God's service there is no room for sadness. These statements seem to be contradictory. Are they? If they are, which one do you think is correct? Could they both apply?

4 The last quotation refers to the necessity of a clean heart. How do we introduce idols into the temple of the heart?

Philosophy

"The word 'philosophy' means 'love of knowledge.' The Jewish philosophers pondered over the meaning of life and tried to analyze how we may apply our knowledge of God and the Torah to life. Their writings are frequently difficult to understand. However, they gave to succeeding generations a treasure of moral and spiritual values.

"In addition to Maimonides, among the outstanding Jewish philosophers were: Saadia, Joseph Albo, Ibn Daud, Yehudah Halevi, Solomon Ibn Gabirol, and Crescas.

Saadia (Ben Joseph) Gaon

"Saadia was born in Egypt in 892. When he was 36 years old, he became the head *(Gaon)* of the Babylonian Academy at Sura. His most important work was *Emunot VeDe'ot*, Faiths and Beliefs, which for the first time offered the philosophy of the teachings of Judaism.

At a time when Jews were tempted to embrace the Moslem religion, Saadia strengthened them in their Jewish faith by showing them that they must resist temptation and face the realities of life by the practical application of Jewish ethics.

"Maimonides later summed up the important contribution of Saadia with this statement: 'Were it not for Saadia, the Torah would almost have disappeared from the midst of Israel; for it was he who made manifest what was obscure therein, made strong what had weakened, and made it known far and wide by word of mouth and in writing.'

"The following are excerpts from Saadia's philosophy:

The Golden Mean

Which is the golden mean? To engage both in the service of the Creator, and in making provision for the maintenance of his household and of himself. A man's chief striving, however, should be centered in the Torah, and in the service of God; and then it will be well with him, both in this world and in the world to come.

God is Not A Man

Such terms as head, eye, ear, mouth, lip, face, hand, heart, bowels, foot, which are used in relation to God in the Bible, are figurative. For it is the custom of language to apply such terms metaphorically to certain ideas like elevation, providence, acceptance, declaration, command, favor, anger, power, wisdom, mercy, dominion. Language would be a very inadequate instrument if it confined itself to the literal meaning of the words it uses; and in the case of God we should be limited to the statement that He is.

1 If God is not a man, why do we ascribe sex to Him and refer to God as Father, King, Lord?

2 What is meant by the statement that "The Torah speaks in the language of man"?

3 Do you think that God sees with eyes, hears with ears, and actually speaks with a voice? If not, how then does God reveal Himself to man?

Yehudah Halevi

"This poet and philosopher was born in Toledo, Spain, in 1085. Like Maimonides, he was a skilled physician and a brilliant philosopher. His most famous work, *The Kuzari*, presents an imaginary dialogue between the King of the Khazars and a Jew who had been called to teach the principles of Judaism. So convincing was the argument, that the King of the Khazars became a convert to Judaism.

Yehudah Halevi insisted upon the close relationship of Judaism with the Jewish people. He pointed out that Christianity and Islam are centered upon their founders, while Judaism is the religious expression of the Jewish people. In *The Kuzari* he explains this, saying:

The People of God

If there were no Israelites there would be no Torah. They did not derive their high position from Moses, but Moses received his for their sake.... We are not called the people of Moses, but the people of God.

Three Elements

Our religion has three elements: fear, love, and joy—and by each of these we can draw nearer to God.

The Heart of the Nations

Thus Israel has been designed to function as the "heart" of the nations, reacting to all the ailments in the body of mankind, while at the same time stimulating its conscience.

1 Halevi taught that Jewish suffering is not without purpose. In your opinion, what purpose has been served by Jewish suffering? What did Isaiah mean when he called Israel "the suffering servant of God"?

2 What is meant by the concept of the Jewish people? Is it proper to refer to the peoplehood of Israel?

3 How can we draw nearer to God by fear, love and joy?

Joseph Albo

"It is believed that Joseph Albo was born about 1380 in the town of Monreal in Aragon. He is remembered because of his philosophic work called *Sefer Ha-'Ikkarim,* Book of Principles. In this, he considers the existence of God, divine revelation and divine justice. Albo defends Judaism against the criticism of the philosophers, and shows how the moral and spiritual teachings of Judaism may be used and applied to life."

Love of God

Love of God gives joy and delight to the soul. Ordinarily, love of a thing that cannot be obtained or that is difficult of attainment causes trouble and confusion to the soul, which casts about for means to obtain the object of its love. And for this reason lovers are always in pain and sorrow until they obtain the object of their love. But the love of God does not cause trouble or confusion to the soul, although God is not a thing that can be obtained. The reason is because the little of Him that man can attain gives wonderful joy and pleasure and delight to the soul.

God Speaks Through Silence

And to indicate that God's essence is absolutely unknown and absolutely simple, in a manner inconceivable, the text says, "And after the fire a still, small voice," pointing to the impossibility of understanding God's essence, so much so that the only way to speak of Him or of the attributes of His perfection is by way of negation, which is the still, small voice. The literal meaning of the biblical expression is, "a voice of *fine* silence," fine silence being an allusion to the subtle distinction to be observed in the understanding of the various negative attributes... of God.

God Is Not A Body

It has already been proved demonstratively that God is neither body nor a force residing in body. It follows that we must deny God all bodily accidents and corporeal affections. It is necessary therefore to give a reason for the expressions found in all the Prophets that God is jealous, wrathful, vengeful and bearing grudge.

The explanation is this. The purpose of the prophets is to lead all mankind to worship God and to love Him. But the masses of the people cannot be made to humble themselves for service except from fear of punishment. Therefore it was necessary for the prophets to speak in a language understood by the generality of the people.

Happiness

Belief in God and in His Torah brings man to eternal happiness and causes his soul to cleave to the spiritual substance. This is proved by experience, as we know from continuous tradition.

Judaism As A Way of Thinking

Rabbi Mayer closed his notebook. "I am not going to ask you to discuss the quotations from the Book of Principles in class," he said, "because the ideas and beliefs they suggest will be the subject of our class discussion in a few weeks. Joseph Albo wrote about Jewish beliefs, the nature of God, the after-life and the Messianic hope. To him, Judaism was not only a way of life, it was also a way of thinking and believing.

"Soon I am going to ask you whether Judaism has a creed, something we must believe to be good Jews. In the meanwhile, I hope that you will think a little more about how Judaism taught moral and spiritual values through the writings of moralists, mystics and philosophers.

"When you talk to your teacher, Joel, explain to her that we believe that moral and spiritual values are best taught through the synagogue, the home, and the religious school. Christians should learn moral and spiritual values through the church, the home and the Sunday school. In that way, Catholics, Protestants, and Jews may teach the ethical duties to God and man—each in their own way, without the danger of making one faith seem superior or inferior. If we do this, then the public schools will be kept free of the sectarian religious doctrines that frequently stir up controversy, misunderstanding and enmity."

Rabbi Mayer opened his notebook again. "Perhaps this is the best answer of all. Professor L. P. Jack, writing in *Living Universe*, said this about the role of the schools in teaching the values of religion:

"*We teach it in arithmetic, by accuracy.*
We teach it in language, by learning to say what we mean—'yea, yea, and nay, nay.'
We teach it in geography, by breadth of mind.
We teach it in handicraft, by thoroughness.
We teach it in astronomy, by reverence.
We teach it in the playground, by fair play.
We teach it by kindness to animals, kindness to servants, by good manners to one another, and by truthfulness in all things."

QUESTIONS FOR DISCUSSION

1 What is the modern significance of the following statements from moralistic literature:

a "If the heart does not know what the lips utter, it is no prayer." (Sefer Hasidim)

b "Poverty, sickness and terror are easier to bear with faith." (Solomon Ibn Gabirol)

c "To avoid an insult, you may tell a white lie." (Sefer Hasidim)

d "To triumph through unrighteousness is to be defeated." (Solomon Ibn Gabirol)

e "Accustom thyself to habitual goodness, for a man's character is what habit makes it." (Maimonides)

f "A gambler always loses. He loses money, dignity, and time. And if he wins, he weaves a spider's web around himself." (Maimonides)

2 The philosopher Philo said: "To be pious toward God is to be loving towards men." How may this be applied today?

3 In the *Sefer Hasidim*, Judah the Pious said: "He who sins not among the wicked is a better man than he who sins not among the righteous." What did he mean?

4 Moses Ibn Ezra said: "Every man must strive first for the improvement of his own character, and then of the character of others." What does this suggest to you?

5 What is the difference between taking revenge and bearing a grudge?

6 Do you agree or disagree with this statement made by Maimonides: "If I find the road narrow and can see no other way of teaching the well-established truth except by pleasing one intelligent man and displeasing ten thousand fools, I prefer to address myself to the one man and take no notice whatever of the contemplation of the multitudes." What are your reasons? Do you think this statement is democratic? Is it practical?

7 What do you think Saadia meant when he wrote: "Our nation is a nation only by virtue of its Torah"?

8 Explain what Ibn Daud meant when he said: "The aim of philosophic theory is the practical realization of all moral purposes, and this is the essence of religion."

9 In 1670, Spinoza said: "I do not know how to teach philosophy without becoming a disturber of established religion." What do you think he meant? How can philosophy disturb established religion? Do you think that it is a good thing for established religion to be disturbed? Why?

10 Do you think a person can come to a real religious faith without doubt? M. R. Cohen, a modern philosopher said: "The business of the philosopher is well done if he succeeds in raising genuine doubts." What is your opinion?

11 Why do you think that mysticism has ever flourished during periods of suffering and strife?

THINGS TO DO

1 Discuss in class whether it is possible to be called religious if a person practices ethical, moral and spiritual values but doesn't believe in God or affiliate with the synagogue.

2 Moses Maimonides wrote a "Guide for the Perplexed." Write an essay offering a guide for the perplexed of our times.

3 Using the Jewish Encyclopedia, look up the moralistic work of Judah the Pious called *Sefer Hasidim.* Write a paragraph about the author and the book.

4 Identify Solomon Ibn Gabirol, Moses Ibn Ezra, Crescas, Ibn Daud, Philo and Israel Salanter. What major contribution did each one make?

5 Look up the meaning of mystic, moral, spiritual, and esoteric.

6 Luzzato declared that "the evil that befalls the sluggard comes not at once, but gradually and unawares. He is drawn into one evil after another until he finds himself steeped in wrongdoing." Write an imaginary story illustrating this statement.

7 Write a short summary of the life of Baruch Spinoza. Include one paragraph from his book on ethics.

SELECTED QUOTATIONS

Truth

Our Sages said: "Truth is the seal of the Holy One, blessed be He" (Shab. 55a). Since truth has been chosen by the Holy One, blessed be He, as His seal, how hateful must untruth be to Him! The Holy One, blessed be He, has admonished us strongly concerning the need of speaking the truth. "Speak ye every man the truth to his neighbour" (Zech. 8.16)....

Rab Safra had an article for sale. As he was reading the *Shema*, a man came to him and said, "Wilt thou sell me this thing for such and such a price?" Rab Safra made no reply, but went on reading the *Shema*. The prospective buyer, thinking Rab Safra did not want to sell the article for the price named, offered more. But when Rab Safra had ended the *Shema*, he said to the stranger, "You may have the article at the price which you mentioned first; for it was at that price I had decided to sell it" (Mak. 24a, and Rashi). Learn from this example how far-reaching is the duty of telling the truth!

MOSES HAYIM LUZZATO
Mesillat Yesharim

Revenge and Bearing a Grudge

The difference between taking revenge and bearing a grudge is well known. To take revenge is to return evil for evil. To bear a grudge is to remind a man of the evil he has done to you though you repay him with good (Yoma 23a).

MOSES HAYIM LUZZATO
Mesillat Yesharim

The Kusari

If, by some catastrophe, all Jewish books from the Bible to the last Yiddish daily were lost, and only the Book of the *Kusari* were left, it would be possible for the historian to construct with fidelity the diverse strands of thought and sentiment which enter into the making of the traditional Jewish mentality. For Yehudah Halevi, the author of this volume, did not set out to defend the philosophy of the Jewish religion against the challenge of the metaphysicians and logicians of his day. He began and ended his quest with the concerns of the living Jewish people, so that his volume faithfully reproduces that cluster of ideas and feelings which rose to the surface of consciousness, whenever intelligent Jews reflected on the peculiar destiny of their people among the nations.

RABBI JACOB B. AGUS

The Goodness of God's Work

Men frequently think that the evils in the world are more numerous than the good things; many sayings and songs of the nations dwell on this ideal. They say that the good is found only exceptionally, while evil things are numerous and lasting. The origin of this error is to be found in the circumstances that men judge of the whole universe by examining one single person only. If anything happens to him contrary to his expectation, forthwith they conclude that the whole universe is evil. All mankind at present in existence forms only an infinitesimal portion of the permanent universe. It is of great advantage that man should know his station. Numerous evils to which persons are exposed are due to the defects existing in the persons themselves. We seek relief from our own faults; we suffer from evils which we inflict on ourselves, and we ascribe them to God who is far from connected with them.

MOSES MAIMONIDES

Belief and Happiness

Not all belief leads to happiness. Thus belief in the impossible does not produce happiness. No one doubts that belief which makes a man happy must be belief in the truth, not belief that a non-existent thing exists or that an existing thing does not exist.

JOSEPH ALBO
Sefer Ha-'Ikkarim

Three Things Conspire

Three things conspire together in mine eyes
To bring the remembrance of Thee ever before me,

And I possess them as faithful witnesses:
Thy heavens, for whose sake I recall Thy name,
The earth I live on, that rouseth my thought
With its expanse which recalleth the expander of
my pedestal,
And the musing of my heart when I look within
the depths of myself.
Bless the Lord, O my soul, for ever and aye!

SOLOMON IBN GABIROL

To Be In Sum, A Man

There are many advantages which Jews may derive from a knowledge and love of Judaism. It can give them a high, clear, religious faith. It can supply them with a system of ethical values, personal and social, idealistic and practical at the same time. It can grace their lives with poetic observances and with the treasures of an ancient tradition. It can make them, in sum, nobler, stronger, better human beings and more valuable citizens.

But one service Judaism performs for Jews which is often overlooked: it is the first function of a human being to respect himself, to stand erect before the world, to injure none, to help all, but to allow none to injure him–to be in sum, a man.

RABBI MILTON STEINBERG

Nothing is Hidden From God

Wicked men think that the eye of God sees nothing but the outer world through the co-operation of the sun. They do not know that He surveys the unseen even before the seen, for He Himself is His own light.

PHILO

SUGGESTED READINGS

Albo, Joseph, *Sefer Ha-'Ikkarim*, edited by Isaac Husik
Bachya Ibn Pakuda, *Duties of the Heart*, Translated by Moses Hyamson
Bokser, Ben Zion, *The Legacy of Maimonides*

Bokser, Ben Zion, *From The World of the Cabbalah*

Caplan & Ribalow, *Great Jewish Books*, Yehuda Halevi, pp. 131-146; Maimonides, pp. 159-179; The Zohar, pp. 191-209.

Cohen, A., *Choice of Pearls, Solomon Ibn Gabirol*

Druck, David, *Saadya Gaon*

Friedlander, M., *Guide For The Perplexed, Maimonides*

Glatzer, Nachum, *The Book of Splendor*

Huzik, Isaac, *History of Medieval Jewish Philosophy*

Levy, Hans, *Philosophia Judaica: Philo*

Luzzato, Moses Hayim, *Mesillat Yesharim (The Path of the Upright)*, By Mordecai M. Kaplan

Saadya, *Emunot Vadayot*

Scholem, Gershom G., *Major Trends in Jewish Mysticism*

Scholem, Gershom G., *Zohar: The Book of Splendor*

Universal Jewish Encyclopedia, Bachya Ibn Pakuda, Vol. 2, pp. 34-35; Maimonides, Vol. 7, pp. 287-295; Moses Hayim Luzzato, Vol. 7, pp. 246-247; Cabala, Vol. 2, pp. 614-620; Saadia, Vol. 9, pp. 289-291; Yehuda Halevi, Vol. 6, pp. 225-229; Joseph Albo, Vol. 1, pp. 161-162.

7

THE VOICE OF JOY

The Ethics of Hasidism

Promise of Action

"The whole religious school curriculum should be changed, textbooks and all," said Paula. "Maybe there will be some action after tomorrow night!"

"What's happening tomorrow night?" Charles asked.

Paula ignored the question, and continued talking to Sandra. "It's about time that we stop suffering as Jews. I get tired of all this studying about how Jews were killed in one country, and how Jews were driven out of another country."

"But it did happen, Paula. As much as we don't like to hear about it, persecution is part of our history, and we should know the facts," retorted Sandra. "I'll ask the Rabbi what he thinks."

Raising her hand, she asked: "What do you think of the subject for the religious school parent-teachers' meeting tomorrow night, Rabbi?"

Larry chortled. "I'll bet the Rabbi picked the subject himself just to start a lively discussion."

Rabbi Mayer smiled. "No, I didn't pick the subject, although I think it is an important one which should be considered thoughtfully."

"What's going on around here?" asked Charles. "What subject? What meeting? What's happening?"

"You sound as though you're asking the four questions at a Passover Seder, Charles," said the Rabbi. "Perhaps I can answer all of them by giving the reasons for the meeting and its subject.

"Last month, following our adult study course, one parent suggested that we eliminate all references to the persecution of the Jew from our religious school text-books. 'There is too much emphasis,' he said, 'on the burden of being a Jew. It is unwise and even harmful to teach children the sorrow Jews have experienced throughout history.'

"Before he was through speaking, however, another parent disagreed. She said that we should not blind ourselves to the facts of history, and that if the students weren't taught about prejudice in the past, they would be shocked and unprepared for any prejudice they might encounter. What's more, she said, the important thing is that the Jews survived the persecution of the past, and were made stronger in their faith because of their suffering.

"Then all the parents started to give their opinions. There was so much interest in the subject that a detailed discussion was arranged for the next parent-teachers' meeting.

"Therefore, when we meet tomorrow night we will discuss the question: 'Is There Too Much Suffering Identified With Judaism?' "

WHAT DO YOU THINK?

1 Do you think there is too much emphasis on the suffering and persecution of the Jew in our textbooks? If your answer is "yes," do you believe the facts should be ignored, toned-down, or not considered until the student is an adult?

2 When you read about discrimination against the Jew in history, does it leave you:

a Angry
b More devoted to being a Jew
c Ashamed of being a Jew
d Indifferent

3 How would you answer those who apply the statement, "where there's smoke there's fire," to imply that the Jews brought their troubles on themselves?

4 In what way did the suffering endured by the Jew throughout history make him stronger and more religious?

5 What would be the status of Jews today if there had been no persecution, suffering, and discrimination?

6 If you were to attend the Parent-Teachers' Meeting, what would you say about the topic of Jewish suffering?

7 If he were asked, do you think the average Jewish student would consider Judaism as a religion of sorrow or joy?

The Religion of Joyful Reverence

"Frankly," said Rabbi Mayer, "I'm glad that this topic has been selected for discussion. Too many people, Jews and Christians, identify Judaism with suffering, persecution and oppression, forgetting the joy of Jewish life and the sacred privilege of being a Jew. Judaism is not a burden we must bear or a religion of tears and sorrow. That is why I agree with parents who feel that it is unwise to place too much emphasis on suffering in our textbooks."

"Do you mean," asked Joseph, "that we should eliminate all references to the persecution of Jews? Just forget about the discrimination in our history?"

"Not at all, Joseph. Certainly we can't ignore history. But the primary emphasis of Jewish history is not suffering, or persecution. Despite powerful enemies and repeated efforts to destroy the Jew, Judaism survived and emerged strengthened, as a joyous affirmation of man's love for God and God's love for man. That is why the Hasidim made such an important contribution to Jewish thinking."

"The Hasidim!" exclaimed Michael. "I don't mean to be disrespectful, Rabbi, but last year in another class when we were told about the Hasidim, it sounded silly to me. I don't see what it has to do with living as a Jew today."

"Let me explain, Michael. Just as we are now discussing persecution and suffering in Jewish life, so at another period of our history there were those who felt that it was wrong to identify Judaism with sorrow and to express our love for God with tears alone. To them, the real service of God was through joyous devotion. They believed that Judaism must teach us to hear the Still, Small Voice in song and fervent worship, the giving of charity and deeds of loving kindness to our fellowmen. And so, a new philosophy of Jewish life and worship swept through Europe in the 18th Century.

"Founded by Israel Baal Shem Tov, 'the man of the good name,' this new movement was called 'Hasidism,' and emphasized the joy of worship, the happiness of being a Jew and the wondrous privilege of obeying God's commandments. The Hasidim opposed those who believed in the 'letter of the law.' They did not think that a Jew had to be a scholar in order to come close to God or worship God with sincere reverence. They insisted that routine worship was often cold and formal. It lacked *Kavanah,* sincere devotion. To the Hasidim, it was important to rejoice and sing, to dance and even shout their love of God.

"To Israel Baal Shem Tov, or the 'Besht,' as he was affectionately called, God is not only the Creator of heaven and earth, He is also the Master of the Universe, who created delight and joy. To him and to his disciples a Jew who does not rejoice in fulfilling the commandments of God, a Jew who does not exult in his relationship to the Holy One, has failed to grasp the true meaning of the Jewish faith."

The Crowded Synagogue

"The Hasidim believed that prayer is the means by which man communicates with God, and God talks to man. Therefore, prayer must be sincere and whole-hearted, and not a meaningless mumbling of words or formal supplications. Once the Baal Shem stopped on the threshold of a house of prayer and refused to enter. 'I cannot go in,' he said. 'It is crowded with teachings and prayers from wall to wall up to the ceiling. How could there be room for me?' And when he saw that those around him were staring at him and did not know what he meant, he added: 'The words from the lips of those whose teaching and praying does not come from the heart cannot rise, but fill the house from wall to wall and from floor to ceiling.'

"Beautiful words are not enough. God doesn't want words without sincerity. God wants the prayer that is uttered with *Kavanah*, joyous sincerity, with true meaning. That is why the Baal Shem could not enter the synagogue. It was so filled with teachings and prayer that came from the lips only, that there was no room for him.

"Only those prayers that come from the heart rise and find their way to God. That is why when another Hasidic teacher, the Tzanzer Rabbi was asked: 'What do you do before praying?' 'I pray,' was the reply, 'that I may be able to pray properly—with all my heart.'

"Thus, at a time when scholars were insisting upon formal prayer, and doted upon complicated legal interpretations of the Talmud, the Hasidim spoke to the common man, who yearned to love God with joy. Through the Zadik, a holy man who devoted his entire life to unity with God and with Israel, the people were taught that the real significance of prayer is its inner meaning, the enthusiasm, love and sincerity of a reaching soul. Even a silent prayer in which one directs his whole being to God, can be more meaningful than a prayer of beautiful words.

"The followers of the 'Besht' were called Hasidim, pious ones. When a Hasid prayed, he prayed with his entire body—he sang, danced and even whistled.

The Whistle

"The saintly Baal Shem knew that every heart could find its way to its Creator, if it went out to Him. He tried to make his devotions a complete surrender, as though he were offering his heart in his hands. Once on the Day of Atonement he poured his soul forth in prayer, but somehow he felt that genuine, heartfelt prayer was absent. Neither he nor any member of his congregation was able to offer it. The time for breaking the fast had long passed. Yet he and all the devout around him were still searching their souls for the prayer that would surely find its way to heaven.

"It chanced that an ignorant shepherd boy came down from the hills. Attracted by the chanting that came to him from the synagogue, he entered. There he saw a multitude engrossed in their devotions. The boy felt a sudden urge to join in the prayers. He wanted to thank God that he was alive. In his childish way he did the only thing he could do; put his fingers into his mouth, and gave a long shrill whistle.

"The congregation looked up, scandalized at the shamefaced boy who now realized what an awful thing he had done. But Rabbi Israel turned with a happy smile to the congregation: 'Our devotions are over. At last we were fortunate enough to offer an unselfish, heartfelt prayer in our midst.'

Religious Hide and Seek

"The Hasidim taught that true happiness is not found in material possessions, but in the joy of the religious life, as man goes forth in search of God.

"A story tells of a little boy playing hide and seek with his friends. For some reason they stopped playing while he was hiding. He began to cry. His grandfather came out of the house to see what was troubling him and said: 'Do not weep, my child, because the boys did not come to find you. Perhaps you can learn from this disappointment. All of life is like a game between God and man, only it is God who is weeping. For man is not playing the game fairly. God is waiting to be found, and men have gone off in search of other things.'

"God is waiting to be found–but where shall man find him? Where is the dwelling place of God? This was the question the Rabbi of Kitzk asked a number of learned scholars. They laughed at him. What a thing to ask! But the pious Rabbi answered his own question. He said: 'God dwells wherever man lets Him in.'

"Man can find God if he will seek holiness, justice and truth. God is waiting to be found. The Still, Small Voice is calling, but men have gone off in the search of other things and aren't listening. It was the Hasidim who taught that since the whole world is filled with the glory of God, a person doesn't have to be a great scholar to find Him –for God dwells wherever man lets Him in.

"This isn't just a lesson in a challenging aspect of Jewish literature," said Rabbi Mayer. "These teachings of the Hasidim should make us think about applying Judaism to our own lives. We should consider how we can let God in–into our thoughts, our actions and our everyday experiences.

"Consider for a moment whether or not your prayers are words read from a book, or an enthusiastic expression of your love of God.

"Ask yourself whether you play the game of hide and seek with God. God is waiting to be found. Do you truly search for God? Do you take the time to let God influence what you say and how you act?"

"But Rabbi," Albert protested, "it's not easy to let God in. Most of the time we have to think of homework, school activities, athletics and lots of other things."

Rabbi Mayer smiled. "What you say is true, but the Hasidim also lived normal lives. They, too, had obligations and responsibilities. Don't think of them as saints without faults, men who went into a trance and thus entered into communion with God. They believed that God could be found in everything, since God is in everything. But a person has to *want* to find God, and make the effort to live by God's commandments, and then, by disciplining his character, he can attain to a state of holiness.

"For example, the Hasidim believed that to follow the Jewish way of life we must learn to control the tendency to anger, hatred or sin. God has blessed us with the freedom of will to choose good and reject evil. We may conquer ourselves only if we learn to discipline our temper, and try to control the inclination to do wrong.

The Rabbi and the Acrobats

"One day a group of acrobats gave a performance in a town. They stretched a rope across the river and one of them walked the rope to the opposite bank. The people came running to behold this thrilling sight, and in the midst of the crowd stood the Baal Shem Tov himself. His disciples were astonished and asked why he was there. This is what he answered. 'I went to see how a man might cross the chasm between two heights. And as I watched him, I reflected that if man would submit his soul to the discipline to which the acrobat submitted his body, what deep abysses might he not cross upon the tenuous cord of life!'

The Jewish Way of Life

"A man expressed the wish, in the presence of the Belzer Rabbi, to die like a good Jew. The Rabbi commented: 'Such a wish is wrong.

It is like the wish of Balaam: "May my soul die the death of the righteous!" Desire rather that you may live like a good Jew, and it will follow as a consequence that you will die like a good Jew.'

"The Hasidim insisted that Judaism is a way of life, not a preparation for death. All of life must be sanctified with holiness—but that does not mean that man must be chained to sorrow or that religion requires us to be solemn and sad. Holiness is also achieved through laughter and love. The Jew joyfully accepts the obligations of life, and the commandments of God. He is to serve and love God in everything he says and does. This is what makes life holy, and that is why Rabbi Shelomo asked: 'What is the worst thing the evil urge can achieve?' And he answered: 'To make man forget that he is the son of a King.' If Jews will remember that they are children of the King of all Kings, they will try to conduct themselves at all times so that they may reflect honor upon the King of the Universe.

The Holiness of Man

"The Hasidic rabbis taught that since man is created in the divine image, every human being is sacred, and precious to God. The infinite love of God for His children is beyond our ability to comprehend. Even the sinners are not beyond God's compassion. Rabbi Shelomo once said: 'If only I could love the greatest Zadik, the most saintly rabbi, as much as God loves the greatest ne'er-do-well.'

"Remembering that we worship God by imitating His attributes of mercy and love, the Hasidim taught us that we must never hate others even though they may wrong us.

"One night, thieves entered Rabbi Wolf's house and took whatever they happened to find. From his room, the Zadik watched them, but did nothing to stop them. They took some utensils, and among them a cup from which a sick man had sipped that evening. Rabbi Wolf ran after them. 'My good people,' he said, 'whatever you have found here, I beg you to regard as gifts from me. I do not begrudge these things to you. But please be careful. The breath of a sick man is clinging to that cup, and you might catch his disease.'

"From then on, he said every evening before going to bed: 'All my possessions are common property,' so that if thieves come again they would not be guilty of theft.

"Such saintliness is difficult for us to understand–but what did earthly possessions mean to a Zadik? His whole life was devoted to worshipping God by loving his fellow-man; even his enemies. That is why Rabbi Michal gave this command to his sons: 'Pray for your enemies that all may be well with them. And should you think this is not serving God, remember that this is indeed the most difficult prayer of all.' Man, even though he may sin, is created in the divine image. It is only by helping God's children, by showing love to every human being, even to our enemies, by conquering selfishness, envy and hatred, that we truly show our love of God.

Social Justice

"The prophet Isaiah taught that God is exalted through justice and sanctified through righteousness. This was accepted literally in the Hasidic tradition, and the Zadik and his disciples worshipped God not only with their prayers, but with the goodness and kindness of their deeds. They believed that we can find God through ethical action, by the application of prophetic justice to every aspect of life.

"Rabbi Wolf's wife once had a quarrel with her servant. She accused the girl of having broken a dish and wanted her to pay for the damage. The girl denied having done what she was accused of, and refused to replace the article. The quarrel became heated. Finally the wife of the Rabbi decided to refer the matter to the court of arbitration, and quickly dressed for the visit. When Rabbi Wolf saw this, he too put on his Sabbath clothes. When his wife asked why, he told her that he intended accompanying her. She objected to this on the grounds that this was not fitting for him, and that besides, she knew very well what to say to the court. 'You know,' the Zadik replied, 'but the poor orphan, your servant, in whose behalf I am coming, does not know, and who is there to defend her cause except me?'

"Just as God does not discriminate against His children because of their race or station in life, so those who would attempt to imitate the moral attributes of God must endeavor to apply the standards of justice and mercy to every human being, master or servant, rich or poor, wise or simple. Judaism summons us to respect the worth and dignity of all men, regardless of their religious faith, their race or their nationality. Through the unity of God we are to strive for the unity of all mankind, remembering that God is exalted through justice and sanctified through righteousness.

Humility

"A man came to a Hasidic rabbi and asked to be taught humility. As he spoke, the clock struck the hour.

"The Rabbi commented: 'From the sound of the clock we can receive ample instruction regarding the submission of the heart.' Each of us should say to himself: 'Another hour of my life has departed; have I accomplished any improvement of my soul within it?'

"Each individual must learn to use time wisely, reverently and, above all, with humility. He must learn to discipline himself against false pride, and conquer his arrogance so that he will not look down upon anyone as inferior or unworthy of his love. Are not all men God's children? Are they not created in the divine image?

"And so, the Hasidim told of a king who attired himself in old garments, lived in a small hut, and forbade anyone to revere him. But when he honestly examined himself, the king found himself prouder of his seeming humility than ever before. A philosopher thereupon remarked to him: 'Dress like a king; live like a king; allow the people to show due respect to you; but be humble in your inmost heart.'

"It is the sincere humility of heart that enables man to comprehend the infinity of God, and thus discipline his soul to worship the Holy One, Blessed Be He.

The Purpose of Suffering

"Even though the Hasidim emphasized the joy of religious life, and worshipped God with exaltation, they were not free of persecution and suffering. Beset by enemies, crushed by tyranny, they never yielded to despair. If they were oppressed and forced to suffer, then they prayed that they might use that suffering to show their love of God.

"One of the most touching prayers in our Jewish tradition is the prayer of Rabbi Levi Yitzchok, who lifted his voice saying: 'Lord of the World.... I do not beg You to reveal to me the secret of Your ways—I could not bear it. But show me one thing; show me what my present suffering means to me, what it demands of me, what You, Lord of the World, are telling me by way of it. It is not why I suffer that I wish to know, but only whether I suffer for Your sake.'

"It was through suffering that the Hasidim learned to respond to human needs more tenderly. Suffering did not embitter them. Rather, it sensitized them and motivated them to show compassion for the sick, assist the poor, provide for the orphan, and respond to those who cried out for help.

"When they were subjected to suffering or grief, the Hasidim never protested against God. Who were they to understand the secret of God's ways? Who were they to question the wisdom of God's providence? Instead of protesting, they made pain a discipline, and suffering a means of self-control. The more they suffered, the more they could understand with the Sassover Rabbi that 'to love, truly to love, means to know what brings pain to your fellow-man,' and that by experiencing his pain you learn to understand him and love him the more. Just as a mother's pain makes her love her child all the more, so must pain and suffering bring us closer to God and make us love Him all the more, too.

The Music of Judaism

"The Baal Shem told this story: 'Once a fiddler played so sweetly that all who heard him began to dance, and whoever came near enough to hear joined in the dance. Then a deaf man who knew nothing of music happened along, and the dancing seemed the senseless action of madmen.'

"The Hasidim taught that the same is true with the music of Judaism. Those who are deaf to the Song of all Songs, that sings of Israel's love for God and God's love for Israel, cannot understand the meaning of Judaism. To them, prayer, worship, the study of Torah and the practice of the *mitzvoth* seem the action of madmen—senseless, confused and in bad taste.

"The essence, the holy purpose of the Hasidic movement, is to sensitize us to hear and understand the music of divinity by attuning our hearts to God, even as we proclaim: 'The Lord is my strength and my song.' That is why Levi Yitzchok, the Compassionate One, used to sing this song, expressing his all-consuming love for the Master of the Universe:

Where I wander—You!
Where I ponder—You!
Only You, always You!
When I am gladdened—You!
When I am saddened—You!
Sky is You! Earth is You!
You above! You below!
In every trend, at every end,
Only You, You again, always You!
You! You! You!

"It was addressed to a God who was close to him, part of him, more precious to him than any dear one, to whom he prayed, and talked and sang—You, O God, ever You, always You.

"We can understand why the followers of the Hasidic movement obeyed the command to 'Rejoice in the Lord.' This rejoicing is the melody of divine love that has echoed through the ages. This is the music of holiness that attunes Israel to the infinite.

A Vision of Humanity

"The Hasidic movement extended its vision beyond the Jewish people and faith, to behold all men. Although for Israel, the teachings of the Hasidic Rabbis were not limited to Jews, but were meant to apply to all peoples and all faiths.

"Because he is privileged to be identified with the covenant made at Sinai, the Jew must ever remember that he is bound to God in love. It is because of that covenant, and his love for God, the Father of all, that he must extend his love to every human being created as each is, in the image of God.

"A rich but miserly man came to consult a Zadik. Pointing to the window facing the street, the latter said, 'What do you see out there?'

'People,' answered the rich man.

The Zadik then took him by the hand and led him to a mirror. 'What do you see now?' he asked.

'Now I see myself,' answered the rich man.

Then the Zadik said: 'Behold, in the window there is glass, and in the mirror there is glass. But the glass of the mirror is covered with silver, and no sooner is the silver added than you cease to see others but see only yourself.'

"Perhaps that is the reason why the Hasidim were so free from the desire to acquire material possessions. These were of the moment. The Jew was summoned to behold people and life through the perspective of eternity; to identify himself with values that were spiritually eternal.

"Poverty was not regarded as a liability, but as a means of disciplining the soul to sympathize with others and to behold their needs. It was not the quest for gold that concerned the Hasidim. It was the quest for God that animated their endeavors and filled them with a sense of divine purpose. If a person is interested in himself alone—his needs, his ambitions, his material desires—how can he go beyond himself to devote his life to service to others? How can he even see others, if his vision is limited to himself? We must have a vision of humanity to challenge us to labor for a sacred cause and to fulfil the destiny of Israel as servants of the holy God.

The Challenge of Faith

"Although the Hasidic teachers beheld the vision of a united humanity through the window of their faith, they were not satisfied with vague statements. They sought ways to make this vision a reality. Where shall a man begin to fulfil the sacred mission of Israel?

"The Rabbi of Zans used to say, 'In my youth, when I was fired with the love of God, I thought I would convert the whole world to God. I soon discovered that it would be quite enough to convert the people of my town, and I tried for a long time but did not succeed. Then I realized that my program was still too ambitious, and I concentrated on those in my household. But I could not convert them, either. Finally, the truth dawned on me. I must work on myself to give true service to God, but I did not accomplish even this.'

"It is only when a child of God recognizes that the improvement of society begins with himself that he is ready to contribute to the fulfilment of Israel's destiny of building God's kingdom on earth."

Rabbi Mayer closed his notebook. "I'm wondering," he said, "if you still think that Hasidism has nothing to do with living as a Jew today?"

Michael grinned. "I suppose that I was sort of against the study of Hasidism just because I didn't know very much about what it meant and what it taught."

"Yes," said Rabbi Mayer, "the *Zadikim* heard the Still, Small Voice in their own way. Let me sum it up.

"Their way was the way of joy. Through the Hasidim, Jewish life took on a new meaning. The Jew experienced an indescribable yearning to come closer to the source of all love and light. To those chained to the letter of the law, to those who were not great students of the Torah, the Hasidic movement offered a rapturous opportunity to search for God and find Him in joyous worship and exalted living. The influence of the Hasidic movement is still with us and is significant in our own time. We regard Judaism not as a burden, not in terms of persecution or oppression, but as a happy means of worshipping our God and living by the teachings of an eternal faith."

HOW WOULD YOU INTERPRET THE FOLLOWING?

1 Rabbi Leib said: "I didn't go to Rabbi Dov Ber to hear Torah from him, but to watch him tie his shoelace. It is not as important to teach Torah as to be Torah."

2 The rabbi of Koznitz said to God: "Lord of the world, I beg of you to redeem Israel. And if you do not want to do that, then redeem the Gentiles."

3 Rabbi Levi Yitzchok once came to a town where he was not known. Following the morning prayers, the Rabbi called the young men, saying that he wanted to ask them something. When they came near, he looked gravely into their faces and said: "ma-ma-ma; va-va-va."

"What do you mean?" asked the young men. He answered: "How is it you do not understand this language, which you yourselves have just used in speaking to God?"

The young men were startled, but one of them said: "Have you never seen a child who does not yet know how to put sounds together into words? Have you not heard him make babbling sounds, such as ma-ma-; va-va? All the sages in the world cannot understand him, but the moment his mother comes, she knows exactly what he means."

4 Rabbi Zusya was afraid. His disciples asked why. The Rabbi said, "I will soon die. In the coming world, God will not ask me: 'Why were

you not like Moses?' because I am not Moses. God will not ask me: 'Why were you not like Jeremiah?' because I am not Jeremiah. But when God will ask me: 'Why were you not Zusya?'—what shall I answer?"

5 A young man came to the Riziner and asked to be ordained as a Rav. The Riziner inquired about his daily conduct, and the candidate replied: "I always dress in white; I drink only water; I place tacks in my shoes for self-mortification; I roll naked in the snow; and I order the synagogue caretaker to give me forty stripes daily on my bare back."

Just then a white horse entered the courtyard, drank water, and began rolling in the snow.

"Observe," said the Riziner. "This creature is white; it drinks only water; it has nails in its shoes; it rolls in the snow, and receives more than forty stripes a day. Still it is nothing but a horse."

HOW WOULD YOU APPLY THE FOLLOWING STATEMENTS TO YOUR LIFE AS A JEW?

1 Once on the New Moon of Elul, Rabbi Levi Yitzchok was standing at his window. A Gentile cobbler passed by and asked him, "And have you nothing to mend?"

At once the Zadik sat himself down on the ground and weeping bitterly cried, "Woe is me, for the Day of Judgment is almost here, and I have still not mended myself!"

2 Rabbi Pinchas said: "Whoever says that the words of the Torah are one thing and the words of the world another, must be regarded as a man who denies God."

3 Said the Medzibozer: "As for the wise, what he is, he says; as for the wicked, what he says, he is."

4 A Hasidic rabbi said: "Once I resolved to devote the whole day to the recitation of the entire Book of Psalms. When towards evening I was approaching the end, the warden of my rabbi came and said that the rabbi wished to speak with me. I requested him to inform the rabbi that I would see him soon as I had finished.

But the warden returned and bade me come immediately. The rabbi asked me: 'Why did you not obey my first summons?' I explained the reason.

The rabbi replied: 'I called you to make a collection for a poor Jew. Psalms can be chanted by the angels as well, but mortal men are needed to aid the destitute. Charity is a greater duty than the chanting of psalms, inasmuch as the angels cannot perform charity."

5 The Bratzlaver said: "Declare at all times: 'The world was created for my sake.' Do not declare: 'Of what concern is this to me?' But do your share to add some improvement, to supply something that is missing and to leave the world a little better for your sojourn in it."

6 They asked Pinchas: "Why is it written: 'In the day that God created a man on earth,' and not 'in the day that God created Man on earth'?"

He explained: "You should serve your Maker as though there were only one man on earth, only yourself."

QUESTIONS FOR DISCUSSION

1 In what way can we experience *Oneg Shabbos*, the joy of the Sabbath?

2 Why, in Jewish practice, is wine used for the benediction on occasions of joy?

3 Do you think Jews today find the same joy in their religion as they did in past ages? Give your reasons.

4 Rabbi Shelomo warned against forgetting that we are children of a king. What do you think he really meant? How can you apply his teaching to your own conduct?

5 Do you believe with Rabbi Shelomo that God loves the ne'er-do-wells and sinners? What are your reasons?

6 What practical benefit can come to a person who prays for the welfare of his enemies?

7 Is a person of humility respected or ridiculed in our society today? How much confidence would you have in following a leader who is humble in spirit?

8 Explain how suffering can be made a ladder to God.

9 The Hasidim and their leaders were respected despite their poverty. Do you think a poor but pious man commands the same respect in our society? Give your reasons.

THINGS TO DO

1 Interview a Christian to find out how he reacts to the study of the persecution of the early Christians. Inquire about his attitude toward suffering in Christian history, and the suffering experienced by Jesus. Interview a Jew on his reactions to the persecution of the Jew in Jewish history. Ask him to tell you his attitude toward sermons and study that relate to Jewish suffering. Compare both interviews and analyze.

2 The Christian has made the cross a reverent symbol of glory and piety. To what extent has Judaism made a badge of honor out of symbols of persecution?

3 The prophet Isaiah regarded Israel as "the suffering servant of God." Read and report on the following, giving your interpretation of Isaiah's meaning: Isaiah 53 Chapter 42.1-9; Chapter 44.1-8, 12-25; Isaiah 52.13-15; Chapter 50.6-8; 49.1-6.

4 Using a Concordance, write out seven Biblical verses that allude to joy.

5 The Misnagdim were the opponents of the Hasidim. Do some research on why they disagreed with the Hasidim, and what point of view they took.

6 Find out the significance of the legend about the *lamid vovniks* and then write an essay on "The concept of Saintliness in Judaism."

7 After adequate study and research, write a report on "The Life and Character of Israel Baal Shem Tov."

8 There are Hasidic groups still active in the larger communities of the United States today. Write a report about present-day Hasidism in this country.

9 In the Talmud (Shabbath 30b), there is the following statement: "The spirit of God rests upon man neither in a state of gloom nor in a state of indolence, but solely in the joy of performing a duty."
Give your interpretation of the meaning of this statement.

10 What do you think the Psalmist meant when he said: "I rejoiced when they said unto me, let us go unto the House of the Lord"?

11 Write a paragraph on how the ethics of Hasidism can help us hear the Still, Small Voice today.

SELECTED QUOTATIONS

Falling in Love with God

Then came Rabbi Israel Baal Shem, in the 18th Century, and brought heaven down to earth. He and his disciples, the Hasidim, banished melancholy from the soul and uncovered the ineffable delight of being a Jew. God is not only the creator of earth and heaven. He is also the One "who created delight and joy." "And when we talk about the need of joy," says one of the great Hasidic thinkers, "we do not mean the joy that is felt in fulfilling the commandments, for the ability of spontaneously feeling such a joy is a privilege of illustrious souls and one cannot demand that every Jew be illustrious. What we mean is, to be free of sadness. A Jew who does not rejoice in the fact of his being a Jew is ungrateful toward heaven; it is a sign that he has failed to grasp the meaning of having been born a Jew." Even lowly merriment has its ultimate origin in holiness. The fire of evil can be better fought with flames of ecstasy than through fasting and mortification.

Jewishness was as though reborn. Bible verses, observances, customs, suddenly took on a flavor like that of new grain. A new prohibition was added: "Thou shalt not be old!" The Baal Shem rejuvenated us by a thousand years. The Jews fell in love with the Lord and felt "such yearning for God that it was unbearable."

ABRAHAM HESCHEL,
The Earth is the Lord's

Kaddish of Levi Isaac of Berditshev

Good morning to you, Lord of the world!

I, Levi Isaac, son of Sarah of Berditshev, am coming to you in a legal matter concerning your people of Israel.

What do you want of Israel?

It is always: Command the children of Israel!
It is always: Speak unto the children of Israel!
Merciful Father! How many peoples are there in the world?
Persians, Babylonians, Edomites!
The Russians–what do they say?
Our emperor is the emperor!
The Germans–what do they say?
Our kingdom is the kingdom!
The English–what do they say?
Our kingdom is the kingdom!
But I, Levi Isaac, son of Sarah of Berditshev, say:
Glorified and sanctified be His great name!
And I, Levi Isaac, son of Sarah of Berditshev, say:
I shall not go hence, nor budge from my place until there be a finish, until there be an end of exile–
Glorified and sanctified be His great name!

Meaning of Salvation

To the Jew salvation means redeeming the world from evil. And that can come only through the constant disciplining and refining of the individual, so that he can discern right from wrong and not only discern it but learn to enjoy the good and reject the evil. This is the definition of ancient Hebrew wisdom. To this ultimate end has Jewish learning been directed. This is the message of Israel to mankind.

DR. JOHN J. TEPFER

General's Wish to be Hasid Puzzles New York

Orthodox Jewish circles in the greater New York area are confronted with a new phenomenon–and a problem. Louis Kitchener, a Christian and a former General in the Second C. S. Army, wants to be a Hasid among Hasidim. But the Hasidim in New York are at a loss to know what to do about him. Not yet accepted into the fold, Kitchener is looked upon by Orthodox rabbis and Yeshivah students with awe and wonder. They find it hard to understand why he wants to become a Hasid. Why not just a simple Jew? Theoretically a Christian until he is accepted, Kitchener observes *kashruth*, Shabbath, the holidays and he will never eat without a hat. More than that, he lectures in synagogues, urging the congregants to become better Jews. Only when the Jews return to the Torah, he maintains, can the world be helped. World peace can only come through Judaism, he insists.

Rabbi Israel Ari Hausman of the Bronx Yeshiva Zichron Moshe recently referred to Kitchener as a true Hasid who observes more *mitzvoth* than most Jews.

Born in Texas in 1904, Kitchener's father was a Methodist and his mother a Baptist. He graduated from West Point in 1926. During World War II he served as a commander in the air corps, later becoming active in the Chemical Warfare Department.

NEW YORK A.J.P.

A Humorist's Credo

I am a happy Jew, free and well-adjusted. I have cured myself of possible Jewish schizophrenia (a common disease) through identification with my people. I have found that the more deeply I become identified with the values of my own people, the closer do I come to an understanding of the hopes and desires of mankind as a whole.

When in my TV performances I draw from the folklore of my own people, for example, mama's attitude toward family, children, home, God, I am invariably flooded with mail from non-Jews who ask, "What makes you think your mother was different? My mother used to be the same way."

It takes a great deal of education to make a total Jew, a well-integrated Jew, a happy Jew.

I am always conscious that I am a Jew. I always carry the responsibility of being a Jew. I tell no dialect jokes, no stories that could be offensive to minority groups, no "little Jew" stories. There were no "little Jews" in the fight for Israel's independence, there were no "little Jews" in the Warsaw ghetto, there were no "little Jews" on Okinawa.

There are Jews in my profession who have suggested that I change my name. "You can get much farther that way," they say. True. You can get farther—farther and farther. But how far away do I care to go? And if I am not accepted as a Jew, but as a "neutral," what have I achieved?

SAM LEVENSON

SUGGESTED READINGS

For the Student

Buber, Martin, *Tales of the Hasidim*
Buber, Martin, *The Legend of Israel Baal Shem*
Levin, Meyer, *The Golden Mountain*
Newman, Louis, *The Hasidic Anthology*
Universal Jewish Encyclopedia, Article on "The Baal Shem," Vol. 2, pp. 3-5
Universal Jewish Encyclopedia, Article on "Hasidim," Vol. 5, pp. 237-241
Zangwill, Israel, "The Master of the Name" in *Dreamers of the Ghetto*

For the Teacher

Buber, Martin, *For The Sake Of Heaven*
Eclipse of God
Ten Rungs
Friedman, Maurice S., *Martin Buber, the Life of Dialogue*
Minkin, Jacob S., *The Romance of Hassidism*
Schechter, Solomon, "Hasidim and Hasidism" in *Studies in Judaism*, Vol. 1
Waxman, Meyer, *A History of Jewish Literature*, Vol. III, Chapter I

8

THE VOICE OF THEOLOGY

Ethics of Jewish Beliefs

The Letter

Rabbi Mayer said: "I want to read you a letter I received from a former pupil who is now a university student. The questions he asks are important, because these are the questions that your friends and classmates will ask you in the next few years. He says:

"Dear Rabbi Mayer:

This is the letter I promised myself to send you months ago, but somehow or other I never got to it because of the usual round of fraternity affairs, campus activities, and studying.

You always told us to come to you if we ever had any problems. I wish that I could talk to you in person, but rather than wait for a vacation period, I am going to write you with the hope that you will answer.

My problem is this. When I was in the religious school I guess I didn't take my studies too seriously. I always thought of Judaism as something that applied to the past, and now when I am asked about Jewish beliefs, I'm stumped. My room-mate is a Christian boy. He's a fine person and a good friend, but he asks too many questions—questions I can't always answer. He is very religious and is well-versed on Christian beliefs. Since I am a Jew, he expects me to know all about Judaism. Was he wrong!

Of course, I can tell him about our holidays and some of the things we practiced at home, but when it comes to questions about what Jews believe, I'm lost. The other night we had a bull-session about religion. There were three of us. One was a Catholic and he was never at a loss when we asked him about Catholic beliefs. Larry, my room-mate, is a Protestant, and he held his own when it came to the beliefs of his church. The fellows turned to me for the Jewish point of view. They wanted me to tell them what Judaism believes about God, revelation, the soul, freedom of will, and what happens in the next life. I've made a list of all the questions on another page.

Rabbi Mayer, please brief me on the answer to these questions and tell me what books to read so that I won't be so ignorant about my own religion.

I know that you are busy, and I hate to trouble you with these questions, but the next time we have a discussion, maybe I won't seem like such a dope about my own religion.

Your friend and pupil,
Joseph

P.S. I know. I should have been listening in class. These are probably the very things you discussed—but as the psychologists say, maybe I'm 'maturing'."

Joseph's List

1 Does Judaism have a creed? If so, what is our creed?

2 What is the Jewish conception of God? Does it differ from the Christian idea of God?

3 What do we believe about prayer? Does the Jewish belief in prayer differ from Christian belief?

4 What is the Jewish idea of man? Is man sinful? Do we believe in original sin and baptism? If not, why not?

5 If God is good, why is there so much suffering?

6 Do we believe in miracles?

7 Do we believe in freedom of will?

8 Does Judaism believe in immortality? What do we believe about the soul? Do we believe in heaven and hell? Are we punished and rewarded in the next world?

9 Do we believe in the coming of the Messiah?

10 Do we believe that we are the chosen people?

11 What is meant by "the mission of Israel"?

WHAT DO YOU THINK?

1 How many of the above questions do you think you can answer correctly?

2 Jewish theology means the study of God and questions that relate to God. After looking at these questions, how would you rate your own knowledge of Jewish theology: excellent, good, fair or poor?

3 Write out your answers to Joseph's questions. After you have completed this chapter, rewrite your answers to the questions on Joseph's list and compare them with the first answers that you gave.

Does Judaism Have A Creed?

"During the next few weeks," Rabbi Mayer said, "we are going to consider these questions and attempt to find out about the ethics of Jewish theology. It is important to know the beliefs of Judaism, because what we believe frequently determines our behavior—the way we act and what we do. Judaism is not only a way of living. It is also a way of believing. It is our belief in God that inspires us to obey His commandments. It is our belief in the truth and the holiness of the Torah that enables us to practice its teachings.

"There are some who say 'Christianity is a religion of creed, and Judaism is a religion of deed.' That statement isn't exactly fair to either religion. It is true that Christianity puts more emphasis upon creed than does Judaism, but Christianity does not minimize the importance of ethical behavior. It is true that Judaism puts more emphasis upon deed than does Christianity, but belief is important in Judaism.

"If you will look up the dictionary meaning of 'creed,' you will find that it is 'a statement of essential beliefs, guiding rules or principles.' Does Judaism have such a statement? Ruth, what do you think?"

"I believe we do have a statement of an essential belief," said Ruth. "We call the *Shema* the watchword of the Jewish faith: 'Hear, O Israel, the Lord our God, the Lord is One.' Anyone who is truly a Jew must believe in the unity of God. Wouldn't you say this is part of a Jewish creed?"

"I would, Ruth," answered Rabbi Mayer. "The belief that God is One is the most important teaching of Jewish theology. Later on I want you to consider this question: Suppose someone born a Jew says that he doesn't believe in one God—or in fact, any God. Is he still a Jew? Does he have a right to say that he is of the Jewish faith? Do we have anything in Judaism that says a person has to believe in the *Shema*, or God, or anything else in order to be a Jew? We're not ready to discuss this as yet. Right now, I want to know whether you believe there is a Jewish creed, and if so, what do you think it is?"

"I agree with Ruth," Burton said, "but it seems to me that the Ten Commandments should also be a part of the Jewish creed. Judaism gave these moral laws of right and wrong to all mankind. We say we believe in the Ten Commandments, don't we? If we believe in them as guiding rules, they should be part of a Jewish creed."

"You have a good argument, Burton," said Rabbi Mayer. "However,—"

"Excuse me, Rabbi," Ruth interrupted, "but isn't there a difference between commands and beliefs? The Ten Commandments are commandments, not beliefs."

"But can you obey them if you don't believe in them?" asked Burton.

"I'm glad you are enthused, but let's not have a debate on this. At the proper time, you will have an opportunity to express yourselves fully, and when you do, I wonder what you will say about someone who is born a Jew but says that he doesn't believe in the Ten Commandments. Is he still a Jew? Does he have a right to say that he is of the Jewish faith?

The Christian Creed

"While the question of a Jewish creed is debatable, there is a clearly defined Christian creed. Most of the Protestant denominations include this creed as part of their worship service. It is called the Nicene or the Apostle's Creed."

Rabbi Mayer opened a Christian prayerbook and read:

> *I believe in one God the Father Almighty, Maker of heaven and earth. And of all things visible and invisible:*
>
> *And in one Lord Jesus Christ, the only-begotten Son of God; Begotten of His Father before all worlds, God of God, Light of Light; Very God of very God; Begotten, not made; Being of one substance with the Father; By whom all things were made; Who for us men and for our salvation came down from heaven, And was incarnate by the Holy Ghost of the Virgin Mary, and was made man: And was crucified also for us under Pontius Pilate; He suffered and was buried: And the third day he rose again according to the Scriptures; And*

ascended into heaven, and sitteth on the right hand of the Father: And he shall come again, with glory, to judge both the quick and the dead; Whose kingdom shall have no end.

And I believe in the Holy Ghost, the Lord, and Giver of Life, Who proceedeth from the Father and the Son: Who with the Father and the Son together is worshipped and glorified; Who spake by the Prophets: And I believe one Catholic and Apostolic Church: I acknowledge one Baptism for the remission of sins: And I look for the Resurrection of the dead: And the Life of the world to come. Amen.

"Before we continue our discussion to find out whether or not Judaism has a creed, suppose we discuss the following questions:

1 Is there any part of the Nicene or Apostle's Creed that you can accept?

2 With what aspects would Judaism disagree?

3 If a Protestant Christian refuses to accept this creed, is he regarded as a Christian? Why?

4 If a Jew refuses to accept the *Shema* or the Ten Commandments is he still regarded as a Jew?

5 What is the difference between a Gentile and a Christian?

6 The rabbinic statement declares: "Even though an Israelite sins, he is still an Israelite." Does this also include refusing to believe?

The Thirteen Principles of Faith

"In the 12th Century, the great Jewish philosopher Maimonides summed up the beliefs of Judaism in thirteen principles of faith. This is frequently called a Jewish creed. To this day, we may read Maimonides' thirteen principles of faith in traditional prayerbooks.

"Here are the first five of the thirteen beliefs offered by Maimonides. Read them carefully, and decide whether you believe in them."

1 I believe with perfect faith that the Creator, blessed be His name, is the Author and Guide of everything that has been created, and that He alone has made, does make, and will make all things.

2 I believe with perfect faith that the Creator, blessed be His name, is a Unity, and that there is no unity in any manner like unto His, and that He alone is our God, who was, is, and will be.

3 I believe with perfect faith that the Creator, blessed be His name, is not a body, and that He is free from all the accidents of matter, and that He has not any form whatsoever.

4 I believe with perfect faith that the Creator, blessed be His name, is the first and the last.

5 I believe with perfect faith that to the Creator, blessed be His name, and to Him alone, it is right to pray, and that it is not right to pray to any being besides Him.

As you have probably discovered, the first five principles of faith are concerned with God.

Which of the five principles do you think Christianity would accept? Which would Christianity reject? Give your reasons.

In what way do Judaism and Christianity disagree on the fifth principle?

6 I believe with perfect faith that all the words of the prophets are true.

What is your opinion?

7 I believe with perfect faith that the prophecy of Moses our teacher, peace be unto him, was true, and that he was the chief of the prophets, both of those that preceded and those that followed him.

Do you agree that all the statements made by Moses are true?

Do you agree that Moses was the greatest of all the prophets? If not, who was a greater prophet than Moses? Give your reasons.

8 I believe with perfect faith that the whole Law, now in our possession, is the same that was given to Moses our Teacher, peace be unto him.

9 I believe with perfect faith that this Law will not be changed, and that there will never be any other law from the Creator, blessed be His name.

Will Orthodox and Conservative Judaism still accept the eighth and ninth principles of faith?

Does Reform Judaism accept or reject the eighth and ninth principles?

10 I believe with perfect faith that the Creator, blessed be His name, knows every deed of the children of men, and all their thoughts, as it is said: It is He that fashioneth the hearts of them all, that giveth heed to all their deeds.

How should the belief that God knows all our thoughts and all our deeds influence our actions and our thoughts?

If God knows all our deeds and thoughts, does this mean that we don't have the freedom to choose between right and wrong?

If God knows all our deeds and all our thoughts, why should we pray?

The last three principles of faith have been the subject of a heated controversy between Orthodox and Reform Judaism. Reform Judaism does not accept the literal interpretation of the twelfth and thirteenth principles of faith. What is your opinion?

11 I believe with perfect faith that the Creator, blessed be His name, rewards those that keep His commandments, and punishes those that transgress them.

Why do you agree or disagree with this?

Do you think that you will be rewarded every time you do a kind deed, and punished every time you do an evil deed?

Doesn't it happen that the wrong-doer sometimes gets away with it?

12 I believe with perfect faith in the coming of the Messiah, and though he tarry I will wait daily for his coming.

Do you believe in the coming of a personal Messiah? If not, what do you believe?

13 I believe with perfect faith that there will be a resurrection of the dead at the time when it shall please the Creator, blessed be His name, and exalted be the remembrance of Him forever and ever.

Do you believe that the resurrection of the dead is possible?

What would science say about this idea of the dead coming back to life?

What does Christianity teach about the resurrection of Jesus?

What do Orthodox, Conservative, and Reform Judaism teach about this thirteenth principle of faith?

The Jewish Conception of God

"Actually, there is no generally-accepted, official or authorized creed in Judaism," said Rabbi Mayer, "not even that of Maimonides. The closest that we come to a creed is the belief in the unity of God that all Jews accept, as proclaimed in the *Shema*. Everything in the Jewish religion follows from that belief. When a Christian minister is ordained he is asked whether he believes in the doctrines of the church. When a rabbi is ordained he is not asked what he believes, but he is charged to go forth and teach the Torah, worship the one God, interpret the values and ethics of Judaism to his people, and serve God and man; not only men of his faith, but every human being of every faith, because man is created in the image of God, and therefore, is holy.

"Nowhere does the Bible attempt to prove the existence of God. God was, is, and will be forever. Man has the sacred obligation of obeying God's commandments, listening to the Still, Small Voice, and bringing the teachings of God to the world. There can be no Jewish religion without God, for without God, it has no meaning or purpose.

"When we attempt to explain our belief in God, we start with the *Shema Yisroel,* declaring that God is One. If God is One, we must never worship the sun, moon, or stars, half-gods, man-gods, saints or devils. Since God is One, He alone is the creator, and He alone must be worshipped. If God is our Heavenly Father, then it follows that all men must be regarded as His children.

"There are other attributes or qualities of God. We believe that God is not a body. In Deuteronomy 4:16-19, the children of Israel were told: 'You saw no form at all when the Lord spoke to you at Horeb out of the fire.' God is a spirit, and does not assume any bodily form.

"According to Judaism, God is omniscient, all-knowing; omnipresent, everywhere; omnipotent, all-powerful. He is transcendant, which means that God goes beyond the world, and yet He is imminent, which means that He is in the world. As the prayerbook states so beautifully: 'Thou art as close to us as breathing and yet art farther than the farthermost star.'

"God is not a person, but we worship Him as a personal God. According to Judaism, God is close and near to everyone who truly calls upon Him. He is not only the God of the universe, but the God of every human being. The rabbis taught that God, when proclaiming the Ten Commandments, introduced Himself as 'thy God' in order to teach that 'He is the God of every man, woman and child' (Yalkut Shimoni, 286).

"Some people think that the greatest contribution of Judaism is monotheism, the belief in one God, but that is not accurate. Judaism's greatest contribution was ethical monotheism, the belief in one God of truth, justice, holiness, mercy and love—a God Who demands truth, justice, holiness, mercy and love from those who worship Him.

"God has a relationship to man," said Rabbi Mayer, "and man has duties to God. It isn't enough to say: I believe in God. What does that mean if the belief in God doesn't have anything to do with the way we act and the way we live? What does God want with our words, our offerings, or even our statement of belief, if we don't show our love for Him by living up to His commandments?

"God is just and merciful. Therefore, those who worship Him show their love by a divine imitation—by being just and merciful in their dealings with others. Man must be holy because God is holy.

"God has revealed his moral commandments in the Torah. By obedience to His commandments, we come closer and closer to God. God is revealed in everything around us—in the wonders of nature, in the order of the universe, in the miracle of a leaf and in the glory of love. It is through the Still, Small Voice that we can hear God speaking to us—just as He spoke to Abraham, Jacob and Moses, the prophets and psalmists of Israel. Everything we have studied about the Still, Small Voice helps us to understand the Jewish conception of God, and teaches us that every individual must regard himself as a co-partner of God in the building of a better world, a world of justice, brotherhood and peace."

The Christian Idea of God

"But, Rabbi," said Deborah, "what I don't understand is how our belief in God differs from Christian belief. Will you explain this?"

"Certainly, Deborah. Christianity, too, believes in God as the Creator and the Heavenly Father, but the difference is this: Judaism is a unitarian religion, while Christianity is a trinitarian religion."

"That means, doesn't it," asked Bernard, "that Christianity thinks of God as being divided into three parts?"

"That is right," said Rabbi Mayer, "although Joshua of Nazareth, called Jesus, declared his belief in one God."

"His belief in one God! I'm not doubting your word, Rabbi," said Bernard, "but how do we know this? I always thought that Jesus believed that God was three: The Father, the Son and the Holy Ghost."

"I can understand your confusion, Bernard, but let me read a passage from the Christian Bible. It is from the Gospel according to St. Mark, Chapter 12, verses 28-34."

> *And one of the scribes came and having heard them reasoning together, and perceiving that he had answered them well, asked him: "Which is the first commandment of all?" And Jesus answered him, "The first of all the commandments is: Hear, O Israel, The Lord our God is one Lord. And thou shalt love the Lord thy God with all thy heart, and with all thy soul, and with all thy mind, and with all thy strength; this is the first commandment."*

"That sounds so Jewish!" Ruth exclaimed in surprise.

"It is, Ruth," Rabbi Mayer said. "The first statement is from Deuteronomy 6:4-5, and is the *Shema Yisroel.* The second statement follows the *Shema*, though Jesus added one small phrase. These two statements are in every Jewish worship service.

"It was much later, a long time after the death of Jesus that Christianity began to emphasize the three in one. This means that to Christians, God is to be found in the Father, the Son and the Holy Ghost, which means holy spirit. Jesus was thought to be the only-begotten son of God. In fact, Christianity believes that God became flesh, or as it is called, incarnate, and walked the earth in the person of Jesus.

"This is, of course, a very sketchy summary of Christian belief. Christians believe that God is love, mercy and justice. Judaism would agree. Christians believe that Jesus was more than a man, but God's son, or God Himself. Judaism must disagree. Christianity thinks in terms of a trinity. Judaism thinks in terms of the unity of God. 'He is our God, there is none else.' "

QUESTIONS FOR DISCUSSION

1 If God is not a body, why does the Torah refer to the fingers and hands of God? If God does not speak, why do we refer to the voice of God? What is meant by a still, small voice? How can a voice be still?

2 Balaam said: God is not a man. Look up Numbers 23:19 and explain what he meant. What did Samuel mean in I Sam. 15:29?

3 If God is everywhere, how should the presence of God affect our actions at home, at play, when we are hiking in the woods, and when we are alone?

4 How is it possible for someone your age to "imitate" the attributes of God?

5 What is your reaction to the Christian belief that Jesus is the only begotten son of God? How would you compare this with Jewish teaching?

6 Is there any personality in the Jewish Bible who was revered as a God?

7 What is your reaction to the belief that Jesus became God incarnate, God in the flesh of a man? What does Judaism teach about the God in man?

8 If Jesus said that God is One, how does Christianity explain the belief that God is three in one?

9 In what way can you be a co-partner with God in the building of a better world?

What Do We Believe About Prayer?

"We have already discussed the Jewish belief in prayer," said Rabbi Mayer, "but in answer to Joseph's question, we should review our beliefs and compare them with Christian beliefs.

"Judaism believes that God is near to those who pray, and answers our prayers, but not always in the way that we expect. Mature prayer doesn't ask God for things. It doesn't attempt to coax God to give us material gifts. Prayer is the sincere expression of our inner feelings. We express our gratitude, our hopes, our longings–and above all, the overwhelming plea to be better than we are. We do not ask God to change things. We ask God to change us so that we may change things.

"The aspirational prayer that pleads, 'Create within me a clean heart, O God,' asks God to help us to be strong and pure, to overcome evil, and to practice truth, justice and mercy. Through our prayers, we enter into the presence of God, and we are answered with strength, light and courage.

"Sometimes people ask me to pray for them," Rabbi Mayer said. "Of course, I pray for them, but I would much rather pray WITH them. My prayers are no more precious to God than your prayers–or the prayers of any who call upon God with all their hearts. Rabbis have no special powers to influence God. Every individual is a child of God and must go to his Heavenly Father with his own prayer. The words aren't always too important. It's the sincerity of the prayer that makes it holy and true."

Rochelle raised her hand. "Do you think that God also answers the prayers of Christians, if they pray sincerely? Don't average Christians, who aren't ministers, believe that they, too, come to God?"

"Yes, of course, God answers the prayers of Christians. A Christian doesn't have to be a minister to pray. In Catholicism, it is believed that the priest has more of the spirit of holiness in him, and therefore his prayer might have more influence with God. In the Protestant denominations, the minister is frequently asked to pray for his people, but every individual also utters the prayers that are close to his heart."

"But," Rochelle asked, "is there a difference, between the Jewish and Christian ideas of prayer?"

"Yes, there are differences," Rabbi Mayer said. "Jews pray directly to God, our Heavenly Father. Christians conclude their prayer by saying: 'In Jesus' name we ask it' or 'In the Master's name we ask it.' This is an important difference. Christianity believes that Jesus is the intermediary. Since Jesus is thought to be God's son, it is believed that if his name is brought in, God will be more receptive.

"Those of the Jewish faith will begin: 'O Lord our God,' or 'Heavenly Father,' or 'Our God and God of our Fathers,' and end 'Amen.' We do not pray in the name of Moses, or in the name of any other great teacher of Judaism. A Jew prays directly to God.

"In the Catholic faith, the Holy Mother or various saints are frequently addressed in prayer. In Judaism, however, we pray only to God."

QUESTIONS FOR DISCUSSION

1 Does the prayer: "Blessed art thou, O Lord our God, God of Abraham, Isaac and Jacob" mean that we are praying in the name of Abraham, Isaac and Jacob?

2 Is it wrong for a Christian to end his prayer in the name of Jesus, when the prayer is given in the public schools? If a minister is invited to give a prayer in the synagogue is it wrong for him to end in the name of Jesus?

3 A famous Jewish scholar, Joseph Klausner, stated that the Lord's Prayer is "a remarkable prayer, universal in its appeal, earnest, brief and full of devotion. Every single clause in it, however, is to be found in Jewish prayers and sayings in the Talmud." If this is so, is it proper to recite the Lord's Prayer in school? Is it proper to recite the prayer in the religious school class or in a synagogue service?

4 Is it wrong for a Jew to pray in a Christian church? When a guest in a Christian church, is it proper for a Jew to sing the hymns, kneel and participate in the service?

5 When a Christian visits the synagogue, is it wrong for him to repeat the *Shema Yisroel* with the congregation? Should he rise for the *Shema*, pray and participate in the service even though he believes that God is a trinity?

6 Read through your prayerbook and select the prayers that you think both Christians and Jews might honestly and sincerely repeat together.

What is the Jewish Belief About Man?

"Last year, when we studied the teachings of the Psalms, we discussed the Jewish idea of man."

"I remember," said Norman. "It was about whether or not man is a robot. The Psalmist said that 'man is but little lower than the angels.' "

"What other statements do you recall? Yes Miriam?"

"Man is created in the image of God and therefore man has a part of God within. Since man has a soul, every human being is sacred and precious to God. We have a responsibility to our fellowman, and we must help all who are in need, because they are children of God."

"Well put, Miriam. In just a few sentences you and Norman have summed up the Jewish idea of man.

Original Sin and Baptism

"In order to answer Joseph's question, we will have to know two terms used in Christianity. One is 'original sin.' Christianity believes that man is created in the image of God, and is endowed with a soul. Christian doctrine believes that because Adam and Eve tasted of the fruit of the tree of the knowledge of Good and Evil, they sinned. This sin has been transmitted through the generations. Therefore, most Christian denominations follow the practice of 'Baptism,' the second term. By immersion, or sprinkling with holy water, the original sin is cleansed, and the person becomes spiritually pure. There are differences in practice. Some church groups baptize the child soon after birth. Other groups wait until the child has grown and understands the religious significance of baptism.

"Since we, in Judaism, do not believe that a person inherits any sin, we do not practice baptism. Judaism teaches that a child is born pure and clean, without sin, and believes in serving God through good deeds. Christianity insists upon right actions, but says that salvation also depends upon belief in Jesus. Baptism enables the Christian to partake more fully of the spirit of Jesus. Christianity is vitally concerned with 'the fall of man.' Judaism thinks in terms of the rise of man."

QUESTIONS FOR DISCUSSION

1 What responsibilities does the belief in the sanctity of man place upon you?

2 What is your reaction to the concept of original sin? Do you think that the sin of Adam and Eve is transmitted through the generations? What are your reasons?

3 We find the use of water in Jewish tradition associated with the washing of hands. What is the traditional benediction to be recited when we wash our hands? What is the significance of this blessing?

4 In the Jewish tradition there was the requirement of purification by means of a ritual bath called a *Mikveh*. This is still observed by the Orthodox. Look up the meaning and significance of Mikveh, and discuss whether the idea of baptism came from this Jewish tradition.

5 Some Christian denominations believe that without baptism a person cannot get into heaven. What would Judaism say about this?

6 What do Christians mean by "being saved"? What is the Jewish belief in salvation?

If God is Good and Merciful, Why is there so much Suffering?

"There is something that worries me," Marvin said. "If man is created in the image of God, and the soul is pure and holy, why should there be evil in the world? And one more thing–if God is good and merciful, why should there be sickness and suffering? God has the power to do anything. Why didn't He create a world without evil and suffering?"

"Marvin's questions have perplexed mankind since the beginning of religious thought," said Rabbi Mayer. "There are no simple answers.

"According to Judaism, no one is sinful by nature. Human beings were not created angels, but flesh and blood, imperfect mortals. There is only one perfection, and that is God. Since man is not perfect, human beings stray from the path of God, and disobey His moral laws. That is why sin and evil come into the world. In order to have a world without sin and evil, God would have to create a world of perfect people. But since God is the only one who is perfect, a perfect world would have to be inhabited by God alone.

"Another question that has perplexed man is this: Since God is merciful and good, why should there be suffering and injustice? This problem has been given a name. It is called 'theodicy,' which means, the problem of reconciling God's goodness with the evil and suffering in the world." Rabbi Mayer paused. "Do I see some puzzled looks? It really isn't as complicated as it sounds. Let me give you some examples:

1 Samuel's mother was always good, kind and devoted. She was a pious woman and tried to keep God's commandments. She became ill with an incurable disease. In his grief, Samuel cried out: "God,

my mother is so good. Why do you punish her with a terrible sickness? Please make her well. I know that You are a God of kindness and mercy. Have mercy upon my mother!"

Do you think God should perform a miracle and make her well?
Do you think God was responsible for her becoming ill?

2 Mr. A. had to struggle for everything. His parents were very poor, and in order to get an education he had to work day and night. Finally, he managed to open a store. At first, he prospered, but a fire broke out and destroyed his store. Mr. A. didn't have enough insurance to cover the loss. He went to work for a department store. A higher position was available, but Mr. A. was passed over, and a relative of one of the owners was given the job. Mr. A. was terribly upset. He had worked hard and thought he deserved the promotion. Mr. A. has experienced great tragedy in his life. His only son was killed in Korea during the war. Mr. A. constantly broods over his great loss. At times he has wondered whether God is really just and merciful, to permit such sorrow to come into his life.

Do you think God caused Mr. A.'s troubles?
Should God be blamed because his son was killed in a war?

"In order to create a world without suffering," continued Rabbi Mayer, "God would have to create a human body without the capacity for pain or death. God would have to determine in advance everything that happens, and man wouldn't have the freedom to choose between good and evil.

"A long time ago, Job asked the same questions: Why do the righteous suffer? I have been good, pious and just, and terrible tragedies have been visited upon me and my family. Why, God, why? The Book of Job teaches us that suffering is not a punishment for sins. Frequently, good people suffer, and evil people seem to be rewarded. We learn that suffering is a part of life, and illness strikes both good and evil people. It isn't God that brings sickness. It is the imperfection of the human body, and the conditions of nature. As for those evil people who are rewarded, it only appears to us that they are rewarded. We believe that sooner or later evil is always punished, just as goodness is always rewarded, even though the reward may not come the way we expect, or at the time we expect it. Job finally realizes that he cannot understand God's ways, and that he must trust the infinite wisdom of the Almighty and have faith.

"Scholars and sages have given us many reasons for suffering. They say that suffering alerts us to sickness. Suffering purifies and strengthens character and faith. It is in the nature of a human being to experience suffering. The prophet Isaiah believed that Israel was the suffering servant of God, destined to be purified for a sacred mission.

"Actually, it is beyond man to understand completely the nature of evil or suffering. It is a mystery that belongs to God.

Miracles

"Earlier, I asked you whether you thought God should perform miracles for people who are sick or in danger. Judaism teaches us that God has created the physical and moral laws of the universe. God abides by His own laws. Let me explain what I mean. Suppose a person is in a hurry to do a good deed. Do you think the traffic light should change from red to green just to let the person through? Or if a person is in a hurry to do evil, do you think that the traffic light should refuse to turn from red to green so that he will be detained? That would be nonsense, because there is an automatic mechanism that controls the traffic lights.

"A group of people are walking near a construction job. A brick slips from the hand of a workman. Should God perform a miracle and cause the brick to veer away from a good person who is in its path, and strike an evil person who is rushing to commit a crime?

Nonsense again, you would say. The path of the brick is determined by its weight and the distance it has to fall.

"In the Bible and Talmud, we are taught that miracles are not to be accepted as proof of a teaching.

A Miracle Is No Proof

"One day Rabbi Eliezer disagreed with his colleagues, but they would not heed him. Finally he said: 'If the rule is as I teach it, let this carob-tree give a sign.' And the carob-tree moved back two hundred cubits. But the sages said: 'A carob-tree proves nothing.' So he said: 'If the rule is as I teach it, let the water in this channel give a sign.' And the water in the channel flowed upward instead of downward. But the sages said to him: 'The waters of a channel prove nothing.' Then he said: 'If the law is as I teach it, let the walls of the school decide.' And the walls of the school leaned over as if to fall. Then a divine echo was heard: 'What ails you? Why do you contend with Rabbi Eliezer? The rule has always been what he teaches it to be.' But Rabbi Joshua, rising to his feet, exclaimed: 'It is not in heaven!' (Deut. 30.12). What did he mean by these words? He meant that the Torah is no longer in heaven; it was given to us from Mount Sinai, once for all time, and we need no longer pay heed to a divine voice, for in the Torah, given at Sinai, it is written: 'The opinion of the majority shall prevail.' The prophet Elijah appeared to Rabbi Nathan, who asked him: 'What was God doing at that moment (when Rabbi Joshua denied the value of miracles)?' And the prophet replied: 'God was laughing and saying: "My children have conquered Me." ' (Baba Mezia.)

"The truth of God's power is not dependent upon miracles. Judaism believes that each day God renews the works of creation, and that if we must think in terms of miracles then we should look to the wonder of the human body, the order of the universe, the glory of a flower, the sacrifices that are made for those we love. 'The heavens declare the glory of God, and the earth showeth His handiwork' is the expression of the Psalmist. The survival of the Jewish people despite thousands of years of persecution may be regarded as a miracle, if we wish to think of wonders. Everything around us shows the power and wisdom and wonder of God. We do not have to look to supernatural events to support our faith in God. We do not expect God to perform miracles which break His own natural laws just because we request Him to do so. Which is stronger, faith that depends upon miracles, or a faith that accepts reason, the discoveries of science, and beholds the evidence of God in a humble thorn-bush, a bird soaring through the skies, the moral power that comes to those who listen to the ethical commands of the Still, Small Voice?

Freedom of Will

"One of the fundamental beliefs of Judaism is freedom of will. Without the freedom to make a choice, how can we say that a person is good or evil, right or wrong? If God determines every action, then how can any individual be held responsible for his actions? If God determines everything that happens, then there can be no right or wrong, justice or injustice, morality or immorality.

"Judaism does not behold man as a puppet controlled by a divine power. The idea of moral freedom is expressed early in the Bible when God tells Cain 'Sin coucheth at the door;...but thou mayest rule over it.' Moses speaks in the name of God: 'I have set before thee life and death, the blessing and the curse; therefore choose life, that thou mayest live, thou and thy seed.' (Deut. 30:15-19). Later, Rabbi Akiba taught: 'Everything is in the hands of God except reverence for God' (Berochoth 33b). This means that man's character depends upon his own free choice. No one can force a person to have reverence for God, or compel him to obey God's moral laws.

"The Jewish philosophers Philo, Saadia, Maimonides, and Gersonides insisted that the truly divine in man is his free will, which distinguishes him from the beast. Since the Bible, the Talmud and Jewish philosophy stress freedom of will, Judaism opposes the idea of original sin. Each individual must choose between good and evil, the blessing and the curse. If he obeys the Still, Small Voice, he will choose good and be blessed. If he rejects its teachings and chooses evil, he will be cursed by his own choice.

"Some religions teach that everything that happens is 'predestined,' which means determined in advance. Judaism emphatically opposes the idea of predestination, and maintains that everyone is blessed with freedom of will to choose good and reject evil. Judaism teaches that God has given us the freedom to obey His moral laws and build a society of justice and peace."

QUESTIONS FOR DISCUSSION

1 How would you answer the question: "Why didn't God create a world without evil and suffering?"

2 According to the Hebrew interpretation "sin" means to "miss the mark." How would you explain this? What is your interpretation of a sin? If no other person is hurt by what you do, except yourself, is it a sin?

3 Sometimes what seems to us to be "good" may be "evil," and what seems to be "evil" may be "good." Give some examples.

4 A little child is killed in an automobile accident because the driver has been speeding. Do you think God is responsible for the child's death?

5 What is your definition of "a miracle"? Do you think God should perform miracles for those who are pious and good? Do you think that faith should be based on miracles?

6 How do you think the so-called miracles in the Bible may be explained? For example, the splitting of the Red Sea, the burning bush, making the sun stand still.

7 If a native of a primitive land came to America and saw television, doors opening by means of an electric beam, etc., do you think he would regard these as miraculous? Do you think of them as miracles? Is it possible that what seems to be a miracle may have a natural, scientific explanation?

8 In Jewish tradition we are taught that there are two inclinations that act within a person: One is called the *yetzer harah*, the evil inclination; the other, the *yetzer hatov*, the good inclination. These battle within man for supremacy. How may we strengthen the good inclination?

9 There can be no morality without freedom. If an officer forces his soldiers to do something evil, should they be held responsible for their actions? If a person is lame, is he wrong if he doesn't walk without limping? How would you apply this same principle to freedom of will and our choice of good and evil?

10 What does the belief in freedom of will have to do with our responsibility to build a better society? How is the doctrine of freedom of will significant to you in your life?

Does Judaism Believe in Immortality?

"Sometimes when I have discussions with my Christian friends," said Miriam, "they bring up the subject of immortality. I know that immortality means the belief in an afterlife, but I'm never sure whether Judaism believes in immortality. Since this is a question on Joseph's list, I wonder whether we may discuss it?"

"Yes, Miriam, this is something you should know," Rabbi Mayer answered. "The question will often come up, and you should have a clear understanding of the Jewish point of view.

"Judaism does believe in immortality, but of the soul, not the body. The Bible states, 'the dust returneth to the earth as it was, but the spirit, the soul, returns unto God who gave it.' (Ecc. 12:7). Since the soul is God within us, eternal and indestructible, the soul never dies. Our prayerbook also reminds us: 'The soul which thou hast given unto me, O God, came pure from Thee. Thou hast formed it. Thou hast created it. Thou hast breathed it into me, and at the appointed time Thou wilt take it from this earth to life everlasting.' "

"But what happens to the soul after a person dies?" asked Burton.

Rabbi Mayer smiled. "That's what we would all like to know, Burton," he said. "I'm afraid, however, that we don't know for certain. This is a mystery that belongs to God. We do believe that when a person dies, his soul returns to God. The when, where, and how—we cannot answer. Since God is our Heavenly Father, the Jew has never feared the afterlife. The soul, which is of God, returns to God, and that is the greatest good that can happen—to become one with divinity. Do you remember the words of the hymn *Adon Olom?* Tell me, how many of you have ever thought of the meaning of the verse: *B'yado afkeed roochee?* The translation is: 'Into thy hands, O God, I commit my soul, both when I wake and when I sleep. And with my soul, my body, too. The Lord is with me. I shall not fear.' This is the heart of the Jewish belief in immortality: 'The Lord is with me. I shall not fear.' "

Heaven and Hell

"But," asked Miriam, "what about heaven and hell?"

"In the Bible," answered Rabbi Mayer, "there are references to *sheol*, or a deep, shadowy place, and *gehinon*, which some interpreted to mean hell. However, today, we do not think of hell as a place of torment and suffering. Suppose you tell me why."

"Could it be," asked Burton, "that because we don't have a body, and a soul is holy and eternal, there isn't anything that can experience pain?"

"That is sound reasoning, Burton. The body returns to the earth, and we don't think of the torment of the body in an afterlife. What other reasons can you suggest? Deborah?"

"It seems to me that if we think of God as our Heavenly Father, a God of love and mercy, what father would want his children to suffer in hell?"

"Deborah's comment is extremely important. Sometimes you may hear it said that the Jewish God is a God of vengeance, and that Judaism is a religion of stern justice. This is not true. We cannot believe that God commits any of His children to suffering in an after-life. Since God is love, mercy and forgiveness, we regard it as blasphemy to associate the suffering and misery of a hell with a God who is called *Rachamana*, the Merciful One.

"Just as we cannot believe in damnation in hell, so Judaism doesn't believe in the physical pleasures of heaven. Without a body we cannot experience the delight of bodily appetites. The idea of a person wearing wings and soaring through space is a juvenile belief. The concept of heaven and hell is predominantly of Persian origin. To Judaism, the greatest joy is the union of the soul with God—that is our heaven."

Retribution

"But if there isn't a hell or a heaven, how are people punished for their sins and rewarded for their goodness?" questioned David. "If a person lives a good and pious life, it seems to me that he should be rewarded in some future life."

"Judaism believes in divine punishment and reward—but in this life, David, and not in a hell or heaven in another life. Those who love God serve Him and obey His laws, but not out of fear of punishment or hope of reward. We don't love our parents with the thought of reward or punishment. We don't do what is right because we expect to be paid back for doing right. As Ben Azai said in the *Ethics of the Fathers:* 'The reward of a good deed is the good deed itself.' Those who do evil are recompensed with evil. Those who do good are recompensed with goodness. This is known as retribution—being paid back. Everything we do has some consequence. If a person does evil, he may not be punished immediately, but he inclines himself to do more evil and damages his character. If a person does good, he may not be rewarded immediately, but he inclines himself to do more good and thus strengthens his character. It is childish to think of avoiding evil and doing good because of bribes and threats.

"When we break the physical laws of the universe, there are usually consequences of a harmful nature. When we break the rules of health, we weaken our bodies. So it is with God's moral laws. When we break them, there are harmful consequences. When we keep them and obey them, there are beneficial consequences.

"Above all, a Jew strives for goodness and holiness because he lives in the presence of his God. God has commanded obedience to His moral laws. The philosopher Hasdai Crescas taught that the righteous yearn for God's love and goodness, and thus find happiness. The love of God and the practice of His laws make a heaven of earth.

"The theologian, Kaufman Kohler, summed up the thinking of Judaism when he wrote: 'Our modern conceptions of time and space admit neither a place or a world period for the reward and punishment of souls, nor the intolerable conception of eternal joy without useful action and eternal agony without any moral purpose. Modern man knows that he bears heaven and hell within his own bosom. Indeed, so much more difficult is the life of duty which knows of no other reward than happiness through harmony with God, the Father of the immortal soul, and of no other punishment than the soul's distress at its inner discord with the primal Source and the divine Ideal of all morality.'

The Resurrection of the Dead

"Before we leave the subject of immortality," said Rabbi Mayer, "there is one other thought that should be discussed further—and that is Maimonides' thirteenth principle of faith: the resurrection of the dead.

"The Bible, with few exceptions, limits its teachings to this world. Rabbinic Judaism, the Talmud and Midrash, however, refer to the doctrine of the resurrection of the dead. The Pharisees believed that a part of the backbone, an almond-shaped bone called *Luz*, never disintegrates, and that when the Messiah comes, and it is time for the resurrection of the dead, the body will be reformed from the nucleus of the *Luz*.

"To this day, Orthodox Judaism believes in the resurrection of the dead. There are references to this in the Orthodox prayerbook. Conservative Judaism reinterprets this idea in terms of a more reasonable approach. Reform Judaism rejects the idea of the resurrection of the dead and in its prayerbook has changed the idea of resurrection to an emphasis upon the immortality of the soul, and the soul's eternal life with God."

Burton said: "It's hard to know just what to believe about these complicated ideas. But what do we believe about the Messiah? You mentioned something about when the Messiah comes. Christians believe that Jesus is the Messiah. What do we believe–and when is the Messiah supposed to come to earth?"

The Messiah

"The idea of the Messiah is extremely important both to Judaism and to Christianity," said Rabbi Mayer. "To understand the belief in the Messiah, we will have to trace its development through three steps.

"The term 'Messiah' comes from the Hebrew word *mashiah* meaning 'anointed.' The Bible applies this to those who were appointed to high offices, and annointed with the sacred oil. Kings and priests were called 'the anointed ones.' This name was given to Saul, the first king of Israel, to David and to the high priest.

"In time, there developed the belief in a Messiah who would be sent by God to redeem Israel and establish God's kingdom on earth. When the Messiah appeared, Israel's suffering would end, the dead would come back to life, and a perfect world would come into being. With the coming of the Messiah the blind would see, the deaf would hear, and the lame would walk. Misery, sickness, war, poverty, and hatred would be no more. The Temple would be rebuilt and the hope was expressed that from 'Zion will go forth the Torah, and the word of the Lord from Jerusalem.'

"It was believed that before the coming of the Messiah the world would be torn with strife, misery, and famine. This was called *hevlay mashiah*, the pangs of the Messiah. Elijah the prophet would reappear on earth as a sign that the Messianic age had arrived. According to Isaiah, the Messiah, surpassing all earthly kings, will rule as 'wonderful counselor, divine hero, everlasting father and prince of peace.'

"Since it was believed that the Messiah would be a descendant of the House of David, Isaiah expressed the Messianic hope, in Chapter XI, that the throne of David would be restored. He prophesied that with the coming of the Messiah, *the wolf shall dwell with the lamb, and the leopard shall lie down with the kid; and the calf and the young lion and the fatling together; and a little child shall lead them. ...They shall not hurt nor destroy in all My holy mountain; for the earth shall be full of the knowledge of the Lord, as the waters cover the sea.*

"In every period of persecution, the belief in a personal Messiah was cherished by the Jewish people. It was especially pronounced during the First Century, when Rome ruled Judea with tyrannical might. The people were not permitted to bear arms, and anyone who was suspected of revolutionary tendencies or regarded as an enemy of Rome, was sentenced to death.

"It was during this time that Joshua of Nazareth was hailed as the long awaited Messiah. John the Baptist was thought to be Elijah heralding the appearance of the 'anointed one.' People asked: 'Is this young prophet really the Messiah?' Since the Messiah was also thought to be the King of the Jews, the Romans regarded Joshua as politically dangerous, and soon ordered his crucifixion. Some Jews believed that he was the Messiah, though most refused to accept him. Those who believed in him were later called Christians."

"How can a Jew be a Christian?" asked Miriam.

"I can understand your confusion, Miriam. Let me try to clarify the matter by referring to terms. First, the Greek name for Joshua is Jesus. The Greek word for Messiah, or annointed one, is *christos* or more familiarly, *christ*. Those Jews who believed that Joshua of Nazareth was the Messiah were known as Messianists, or followers of the Messiah. Translate Joshua the Messiah into Greek and what do you have?"

"I know," said Bernard. "It would be Jesus the Christ!"

"That's right. Now you may be able to answer the question: 'how could some Jews be regarded as Christians?' "

"Wouldn't they be the Jews who believed that Jesus was the Messiah or the Christ?" Miriam asked.

"Yes," answered Rabbi Mayer. "They were still Jews, but they believed that Joshua of Nazareth was the Messiah. Later on, when Paul appeared, those Jews who believed in Joshua of Nazareth as the Messiah joined with the non-Jewish Christians. They separated from Judaism, and a new religion came into being, known as Christianity."

"That ended the Jewish belief in the Messiah, didn't it?" said Burton.

"No, Burton. Most of the Jews refused to accept Jesus as divine, the son of God, but they still hoped that someday the real Messiah would be sent by God. As late as the Seventeenth century we find Jews believing in men who proclaimed themselves as the Messiah. Sabbatai Zevi was one of these false Messiahs, and many Jews were convinced that he was really sent by God, until he disillusioned them by becoming a convert to Islam. There were many other false Messiahs, but the Jewish people continued to hope and pray that the true Messiah would come.

"To this day, Orthodox Judaism believes in the coming of the Messiah. We find this hope expressed in their prayerbook. Conservative Judaism still looks for the coming of a Messiah, with modifications. Reform Judaism does not believe in a personal Messiah, but in a Messianic era, an age of brotherhood, justice and peace. The references to the personal Messiah in the Orthodox prayerbook were omitted from the Reform prayerbook. In their place, there was substituted the hope for redemption rather than a redeemer; for a messianic age rather than a personal Messiah. This is really the third step in the development of the Messiah idea, but...." Rabbi Mayer looked at his watch. "I don't think we will have time to discuss this further today.

"Next week, we will discuss the Messianic age, and the remaining questions on Joseph's list."

Burton raised his hand. "I'm still not sure what Judaism believes about Jesus today. Do we believe in him or don't we?"

"Judaism believes in but one God," said Rabbi Mayer. "We do not worship any other, or pray to anyone besides God. Judaism does not believe that Jesus was the Messiah. We do not believe that he was the only-begotten son of God, or God incarnate, which means God becoming flesh—God as a man. There is a profound difference between the belief in Joshua of Nazareth, a Jewish teacher, and Jesus the Messiah, the Christ. Judaism and Christianity part, not over the teachings of Jesus, because these for the most part were Jewish teachings, but rather over the divinity of Jesus. Judaism says that Jesus was a man. Christianity says that Jesus was and is divine, the only begotten son of God, or God Himself come to earth as a man.

"Orthodox Judaism rejects Jesus as the Messiah, and believes that the Messiah is yet to come. Conservative and Reform Judaism reject Jesus as the Messiah, and in fact, reject all Messiahs. We place our hope in the Messianic age, God's kingdom on earth. Judaism therefore respects the teachings of Jesus, but can never accept the belief that he was the Messiah, or that he is to be worshipped as divine. To us, 'Hear O Israel, the Lord our God the Lord is One,' can never permit the belief that the Lord is two, or three. There is but one God. Every individual, no matter how saintly, how holy, must be regarded as a mortal human being. We have no argument with those who contend that Jesus was a wise and good man. We cannot accept the conviction of those who worship him as the Messiah, the God incarnate."

QUESTIONS FOR DISCUSSION

1 How does the Jewish belief in immortality differ from the Christian belief?

2 Do you believe that people are less good and virtuous if they don't accept the concept of punishment in hell?

3 Before you read of these Jewish beliefs, what was your idea of heaven? Have you changed your opinion?

4 Do you believe that without the belief that their dear ones are in heaven, the mourners are without a source of comfort?

5 A juvenile court judge, social worker and doctor will try to cure and rehabilitate those who have done wrong. Is God less merciful than a judge, social worker or physician? Do you believe that God would want any of His children to suffer in this life or in the next life?

6 Give some examples of how those who break God's moral laws are punished. How are those who observe God's laws rewarded?

7 Spinoza said: "Virtue is its own reward." What did he mean?

8 If there is such a thing as resurrection of the dead, do you think those who believe this would want to die in the prime of life? Would an infant be resurrected an infant? Would an old person come back to life as an old person? What do you think?

9 Maimonides in the *Mishneh Torah* said: "Not immortality, but the power to win eternal life through the knowledge and the love of God is implanted in the human soul." What did he mean?

10 It has been said that Jewish theology is based on *kiddush haShem*, the sanctification of God's Name, and *kiddush hahayim*, the sanctification of life. What does this mean?

11 Professor Mordecai M. Kaplan, in *The Future of the American Jew*, states: "The Torah can still function in the life of the Jew to bring out the best in him, if he learns to approach it in the right way. Though the modern Jew cannot believe that God revealed the Torah to Israel, he cannot deny the historic fact that the Torah revealed God to Israel." What is your opinion of this statement? Do you think God revealed the Torah to Israel at Mt. Sinai?

12 According to tradition, when God gave the Torah to Israel at Mt. Sinai, the children of Israel responded: "We will do and we will obey." Does this mean that in Judaism doing is more important than believing?

13 Conrad Henry Moehlman has said: "Judaism has stressed conduct more than dogma. Judaism has been more interested in this life than in the world to come." Do you agree or disagree? What are your reasons?

14 Rabbi Jose ben Hanina said: "The flax dealer who knows that his flax is good, pounds it, for it becomes more excellent because of the pounding. The more he beats it, the more it glistens. But when he knows that his flax is bad, he does not dare to pound it, for it would split. So God bears down not on the wicked, but the righteous." What do you think?

15 Abraham Lincoln said: "When any church will inscribe over its altar as its sole qualification for membership, 'Thou shalt love the Lord thy God with all thy heart and all thy soul and all thy might, and thy neighbor as thyself,' that church will I join with all my heart and all my soul." Abraham Lincoln never joined a church. With that as his credo, do you think he should have become a Jew?

16 Sherwood Eddy offered a definition of faith: "Faith is not trying to believe something regardless of the evidence. Faith is daring to do something regardless of the consequences." What is your opinion?

17 What is meant by the Jewish Jesus and the Christian Christ?

18 If Jesus may be regarded as a Jewish teacher, why isn't the New Testament a part of the Holy Scriptures of Judaism?

19 Did the belief in the Messiah help the Jews to listen to the Still, Small Voice and practice Jewish ethics?

THINGS TO DO

1 Write out the Nicene Creed. Then pencil out every belief that Judaism cannot accept, and submit your paper to your teacher.

2 Each member of the class should select one of the following theological beliefs, and write an essay describing the Jewish point of view: God, Torah, Prayer, Man, The Soul, Miracles, Freedom of Will, Immortality, The Messiah.

3 Look up the Jewish teaching about revelation. How do Orthodox, Conservative and Reform Judaism differ on the teaching about God's revelation of the Torah?

4 Check through the Orthodox prayerbook and list four references to the resurrection of the dead. List two passages from the Conservative prayerbook that refer to the afterlife. List two passages in the Union prayerbook that indicate how Reform Judaism has changed its belief from the resurrection of the body to the eternal life of the soul.

5 Identify the following and describe the essential contribution of each to JewishTheology: Maimonides, Hasdai Crescas, Samson Raphael Hirsch, Solomon Schechter, Kaufman Kohler, and Joseph Klausner.

6 Write a paragraph on: The Jewish Belief in Satan.

7 Write a paragraph on how the Persian religion influenced the Jewish belief in angels, demons, resurrection, heaven and hell.

8 Discuss in class: If God is omniscient and knows everything, does man really have freedom of will?

9 Give some examples from life showing that evil brings about evil, and goodness brings about goodness.

10 Look up the meaning of vicarious atonement. How does this apply to Judaism and to Christianity?

11 Interview a Christian minister and a rabbi on: What I Believe about the Messiah.

12 To learn more about the first step in the development of the Messiah idea, look up I Samuel 12:3,5; 24:7; Psalm 132:17; Leviticus 4:3,5,16; 6:15; Psalm 105:15; I Chronicles 16:22.

13 Find in the New Testament the statements Jesus made before he died.

14 Write an essay showing that Jesus was born, lived and died as a Jew. If Jesus should come back to earth and visit your community, where would he go to worship; what holydays and festivals would he observe, what language would he speak, and what prayerbook would he use?

15 Discuss in class: which is more important, believing or doing?

16 Will a person of the Jewish faith practice Jewish ethics if he doesn't know and believe in the fundamental teachings of Judaism?

SELECTED QUOTATIONS

A Scientist's Credo

The striving after knowledge for its own sake, the love of justice verging on fanaticism, and the quest for personal independence—there are the motivating traditions of the Jewish people which cause me to regard my adherence thereto as a gift of destiny.... History has imposed upon us a severe struggle. But as long as we remain devoted servants of truth, justice and freedom, we shall not only continue to exist as the oldest of all peoples, but we shall also, as hitherto, create, through productive effort, values which shall contribute to the ennobling of mankind.

ALBERT EINSTEIN, 1879-1955

Faith in a Foxhole

No, Dad, I have not altogether forgotten your prophetic message, of that "still, small voice." It would no doubt please you to learn that it has, in fact, proved helpful to me here, on occasion. In the midst of the sickening muck and sweat and blood of the Nature and man-made *Gehenna* of these Pacific Islands, that "still, small voice," Dad, has enabled me, on occasion, to look beyond all this Desolation, and to find, even here, something encouraging for the human spirit! Among other things, it helped me to direct my thoughts to that grand heroism of so many of our men, who performed their Duty, as they saw it, unafraid of Death! As though Death did not matter, but Duty did! As though Duty was informed with a mystic Destiny that swallows up Death! ...

At those *in extremis* moments, Dad, when one is driven to curse Existence and die, it is good to cup one's inward ear toward that Voice of Great Stillness.... For during those desperate moments, it does somehow help to unite, across the great chasm of the ages, one's inmost being with the suffering, but exultant, immortal spirits of the Jeremiahs and the Jobs of the distant past. Yes, it *does* then inspire one, with them and through them, to "see" beyond the Desolation—a new Israel, and, in the very teeth of personal tragedy, to capture a precious bit of their indefeasible confidence in Existence and of that deep, deathless serenity which was theirs as a result of this mystic trust....

HAROLD SILVER

The Voice Within Us

There is, further, the whole range of mental processes—consciousness, thought, emotion, memory—all so marvelous when we come to think of them. These too are God's witnesses, Bibles within ourselves, inner revelations of the Divine. Think, moreover, of Conscience, or the Moral Sense as it is sometimes called. It is the voice within us that alternately exhorts and warns, a flame in the breast which now scorches and sears it, now warms it with the glow of in exquisite joy.

This power to know good and evil, this mysterious law engraven on the heart's tablets, this conscious possession of a higher self, of an ideal by which in our best moments we measure our acts and our lives—whence has it come? Is it a mere accident, a chance thing in a universe sown thick with signs of deliberate purpose? Or is this too not a manifestation of Divine wisdom and will? Does not the ideal within us correspond with some eternal ideal, some pattern of goodness fashioned by God Himself?

KAUFMAN KOHLER

The Torah

Why was the Torah not given in the land of Israel? In order that the nations of the world should not have the excuse for saying: Because it was given in Israel's land, therefore we have not accepted it.

The *Mekilta*

The Jewish View of Man

In the religious outlook of Judaism, man is not only the creature of earth, but also the child of heaven. In him are united dust and star, flesh and spirit, body and soul. His life presents an arena where beast and angel wage incessant struggle for sovereignty. Passion and reason are ever active in him. He thinks of good and of evil. The way of life and the way of death lie open to him. His prerogative consists in his ability to choose one or the other. Freedom of will, though limited in form, is part of his nature. His mind is his lamp to illumine his way. The more clearly he sees the way of life and the more firmly he clings to it, the higher and nobler is his character. The more he tames the beast and refines his conscience, the truer child of God he becomes.

SAMUEL S. COHON
From *What We Jews Believe*

The Test of Man's Worth

The Divine test of man's worth is not his theology, but his life.

Judaism is not only ethical, but ethics constitutes its essence, its nature—"its beginning, its middle and its end."

When man appears before the Throne of Judgment, the first question he is asked is not—"Have you believed in God?" or, "Have you prayed or performed ritual acts?" but, "Have you dealt honorably, faithfully in all your dealings with your fellowman?"

ISRAEL H. WEISFELD
The Ethics of Israel

Freedom of Will

Judaism has ever emphasized the freedom of the will as one of its chief doctrines. The dignity and greatness of man depends largely upon his freedom, his power of self-determination. He differs from the lower animals in his independence of instinct as the dictator of his actions. He acts from free choice and conscious design, and is able to change his mind at any moment, at any new evidence or even through whim. He is therefore responsible for his every act or omission, even for his every intention. This alone renders him a moral being, a child of God; thus the moral sense rests upon freedom of the will.

KAUFMAN KOHLER

The Religion of Jesus

....When Paul fashioned a new religion around Jesus, the Christ, Jews took cognizance of him. Then, they rejected not Jesus, the Jewish teacher, but Christ the Messiah. There were definite criteria for the advent of the Messiah. He was to usher in the Messianic kingdom of justice, truth and peace. Not Jesus alone, but many other Jews who through the centuries claimed to be the Messiah, were judged and found wanting. Wars, oppression, corruption, continued as before. The real Messiah, they believed, was yet to come. As to Jesus in particular, the Jews were especially repelled by the claim that he had fulfilled the law, which thenceforth could be disregarded....

Finally, Jews have rejected Christianity because of the concepts with which the Church fathers buttressed and embellished the new faith in order to make it acceptable to the pagan Roman world. Completely alien to Jewish thought were such ideas as Immaculate Conception, virgin birth, trinitarianism, Holy Ghost, vicarious atonement, the assumption of Jesus (and later of Mary), and the "fall." The religion *of* Jesus was understandable to them; it was Jewish. The religion *about* Jesus was beyond their recognition. They doubted even that Jesus would recognize it.

RABBI PHILIP S. BERNSTEIN
What The Jews Believe

Will You Accept This?

Very well then, says the Christian, let it be conceded that Jesus is neither God, nor uniquely His son, nor the Messiah, nor a moral prophet, nor even an impeccable human being. Certainly he was, despite his defects, a great man, a gifted and exalted teacher. Will not the Jews accept him as such? To which the answer of Jews runs: Have Jews, except under the extremest provocation, ever quarreled with such a presentation of him?

RABBI MILTON STEINBERG
Basic Judaism

The Day the Messiah Will Come

Rabbi Joshua ben Levi found Elijah standing at the entrance to the cave of Rabbi Simon ben Yichai.

He said to him: "When will the Messiah come?"
Elijah answered, "Today—if you hearken unto His voice!"

(Psalms 95:7)

Salvation

Salvation is attained not by subscription to metaphysical dogmas, but solely by love of God that fulfills itself in action. This is a cardinal truth in Judaism.

HASDAI CRESCAS, *1410*

SUGGESTED READINGS

For the Student

Bernstein, Philip, *What The Jews Believe*
Cohon, Samuel, *What We Jews Believe*
Cronbach, Abraham, *Judaism For Today*
Gittelsohn, Roland, *But Little Lower Than The Angels*
Heller, Bernard, *The Odyssey of a Faith*
Isserman, Ferdinand, *This is Judaism*
Joseph, Morris, *Judaism as Creed and Life*
Kertzer, Morris, *What Is A Jew?*
Steinbach, A., *What is Judaism*
Steinberg, Milton, *Basic Judaism*
Universal Jewish Encyclopedia, "Theology," Vol. 10, pp. 242-244; "Theodicy," pp. 241-242; "Messiah," Vol. 7, pp. 499-506

For the Teacher

Brickner, Barnett, *Answering Your Questions About Jews and Judaism, A Pamphlet*
Cohon, Samuel, *Judaism As A Way of Life*
Cohon, Beryl, *Jacob's Well*
Goldstein, Morris, *Jesus and The Jewish Tradition*
Heschel, Abraham J., *A Philosophy of Judaism*

Kohler, Kaufmann, *Jewish Theology*
Klausner, Joseph, *The Messiah Idea in Judaism*
Sandmel, Samuel, *The Jewish Understanding of the New Testament*
Schechter, Solomon, *Some Aspects of Rabbinic Theology; Studies in Judaism, Third Series*
Silver, Abba Hillel, *Where Judaism Differed*
Zeitlin, Solomon, *Who Crucified Jesus?*

9

THE VOICE OF DEMOCRACY

The Ethics of Social Action

Chosen for what?

"The Messiah idea in Judaism has evolved through three stages. The first was the anointing of kings and priests. The second was the belief in a personal Messiah. We cannot begin to understand the third step of the development of the Messiah idea," said Rabbi Mayer, "without first asking whether the Jews are the chosen people, and then proceeding with a discussion of the attitude of Judaism toward social justice.

"Some people accuse the Jews of being superior and arrogant because of this chosen people concept. I'm afraid that both Jews and

Christians frequently misunderstand what is meant by a chosen people."

"It seems simple enough to me," said Bill. "God picked Israel to be His favorite people."

"In a sense that is correct, Bill," said Rabbi Mayer, "but it is not that simple. If we say that God is the God of all peoples and if we believe that God is the universal Father of all mankind, then how can God have favorites?

"A long time ago, the prophet Amos punctured the arrogance of the children of Israel when they thought that they were superior to other peoples. Speaking in the name of God he said: *Are ye not as the children of the Ethiopians unto me, O children of Israel.* Just as God loves the children of Israel, so he loves the dark-skinned children of Ethiopia. And then Amos continued: 'Have not I brought up Israel out of the land of Egypt? And the Philistines from Caphtor, and Aram from Kir?' Just as God redeemed Israel from the slavery of Egypt, so He redeemed the Philistines from bondage in Caphtor, and the people of Damascus from the captivity of Kir."

Jonathan said: "Now I'm really confused. If what Amos says is true, then why do we say the blessing praising God who has chosen us from among all peoples, and given us His Torah?"

"I'm glad that you asked this question, because it gets to the very heart of the idea of the chosen people. The blessing does not say that God has chosen us for privileges, or for favors, or for power. God chose Israel in order to reveal His Torah through Israel to all mankind. Yes, in that sense, the Jews are the chosen people—chosen to teach God's moral laws to all the peoples of the world.

"Jewish tradition teaches us that before God proclaimed the Ten Commandments on Sinai, He offered the Torah to all the peoples, but they refused it. He then said to the people of Israel:

> *Now, therefore, if ye will hearken unto My voice, indeed, and keep My covenant, then ye shall be Mine own treasure*

from among all peoples, for all the earth is Mine; and ye shall be unto Me a kingdom of priests, and a holy people.

The Choosing People

"Israel was given a choice–either to accept the Torah and become servants of God, teachers of the moral law, and thus a kingdom of priests and a holy people, or to reject the privilege of making a covenant with God and teaching His Torah. Israel accepted a divine relationship with God saying: 'We will do and we will obey.' In that sense, Israel was chosen by God to reveal His moral laws, and become the chosen people. In another sense, Israel was not only a chosen people but a *choosing* people–because Israel chose God; Israel elected to live up to the teachings of God and to serve mankind as well."

"Let me see if I understand," said Jonathan. "The Jews are both a chosen and a choosing people. We are chosen people because God made a covenant with our ancestors and revealed the Torah to them, thus placing upon Israel the obligation of teaching it to the world. We are a choosing people because Israel chose to accept the covenant, the Torah and the mission of serving as teachers of God's moral laws."

"That's right, Jonathan," said Rabbi Mayer. "You see, in making a covenant with God, and in accepting the yoke of the Torah, the Jews were now committed to teach the world to obey the moral laws of God. This meant that the children of Israel would have to battle against evil and fight injustice everywhere. It meant that Jews in every generation, would have to struggle and persist and even suffer in the effort to bring God's teachings to mankind. But, in every age there were those who, for selfish and greedy reasons, did not want justice–and therefore they hated the Jews who constantly opposed them and their ideas. The Jews became a symbol of the moral law–and those who hated the moral law also hated the Jews and their religion. But no matter how strong the opposition, Judaism insists upon social justice and human rights for all peoples regardless of their race, religion or nationality.

Judaism and Social Justice

"This brings us to the question on Joseph's list: 'What is the attitude of Judaism toward social justice?' The answers to this question reveal the grandeur of Jewish belief and Jewish action harmonized into an exalted moral code. In the answers, we find the real meaning of the Still, Small Voice, summoning mankind to obey God's commandments.

"The Jewish attitude toward social justice is based on the conviction that God is a God of holiness, justice and truth—a God Who is worshipped by practising holiness, justice, mercy and truth. God is the Creator and universal Father of all people, and therefore if God is the Father, then all men must be united in the bond of universal brotherhood. But there is another belief of Judaism that is equally essential."

"I think I know what it is," said Eldon. "If God created man in His image, then every man and every woman is sacred and holy because of the soul, which is a part of God within. When we help our fellow-human beings, we help God. When we hurt them, we hurt God."

"Go ahead, Eldon," Rabbi Mayer said. "You seem to have grasped the idea so far."

"God commanded justice through His moral laws," continued Eldon. "What I mean is that social justice is the will of God—and that's why Judaism must always think in terms of justice for all of God's children."

"What you say is basic to the understanding of social justice in Judaism," said the Rabbi. "The Midrash asks the question:

Adam, the First Man

Why was Adam, the first man, created a single individual? To teach us that whoever destroys one human soul, the Torah regards him as if he had destroyed the entire world, and he who sustains one human soul, the Torah regards him as if he had saved the entire world.

Also for the sake of harmony, in order that no man may say to his fellowman, "I am descended from better stock than you are." All men are descended from one common ancestor. Also in order that the scoffers may not say, "many first individuals were created by many gods."

Also in order to manifest the greatness of the Holy One, blessed be He. Human beings mint coins bearing the picture of one original (a king or prince), and all coins are identical. However, the King of Kings, the Holy One, blessed be He, patterned all human beings after the image of Adam, the first man, and yet no two human beings are exactly alike. Because of all the above reasons, every individual is privileged to declare: "For my sake was the entire world created."

"Many years later, the philosopher, Philo, taught that the Ten Commandments were addressed not in the plural but in the singular to teach that 'each single person when he is law-abiding and obedient to God, is equal in worth to a whole nation, even the most populous, or rather to all nations, and if we may go still further, even to the whole world.'

"The belief in the sanctity of the individual is a foundation of the Jewish belief in social justice. It follows that Judaism must never tolerate hatred, cruelty or injustice to any of God's children. To hate or to be prejudiced against a person because of the color of his skin, or his religious faith, or his nationality, is to hate God. All people, whether rich or poor, wise or ignorant, are children of God, and therefore they are deserving of equal opportunities and rights because they are created in the image of God."

WHAT DO YOU THINK?

1 In what sense do you think the Jews are the chosen people?

2 Why do you think that the people of Israel developed such a sensitivity to religion that they were worthy of being chosen to teach God's moral laws to the world?

3 Does the idea of the chosen people place any moral obligations upon modern Jews? What are these obligations?

4 What do you think is meant by "a kingdom of priests and a holy people"? How does that apply to modern Jews?

5 Do you prefer the idea of Israel being a chosen people or a choosing people? Why?

6 How did Israel incur enmity and hatred because of the covenant made with God to teach His moral laws?

7 How should the Jewish belief that all people are children of God influence our attitude toward: the poor, the sick, minority groups such as Negroes, Indians, Puerto Ricans, and foreigners?

Judaism and Democracy

"I'm sure," said Rabbi Mayer, "that you are all aware of the contribution that Judaism has made to our Democracy and the American way of life. The Bible, which was the people's Magna Charta, gave the founding fathers the basis for the moral principles of the new nation. The Pilgrim Fathers used the Jewish festival of Succoth as the model for Thanksgiving. The statement from Leviticus: 'Proclaim Liberty Throughout the Land unto all the inhabitants thereof,' is emblazoned upon the Liberty Bell in Independence Hall, Philadelphia. The Bible was the source material for American democracy from the Mayflower Compact, through the Declaration of Independence and the Constitution, to the present-day beliefs that characterize the American way of life. Men like Thomas Paine, Benjamin Franklin and Samuel Adams emphasized the religious nature of the need to resist political evil by references to the Bible. It was understandable that it should be said that 'Hebraic mortar cemented the foundations of American Democracy.'

"Steeped in the Biblical tradition, those who shaped the political philosophy of American democracy recalled the stirring command: 'Thou shalt not oppress the stranger.' They remembered that the Sabbath must be a day of rest for the free man and the slave. 'Justice, Justice shall ye pursue,' echoed in their hearts.

"Clamoring for freedom, they could feel themselves a part of the exodus from Egypt. They identified themselves with the children of Israel and their liberation from tyranny.

"A State Department booklet titled *The History of the Seal of the United States*, by Gaillard Hunt, reveals that after the Declaration of Independence had been signed, the Continental Congress set itself to the task of adopting an official seal for the new nation. The first design submitted by the committee, composed of Benjamin Franklin, John Adams and Thomas Jefferson, showed 'Pharaoh sitting in an open chariot, a crown on his head and a sword in his hand, passing through the divided waters of the Red Sea in pursuit of the Israelites; rays from a pillar of fire in the cloud, expressive of the Divine Presence and Command, beaming on Moses who, standing on the shore and extending his hand over the Sea causes it to overwhelm Pharaoh.' "

"Did they adopt that as the seal of the United States?" Judith asked.

"No, Judith," said Rabbi Mayer. "However, the spirit of that suggested design has characterized the political structure of America to the present day. Hatred of tyranny, the love of freedom, and the emphasis upon human rights derived from the biblical teaching of the sanctity of man, have been woven into the political design of American democracy.

"Those of the Jewish faith have found true freedom in America. We are free to live by our faith. We are privileged to work with our fellow-Americans to make the dreams of the prophets come true."

QUESTIONS FOR DISCUSSION

1 After looking up the meaning of "democracy" in the dictionary, discuss in class your opinion of "What Makes America a Democracy."

2 What is your opinion of the idea expressed by some that Jews should not seek political office or be "too prominent" in public affairs?

3 Part of the preamble of the Declaration of Independence states: "We hold these truths to be self-evident: That all men are created equal; that they are endowed by their Creator with certain unalienable rights; that among these are life, liberty, and the pursuit of happiness." Where are these thoughts to be found in the Bible? How would you apply this statement to American life today?

4 What do you think George Washington meant when he wrote the following to the Jewish congregation of Newport, R. I., in 1790: "For happily, the Government of the United States, which gives to bigotry no sanction, to persecution no assistance, requires only that they who live under its protection should demean themselves as good citizens, in giving it on all occasions their effectual support."? How can we give our government effectual support? Interpret this statement in terms of American life today.

5 How would you interpret this statement made by Rabbi Bernard Bamberger, of New York: "During February, we honor the memory of some dangerous men. The Founding Fathers, we sometimes forget, fought against institutions and procedures hallowed by tradition and accepted as unchallengeable by the more respectable elements of society. Washington's army was described as 'a rabble in arms'...when we glorify Moses, Washington or Lincoln, we are glorifying those who were responsible for radical change in the life of humanity....The great revolutionaries, the prophets and patriots, did not want change just for the sake of change–they wanted greater righteousness and greater happiness for mankind."

SOME STATEMENTS TO THINK ABOUT

Judaism and Americanism

The phrase, "We must be Americans first, Jews afterwards," which so many of our colleagues are so fond of using, is a mere string of words without real meaning, sound without sense. The system of government prevailing in the United States and the Jewish religion are both built upon the same rock of Old Testament, the Mosaic legislation. The religious and civil duties of the Jewish-American can never, by any possibility, conflict. What makes for the highest interest of the American State is precisely what the Jewish religion teaches.

RABBI ISAAC MAYER WISE

Freedom and Religion

We believe that the national security of our country is rooted in the individual freedom of its citizens....Freedom is not only the moral and spiritual basis of our national life; it is the bulwark of our security.

We are impelled to this conviction by the basic teachings both of Americanism and of Judaism. God can be worshipped and religion can flourish only in an atmosphere of freedom.

Institute on Individual Freedom and National Security, March 15, 1953, sponsored by the Central Conference of American Rabbis

Human Equality in the Jewish Tradition

In the biblical and rabbinic tradition the fundamental concept regarding human equality is that all human beings are equal in their obligations to God. Obligations rest on the individual both as himself and as a member of the community....From the concept of equal obligations to God derives man's unique role as the servant of God.

RABBI LOUIS FINKELSTEIN

The Synagogue and Social Action

Joel raised his hand. "There are some things that I don't understand. What does the chosen people idea have to do with the Jewish contribution to American democracy, and especially with the way we live as Jews and Americans today?"

Rabbi Mayer replied, "When the Jewish people accepted the Torah, Joel, they resolved to build a society based on justice, freedom and peace. They were chosen for a great and a holy purpose. They chose to accept that mission in the land of Israel and in every nation where they lived. Today, we, as modern American Jews, have a mission, too. That mission is to help make the country in which we live a nation of justice, freedom and peace. We believe that the political form of government that comes closest to the will of God and the teachings of Judaism is democracy. Therefore, we have the responsibility, as Jews and as American citizens, of applying the principles of democracy to life."

"But how do we accomplish this?" asked Joel. "Where do we begin?"

"The most logical place to begin," said Rabbi Mayer, "is in the synagogue. It is in the synagogue, where we learn the teachings of the Torah and express our love of God through the inspiration of the prayerbook, that we begin to apply the Jewish principles of social action.

Justice and Judaism

"The relationship of the synagogue to social action is brought out clearly in a book by Albert Vorspan and Rabbi Eugene Lipman. The book is called *Justice and Judaism.* In it we learn why modern Jews must be concerned with problems dealing with housing, education, marriage and the family, crime, punishment, and juvenile delinquency, civic reform, civil rights, civil liberties, immigration and international peace.

"The authors believe that not only must Jews be concerned with social justice, but they also urge each synagogue to have a committee on social action to study and practice the principles of democracy, justice and peace.

"At the end of the book, there are twenty questions and answers on the synagogue and social action. Today, we are not going to consider all of these questions and answers; just a few. They will help us to understand why it is important for the synagogue to be vitally concerned with social action."

What is Synagogue Social Action?

Synagogue social action is the process of translating the principles of Judaism into action in our communities, the nation, and the world, through the synagogue. It is the contemporary expression of the passion for social justice which characterized the prophets of Israel and which is intrinsic to Judaism.

Why Should the Synagogue be Concerned with Social Issues?

Judaism is not merely a set of beliefs; it is a way of life. Judaism is not an other-worldly religion. In our tradition, man is called the co-worker of God in the creation of a better world here and now. In Judaism, social justice is a religious duty. What does God expect of us? Judaism answers: "To do justly, to love mercy, and to walk humbly with thy God."

What National Group Is Concerned with Social Action in Reform Judaism?

The Commission on Social Action of Reform Judaism. It comprises the Union of American Hebrew Congregations, the Central Conference of American Rabbis, the National Federation of Temple Sisterhoods, the National Federation of Temple Youth, and the National Federation of Temple Brotherhoods—the entire family of Reform Judaism.

Do Conservative and Orthodox Judaism Have Programs of Social Action?

Yes. The United Synagogue of America (Conservative) and the Union of Orthodox Jewish Congregations (Orthodox) are also members of the NCRAC. Both groups are developing social action programs nationally and within their congregations. The three Jewish religious bodies work together closely in this area.

Do Christian Groups Have Such Programs?

Yes. In fact, they have set the pace in this direction. The Roman Catholic Church and virtually every Protestant denomination have social action programs functioning nationally and in many local churches.

Isn't Social Action Controversial?

Yes. Some people challenge the idea that the synagogue should go beyond prayer and ritual and the religious school. The Reform movement has overwhelmingly registered its disagreement with that viewpoint. Successive biennial assemblies of the UAHC have stated categorically that the synagogue must be concerned with the moral issues of society, even though controversy may result. Judaism divorced from life is an empty shell which must repel many intelligent, deeply-committed, religious Jews.

Doesn't Social Action Involve a Synagogue in Politics?

Some people talk about politics as if it were a dirty word. But what is it? Webster's *Universal Unabridged Dictionary* defines politics as: "The science of government; that part of *ethics* which consists in the regulation and government of a nation or state, for the preservation of its safety, peace and prosperity... and the protection of its citizens in their rights, with the preservation and improvement of their *morals.*"

Obviously, Judaism, a religion grounded in ethics, must be concerned with politics in this sense. The ethical insights of prophetic Judaism must be applied to the specific social and political problems of our time. Such questions as civil rights, genocide, Point Four, and immigration, have political aspects, but they involve ethical concepts on which Judaism must have something to say.

It is *partisan* politics that the synagogue must and does avoid. It is not our task to further Republicans over Democrats or vice versa, but it is our task to apply the principles we profess in the world in which we live.

How Can a Social Action Program Strengthen the Synagogue?

Social action is Judaism in practice. By giving dynamic vitality to the synagogue, it helps to bridge the gap between prayer and practice, creed and conduct, thus bringing a sense of greater reality to our faith. A synagogue with a well-established social action program said it has: "....given sensitive and social-minded Jews a sense of rootage in the congregation...inspired youth groups with the conviction that the synagogue is as much interested in bettering the future as in preserving its link with the past...given real meaning to the beautiful prayers for democracy, peace and justice in our prayerbooks... helped our membership to a healthier degree of personal integrity."

QUESTIONS FOR DISCUSSION

1 How should the belief that Jews were chosen by God to teach His moral laws help to make us better Americans?

2 What are the ideals of Judaism? What are the ideals of democracy? Are they the same?

3 How can the Synagogue contribute to social justice?

4 Do you think that you should have a committee on social justice in your synagogue? What would be some of the problems that such a committee would take up? Do you think the committee should be limited to study, or should it take action to correct injustice, oppression, prejudice and unrighteousness?

5 Do you think that the Synagogue has a right to deal with controversial problems? If so, in what way?

SOME STATEMENTS TO THINK ABOUT

The Survival of the Synagogue

Surely a religious institution should have a position on the burning question of religion in the public schools. Moreover, the very survival of the synagogue is bound up with questions of race, housing, juvenile crime, education, and recreation in our area. These problems concern us both practically and morally. In the complex issues of social change we shall have to move deliberately, prudently and wisely—but that need not mean timidity and futility.

RABBI BERNARD J. BAMBERGER

God and Social Victory

America must emphasize independence and interdependence. It should come to its God idea not through a feeling of helplessness, but through a feeling of confidence. It will find its God not in defeat but in social victory. It will seek Divinity not primarily through mystical surrender, but through practical moral activity.

RABBI JOSHUA LOTH LIEBMAN

Segregation and Race Relations

"According to Judaism," said Rabbi Mayer, "all men are equal because they are created in the image of God. This means that prejudice against any human being because of his religious faith or color is a sin against God.

"On May 17, 1954, the United States Supreme Court declared that segregation by race in the public schools is illegal. This decision created a great deal of controversy, especially in the south, because many southern people object to what is called 'the mixing of races' in the public schools. They would have Negro children go to Negro schools, and white children go to white schools. This is contrary to the decision of the Supreme Court.

"Since Judaism is opposed to any form of discrimination because of race, the Union of American Hebrew Congregations endorsed the decision of the Supreme Court at its Biennial Assembly in Los Angeles in February, 1955:

Having consistently opposed every form of discrimination because of our fundamental belief in the equality of all men under God, we rejoice in the unanimous decision of the U. S. Supreme Court in the school segregation cases....

As proponents of Judaism which first enunciated the concept of the fatherhood of God and the brotherhood of man, we pledge ourselves to do all within our power to make the decision of the highest court in the land meaningful in our respective communities.

We therefore urge our congregants and congregations in all sections of the country to join with forward-looking racial, religious and civic groups in the community in using their influence to secure acceptance and implementation of the desegregation decisions in every community in our land.

"But should there be any objection to having Negroes in the same school with white children?" asked Sarah indignantly. "After all, they are human beings, and what's more they are Americans."

"I agree with you, Sarah," said Rabbi Mayer, "but there are many people in the south who feel that segregation is part of their way of life. They want to give Negroes good schools and equal opportunities for an education, but insist upon separating the races.

"When the School Boards tried to bring about 'integration,' which means having the white and Negro children together, there were riots in Clinton, Tennessee. Most of these riots were instigated by extremists who refused to abide by law and order. The Governor of Tennessee sent the State Militia to maintain order."

"I think the South should be ashamed of such actions," said Marvin. "After all this is America, and everyone's rights are guaranteed by the Constitution, and what's more..."

"Just a minute, Marvin," interrupted Rabbi Mayer. "Don't condemn the South for the action of some hot-headed extremists. Remember that some communities in the North also resisted integration, and there were disturbances in the North, too. For example, in Milford, Delaware, a leader of the National Association for the Advancement of White People urged a 'strike by parents of white pupils until the Negroes get out of our schools. No matter if it means bloodshed, we'll see it through, no matter what the consequences.'

How Many Bubbles in A Bar of Soap?

"Discrimination and prejudice against the Negro are not limited to opposition to the Supreme Court Decision, but may be evinced in other ways, such as depriving the Negro of the right to vote, preventing him from living in certain residential areas, having discriminatory regulations against him on buses and trains, and limiting his economic opportunities.

"In an official sworn affidavit, a Negro woman declared that on April 11, 1952, she was deprived of the right to vote because, after meeting all of the qualifications for voting she could not answer the question: 'How many bubbles are there in a bar of soap?' Frequently, Negroes are prevented from voting because of poll taxes, literacy tests, and the fear of mob violence.

"We frequently find prejudice against the Negro when he wishes to rent or buy a home in a white neighborhood. Some communities make what is known as 'restrictive covenants,' which means a ruling forbidding Negroes from living in certain districts. The United States Supreme Court has declared that 'restrictive covenants' cannot be enforced, and that deliberately planned racial segregation in housing is not legal.

"In some communities, the purchase of homes by Negroes has resulted in violence. A mob stormed the home of a Philadelphia Negro when he bought an abandoned store in a white neighborhood and made it over into a home. In Chicago, a mob hurled bricks and crude bombs at the home of a Negro because he had moved into Trumbell Park, an all-white housing project. In a West Coast city, a Negro and his two children were burned to death when neighbors set his house afire two days after Christmas. There have been other race riots in Detroit, Cleveland, and St. Louis.

"Frequently, Negroes are denied the privilege of getting jobs with higher salaries. Some department stores and other businesses will refuse to hire Negro clerks. As a result of such discrimination, many Negroes who are educated and trained for more skilled positions, are compelled to take poorly-paid jobs. Because of their limited income, Negroes are compelled to live in unsanitary slum areas.

"Efforts are being made to clean up these slum areas and to build government housing projects that will enable the Negro to enjoy a higher standard of living, but there is still a great deal of work to be done to give the Negro the rights and liberties he deserves as an American citizen.

Accentuate the Positive

"Optimism has ever been a characteristic of the Jewish faith," said Rabbi Mayer, "so instead of concentrating on the negative efforts of the unAmerican fanatics, we should not forget those who have been bravely working for Negro rights. Not only the National Association for the Advancement of Colored People, but other organizations have come into being to strengthen the decision of the Supreme Court, and to give Negroes their rights as Americans. In Milford, Delaware, the hot-heads and the extremists did not win out, and today Negro children and white children are integrated in the public schools. In a step-by-step plan, St. Louis desegregated its schools without friction. Kentucky integrated most of its schools.

"In many communities, local Human Relations groups have helped to educate the people of their cities and show the importance of bringing more light and less heat to the problem of race relations. Catholic authorities have announced plans to integrate parochial schools in New Orleans, Nashville, and San Antonio. Protestant, Catholic, and Jewish organizations have endorsed the decision of the

Supreme Court—not only on the question of the integration of the schools, but the right of Negroes to unrestricted use of buses and trains. Parent-teacher groups, civic organizations and women's clubs have joined with Americans of every race, every religious faith, to end segregation, to destroy race prejudice, and to contribute to the realization of the American dream."

QUESTIONS FOR DISCUSSION

1 Why does Judaism oppose race prejudice?

2 What is your opinion of the wisdom of the Surpreme Court Decision about desegregating our public schools? Do you favor or oppose the decision? What are your reasons?

3 Give your reasons why you personally favor or oppose the mixing of races in your school? Do your reasons apply to Chinese, Japanese, Mexicans, Puerto Ricans, and Hindus?

4 If you or a member of your family were ill and a blood transfusion was required, would you object to a Negro giving blood? Is there such a thing as Negro blood or white blood? What are the real blood types?

5 How do Amendments XIV and XV of the Constitution relate to the problem of race prejudice and Negro rights?

6 Why should Jews be particularly concerned about prejudice against Negroes? Why should Americans be concerned about prejudice against Negroes? Is there a relationship between anti-Semitism and prejudice against the Negro?

7 Would you object if a Negro or a Chinese family wanted to move next door to you?

8 Walter White, a Negro leader, in his autobiography, *How Far The Promised Land?*, wrote: "During World War II, youngsters were asked how Hitler could be punished. Said one: 'Paint him black and send him to the United States.' " What is your opinion of that statement?

9 Those who oppose desegregation argue that the mixing of Negroes and whites in the public schools will contribute to inter-racial marriages. What do you think?

10 If Amos and Isaiah lived today, what do you think they would say about segregation and prejudice against the Negro?

11 Do you think that your rabbi should speak courageously on race prejudice, even though his views may not be popular with the congregation? Why?

SOME STATEMENTS TO THINK ABOUT

Justice, Justice Shalt Thou Pursue

We cannot deny that we live in a day when mankind looks to America for leadership in the struggle for freedom. The denial of justice to any of our citizens dims our moral standing and prestige among the nations. When this denial of Justice is predicated on the color of a man's skin, we make suspect the whole concept of democracy in the eyes of the billion colored people whose friendship we want and need.

Commission on Justice and Peace of the Central Conference of American Rabbis

The Right of Protest

....We have known humiliation, we have known abusive language, we have been plunged into the abyss of oppression, and we decided to rise up only with the weapon of protest. It is one of the greatest glories of America that we have the right of protest.

If we are arrested every day, if we are exploited every day, if we are trampled over every day, don't ever let anyone pull you so low as to hate him. We must use the weapon of love. We must have compassion and understanding for those who hate us. We must realize so many people are taught to hate us that they are not totally responsible for their hate. But we stand in life at midnight; we are always on the threshold of a new dawn.

REVEREND MARTIN LUTHER KING, JR.
(a statement made a few hours after his arrest as a leader of Negro passive resistance against the city's bus lines in Montgomery, Alabama)

The Christian Church Speaks Against Segregation

We urge Christian statesmen and leaders in our churches to use their leadership in positive thought and planning to the end that this crisis in our national history shall not be made the occasion for new and bitter prejudices, but a movement toward a united nation embodying and proclaiming a democracy that will commend freedom to all peoples.

Southern Baptist Christian Life Commission

We sincerely hope that the day will come when the ideal of Christian brotherhood will displace from our Southern scene all traces of the blight of racism. Let us Catholics, true to our convictions, set the pattern.

The Catholic Committee of the South

Courage in Action

Dateline: December 10, 1956

CLINTON, TENN.—The Rev. Paul W. Turner, who was beaten here last Tuesday for escorting Negro children to Clinton High School, said yesterday, "there is no color line around the cross of Jesus."

This minister of the white race, in a sermon to 650 members of his congregation who packed the First Baptist Church, said: "Give up our constitution and nothing you now cherish is of any value whatsoever. When mobs flout the law, the terrible results are a Phenix City, Alabama, or a Cicero, Illinois.... Where anarchy prevails, no one has any freedom whatever."

Poison of Prejudice

It is curious that most worthy people who have been attacking racial prejudice in this country have not used one argument which history has again and again proved to be true. They think only of the victim of racial prejudice, his sufferings, his wrongs, and the damage done to his dignity as a man. They forget what happens psychologically to the prejudiced man or woman....

There is no snake in the breast more dangerous than unreasoning hate and nurtured contempt. It is the most poisonous kind of compensation for failure, or for lack of self-confidence. Despise a race, or hate a race, or dislike a race, and the poison will come out like invisible boils....

Racial prejudice has killed the bodies of millions in the last few years. We cannot forget that. But it is still warping the spirits and cramping the minds of tens of millions of the prejudiced.

HENRY SEIDEL CANBY

Civil Liberties

"One of the most important requirements of the American way of life," said Rabbi Mayer, "is the Bill of Rights. This is the first Ten Amendments to the Constitution, ratified by the various states, and on December 15, 1791, made a part of the Constitution of the United States.

"I'm sure that you have heard of the Bill of Rights, but do you know what these rights are?"

Mark raised his hand. "I believe that they guarantee the freedom of the American citizen, and protect his right to speak, write and live in a land of liberty."

"That is a general description, Mark, and essentially correct. However, these rights are important enough for us to take the time to consider what they really are. These are the first Ten Amendments:"

Amendment I–Freedom of Religion, Speech, and the Press; Right of Assembly and Petition
Amendment II–Right to Keep and Bear Arms
Amendment III–Quartering of Soldiers
Amendment IV–Regulation of Right of Search and Seizure
Amendment V–Protection of Persons and Their Property
Amendment VI–Rights of Persons Accused of Crime
Amendment VII–Right of Trial by Jury in Suits at Common Law
Amendment VIII–Protection Against Excessive Bail and Punishments
Amendment IX–Constitution Does Not List all Individual Rights
Amendment X–Powers Reserved to the States and the People

"These are the guarantee of the rights and liberties of the American people," said Rabbi Mayer. "Try to imagine what our democracy would be without them. Think of what it might be like to live in a country where the citizen can't worship God according to his convictions; where there is no free speech, and government spies report on the statements you make. Imagine a country where the press is not free, and the newspapers must report only what the government commands them to publish; a country where you cannot meet with others without government permission, and there is no possibility of seeking justice if you feel that you have been wronged."

"I don't see why people would want to live in such a country," said Sarah. "That sounds just like Fascism and Communism. Why don't the people rise up and rebel against such tyranny?"

"I'm sure that they would like to, and sometimes they do," answered the Rabbi. "But remember that only the governments of those countries have the right to issue arms; that soldiers can be quartered in every home in war or in peace; and that agents can come into your house without a warrant and search your possessions.

"Sometimes we forget how fortunate we are to live in a free nation. In America no person is compelled to be a witness against himself, and no one can be deprived of life, liberty or property without due process of law. In Communist countries, people are accused and sentenced to imprisonment or death without a free trial. They may never know what they are accused of. In America, the rights of persons accused of a crime are zealously protected. They have a right to a public trial, and must be informed of the charges made against them—and in addition, they have the right to the assistance of counsel for their defense."

Jerry shuddered. "It scares me to think of what could happen to a person without these rights. I'm sure glad that I'm living in America, and not in one of those police states where the people are deprived of their rights—just like that." Jerry snapped his fingers.

"I think that we are all glad that we are living here, Jerry," said Rabbi Mayer. "Being an American is important—and keeping America free, just, and democratic is even more important. Sometimes people forget what America really means, and because of selfish interests, fear, ignorance or prejudice they ignore the Bill of Rights. That's why we have to be alert to any effort that would deprive Americans of their rights and liberties."

"Who would want to do that?" Melvin asked. "You mean people who are enemies of America—people who want to destroy our way of life and our system of government."

"No, Melvin," answered Rabbi Mayer. "They do not regard themselves as enemies of America. It is true that there are extremist groups who want to change our system of government. Sometimes, however, those who regard themselves as good Americans use their love of America to propose measures that endanger the rights of other Americans."

Melvin seemed puzzled.

"I'm not sure that I understand," he said. "What are some examples of those who love America but endanger civil liberties?"

"Let me put it this way," said Rabbi Mayer. "Suppose you expressed political views that were a bit different; views that were not exactly like the views expressed by the majority. Suppose you were accused of being a communist because you once belonged to a liberal organization, or you once knew somebody who was later suspected of being a radical, and you lost your job. Suppose the people in your community heard about this and began to suspect you—without giving you a chance to defend yourself.

"During a period of apprehension and fear," continued the Rabbi, "people become unduly suspicious. We have had government workers fired from their jobs as 'security risks.' A Congressional investigating committee for a while forgot the bill of rights, and created suspicion and fear.

Black Silence of Fear

"That is what Justice William O. Douglas meant when he wrote an article called 'Black Silence of Fear.' In part, this is what he said:

> Irresponsible talk by irresponsible people has fanned the flames of fear. Accusations have been loosely made. Character assassinations have become common.
>
> Suspicion has taken the place of good will.... Once we had confidence in each other. Now there is suspicion. Innocent acts become tell-tale marks of disloyalty. The coincidence that an idea parallels Soviet Russia's policy for a moment of time settles...an aura of suspicion around a person....

"Justice Douglas wrote that article on January 23, 1952, and at that time there was an atmosphere of fear and suspicion in America.

"Committees set themselves up as authorities and removed books from Public Libraries, burning them as dangerous. Teachers and Professors were afraid to speak out on controversial subjects, because of the fear of being labeled radicals. State and government employees had to take 'loyalty oaths,' and even the churches and synagogues in some states were asked to take these loyalty oaths in order to receive tax-exemption.

"The situation became so serious that President Dwight D. Eisenhower urged the American people:

> Don't join the book burners. Don't think you are going to conceal faults by concealing evidence that they ever existed. Don't be afraid to go in your library and read every book as long as any document does not offend our own ideas of decency. That should be the only censorship.
>
> How will we defeat communism unless we know what it is—what it teaches? ...
>
> Now we have got to fight it with something better. Not try to conceal the thinking of our own people. They are part of America. And even if they think ideas that are contrary to ours they have a right to have them, a right to record them, and a right to have them in places where they are accessible to others. It is unquestioned or it is not America.

"The American people refused to be pressured into hysteria and fear. But we must ever be on guard against the possibility that Americans will be deprived of the sacred heritage of freedom of religion, freedom of speech, freedom of the press, and freedom from fear. Those who love America must never become indifferent to the attack upon civil rights and liberties.

"There are other problems that call for social action today. Some of these problems are directly related to civil rights and liberties. Others are not. What are some of these social problems?"

Housing

Joel raised his hand. "In our high school class last week, we discussed slum clearance and housing. Would that be one?"

"Yes, Joel, that is definitely a problem. Many communities in the United States have developed citizens' housing associations to deal with the unsightly and unsanitary evil of slums. A great deal has to be done to combat sickness, disease and the miserable standard of living that characterize the slums.

"In 1937, President Franklin D. Roosevelt said: 'I see one third of a nation ill-housed, ill-fed, ill-clothed.' Eleven years later, the President's Committee on Civil Rights issued a report pointing out the dangers and the problems created by housing needs.

"Every American should have the opportunity of buying or renting a home anywhere. However, we know that in some communities there are efforts to keep out of certain neighborhoods those of the Jewish faith, Negroes, Puerto Ricans, Mexicans and Japanese or Chinese Americans."

Crime

"Another reason why we should be concerned with housing," said Joel, "is that slums are a breeding-place for crime."

"And juvenile delinquency, too," added Jonathan.

"What you say is true," said Rabbi Mayer. "Every time we pick up a newspaper we read about violence, murder, armed robbery, kidnapping and burglary. Juvenile delinquency, too, is on the increase. Parents, churches, synagogues, civic groups and law enforcement agencies are deeply concerned about the problem of juvenile delinquency.

"Crime and juvenile delinquency are not limited to the slums, however. Those from middle and high income groups are also involved. As a result, special congressional committees have been studying the effects of comic and crime books, television and the motion pictures upon juvenile delinquency. Special juvenile court judges and family courts have been set up to combat the alarming spread of juvenile delinquency. The social scientists in their research have indicated that the number of Jewish juvenile delinquents is small. In just a little while, I'm going to ask you why Jewish children are less prone to delinquency.

"Organized crime is still a major problem. Rackets, confidence men, swindlers take millions from the public every year. Innocent people are preyed upon and compelled to pay 'protection' to operate their businesses. The selling of dope—especially to minors—demands the continuous vigilance of narcotics agents. Gambling syndicates, bookies, lottery and numbers rackets are evils that must be stamped out.

"The church and the synagogue cannot afford to ignore the controversial questions of prison reform and capital punishment. Experts on criminology believe that our prison system is a failure, primarily because the objective is punishment, rather than rehabilitation and cure. Reform schools, prisons, and detention homes, instead of removing the causes of crime, frequently embitter the offender, teach him additional lessons in crime and lead to further crimes. The conditions of prisons and the treatment of prisoners are sometimes so intolerable that the public is shocked when the facts are known.

"Six states of our nation have abolished capital punishment. Other states are studying the possibility of abolishing the death sentence. Sometimes innocent people are executed legally on the basis of circumstantial evidence. Errors do occur, and innocent men and women are convicted. It is not without cause that capital punishment has been called 'legalized murder,' and religion may well question the right of the state to take a human life.

Unemployment

"In 1929 an economic crisis occurred in the United States. At the peak of the depression it was estimated that 15 million men and women were unemployed and that fully 25 million people in America were living in a state of destitution.

"The churches and the synagogues together with social and government agencies brought influence to bear upon the problem, and as a result legislation was created to provide unemployment insurance, minimum wage laws, federal child labor laws, old age insurance, pensions, and state and federal construction projects.

"Unemployment frequently leads to crime. The incidence of crime takes a sharp jump during periods of depression and unemployment. Men who otherwise might be law-abiding citizens are tempted to go beyond the law in order to provide food and shelter for their dear ones. It is difficult for a person to think about the moral and spiritual values of life when his stomach is empty and the prospects of employment are dark.

"Even in our own day, at a time of prosperity, it is startling to know that people are starving. It is shocking to read the statement of Trygve Lie, former Secretary-General of the United Nations, telling us that nearly one-third of the entire human family is hungry, with millions upon millions of children born to live their few years of pain and privation without having ever experienced the satisfaction of having enough to satisfy their gnawing hunger.

Labor-Management Relations

"Even those who are employed sometimes encounter trouble because of conflicts between labor and management. During the last fifty years the labor movement has grown strong, and unions have risen up to protect the rights of the workingman and enable him to receive a living wage.

"Strikes and labor disputes cause hardship to both labor and management. Men and women are thrown out of work, and businesses and factories are compelled to shut down. The government has been of great assistance in arbitrating many of these disputes, but the conflict between labor and management is still a problem that demands careful thought and planned social action.

"While our sympathies go out to the laboring men, we must never forget that without capital and management the American system of free enterprise could not survive. Our system of free enterprise and competitive business has created living conditions that are the envy of the whole world. Justice is due not only to the laboring man, but to management as well.

Health and Public Welfare

"Sickness and poor health are problems that not only cost the nation great sums economically, but also deprive the individual of happiness and life itself. The church and the synagogue cannot afford to sit back and ignore the health problems that confront our nation.

"Government and private research groups are spending billions of dollars to rid the nation of the scourge of disease. Polio has now been checked, thanks to Dr. Jonas Salk and his vaccine. Wonder drugs have reduced the death toll, and the discoveries of science continue to bring renewed health and life to millions of people. However, we still have many problems to solve. Some of these problems are the prevention of physical disease; the provision of hospitalization and medical care for those in need; the establishment of more clinics for the poor, better equipped hospitals especially in rural areas, and further compensation for industrial accidents.

"One of the major threats confronting America is the increase of mental illness. There is a compelling need for the prevention and treatment of mental illness, more hospitals for the mentally ill, and funds for the establishment of mental health and child guidance clinics in our cities and rural communities."

Miriam said: "There doesn't seem to be an end to the number of problems that have to be solved. A person feels helpless at the very thought of all that has to be done."

"We have many problems," said Rabbi Mayer, "but we never lose hope. There is too much to be done. Since religion must enter into every aspect of life, it is the business of religion to be concerned with all of the problems that concern our society. Judaism has a special responsibility, because we say that religion is a way of life, and because we believe that we have a commitment to God to fight injustice, eradicate evil, and bring health, justice, freedom and peace to all mankind. Therefore, when people say that Judaism should stay out of politics, and that the Synagogue should have nothing to do with social action, they show that they know very little about the spirit and the purpose of our Jewish faith.

Other Problems

"There are other problems that should be considered. Right now, we can only mention them. Perhaps later we will be able to consider them in detail. The question of immigration has yet to be solved. At one time, America opened its doors to immigrants, and our immigration policy encouraged those of Europe to seek the hospitality of our shores. In recent years, efforts have been made to reduce quotas and thus prevent immigrants from coming to America. There are many who question the wisdom of laws which shut out many worthy people who want to emigrate to the United States.

"We have problems of education, too. There is a need for more adequate schools and equipment, competent teachers, and special instruction for handicapped and exceptional children.

"We must provide recreational facilities for children and adults and give the underprivileged the opportunity for wholesome entertainment and recreation.

"Today, many communities are instituting centers for the aged, and offering the older persons an opportunity to be useful, to engage in constructive work and play. Unfortunately, we sometimes forget the aged, and there are many elderly people who feel that they have been abandoned."

Social Action and the Still, Small Voice

Rabbi Mayer paused for a moment and then said, "By now, I hope you see how important it is to apply the message of the prophets to our modern society. Just as the prophets were interested in every aspect of life, politics, economics, education, social welfare, justice and peace, so we, the spiritual descendants of the prophets, must apply religion to solve the problems that confront our world. The Bible, rabbinic literature, the prayerbook and the synagogue must inspire us to sanctify life with holiness, study carefully and deliberately the injustices of our society, and then take action to bring justice and righteousness to those of every race and every religious faith, the rich and the poor, the educated and the unschooled, the healthy and the afflicted.

"Our ancestors made a covenant with God at Sinai to accept the Torah. When they accepted the Torah they also took upon themselves the obligations of fulfilling its teachings. This covenant is just as binding upon us today as it was to the children of Israel who heard the voice of God at Sinai.

"We must not wait for a supernatural Messiah to appear to solve our problems miraculously, but seek social justice here and now."

"But, Rabbi," said David, "I thought that we believed in the coming of the Messiah."

"No, David," said Rabbi Mayer, "Conservative and Reform Jews do not literally believe in the coming of a personal Messiah to solve the problems of society and of the world. It is only when we understand the third step in the development of the Messiah idea that we really understand the mission of Israel, and our role as a choosing people dedicated to the service of God. Up to this time, we were not ready to study the third and most important step. First, we had to examine and understand the ethics of social action. Now we are prepared to advance to the study of the most exalted purpose of our religious faith—the mission of Israel, which is to bring into reality the Messianic Age, a Kingdom of God on earth."

QUESTIONS FOR DISCUSSION

1 How should the Bill of Rights be used and practiced by someone your age? In what way does the Bill of Rights apply to the problems of youth?

2 Do you think that reading about communism will strengthen or weaken the influence of communism in America? The Communist Party in America was outlawed by an Act of Congress. Do you think this was a violation of civil rights?

3 Why do you think that the rate of juvenile delinquency is so low among Jews? In what way does the Jewish religion prevent criminal tendencies among Jews?

4 What is your opinion about capital punishment? Will the abolition of capital punishment cause an increase in crime?

5 Jewish law prohibits the death sentence based on circumstantial evidence, and requires two eye-witnesses to the crime. What do you think? Is this too lenient?

6 Do you think that an unemployed person who commits a crime to feed his family is justified? Should he be punished for theft if his children are hungry?

7 Do you think that labor unions have a right to call a strike during a war or a national emergency? Does the government have a right to send soldiers to run mills and factories if vital war materials are needed and the workers go on strike? In what way does labor sometimes take advantage of management? Do you favor or oppose labor unions? What are your reasons? Does a man have a right not to join a union if he doesn't want to? In what way does management sometimes take advantage of labor?

8 Do you think that censorship of books, magazines and newspapers is ever justified? What are the advantages and the dangers of censorship?

9 Should the State spend large sums of money on the feeble-minded, the insane, the aged, and the incurable? Would it be better to take that money and give added help to those who might be able to contribute something of value to society?

10 Do you think that our immigration laws should be relaxed? Are there dangers of having immigrants compete for jobs with native Americans if too many enter? Do you think the government should keep former Nazis and suspected communists out of our country? Suppose these people say that they have given up those political beliefs, should we forgive them and permit them to come to America?

11 Do you think that the Synagogue should avoid controversial problems that relate to social action and concentrate on Jewish education and worship?

12 If your rabbi becomes involved in a controversy over social justice, do you think he should be asked to drop the matter for the sake of harmony and peace in the congregation and in the community?

THINGS TO DO

1 Imagine that a political convention is being held in Biblical days, and that you are a member of a platform committee to draw up a plank on civil rights. Taking quotations from the Bible, what would this civil rights plank declare?

2 Look up the dictionary meaning of the terms: radical, revolutionary, communist, socialist, fascist, bigot, and liberal.

3 In the Jefferson Memorial, we read this quotation: "I have sworn upon the altar of God, eternal hostility against any form of tyranny over the mind of man." What would Thomas Jefferson say about censorship, book burning and congressional investigations if he lived today?

4 Write to the American Civil Liberties Union, 170 Fifth Avenue, New York 10, New York, for a statement of its principles.

5 Write a paragraph contrasting the civil liberties enjoyed by the citizens of the United States with civil liberties under communism.

6 Find out about the need for slum clearance in your community, and the problems that are created by slums.

7 Write an essay on the biblical and rabbinic attitude toward capital punishment.

8 List the names of two men who were unjustly condemned to death by capital punishment, and later found innocent.

9 Write to the following organizations for information on their purpose and program:

National Community Relations Advisory Council
9 East 48th Street, New York, N. Y.

National Religion and Labor Foundation
3494½ N. High Street, Columbus, Ohio

National Association for the Advancement of Colored People
20 West 40th Street, New York, New York

National Probation and Parole Association
1790 Broadway, New York, N. Y.

National Committee on Immigration and Citizenship
40 East 40th Street, New York, N. Y.

National Committee Against Discrimination in Housing
35 West 32nd Street, New York, N. Y.

10 Write to the Community Relations Service, 386 Fourth Avenue,

New York 16, N. Y., and ask for copies of *The People Take the Lead.* Analyze and discuss in class the progress being made in civil liberties.

11 Obtain a copy of the *Universal Declaration of Human Rights,* issued by the United Nations. How does this compare with the Bill of Rights of the Constitution? Write an essay on your idea of what the world would be like if we lived by this declaration of the United Nations.

SELECTED QUOTATIONS

The Covenant

Israel, through its historic Sinaitic covenant, established a special moral relationship to God. Through this covenant, Israel voluntarily covenanted itself, obligated itself, assumed as its unique national duty for all time, to be a "holy people" unto God, a people just and humane, loving God and following His law....From this "peculiar" historic relationship to God, then, flows Israel's chief national duty; to be this holy people unto God, and its supreme motive; to be faithful and loyal "with all thy heart and all thy soul" to its "appointment"–its historic role as a holy people.

MAXWELL SILVER

Judaism and Democracy

In our Bible the essence of the democratic process is discerned. Rabbinic and Mediaeval Judaism are marked by the continued insistence on every man's right to life, liberty, and the pursuit of happiness, which are also at the very core of the American design for living. The devotion to one God, the respect for the individual person, the regard for the sacredness of human life, the establishment of checks and balances to insure justice and freedom of opportunity, the ennoblement of learning as the patrimony of the common man–all these are as much of our continuing Jewish lore as they are of the Declaration of Independence, the Constitution of the United States and the vast body of American law.

Conference on Judaism and American Democracy

Lofty Pronouncements

Your Commission on Justice and Peace acknowledges with humility that its greatest failure to date has been in the area of implementing the social idealism of our people within our own congregations. With exceptions as notable as they are rare, we have limited ourselves to lofty pronouncements, but have not devised ways and means of teaching the practical application of these pronouncements to our people or of activating them in the search for a decent society.

Commission on Justice and Peace, 1951

A Little Rebellion

I hold...that a little rebellion, now and then, is a good thing, and as necessary in the political world as storms in the physical...It is a medicine necessary for the sound health of government.

God forbid that we should ever be twenty years without such a rebellion....

THOMAS JEFFERSON

Justice Will Prevail

I am not discouraged. Things will right themselves. The pendulum swings one way and then the other. But the steady pull of gravitation is toward the center of the earth. Any structure must be plumb if it is to endure, or the building will fall.

So it is with the nations. Wrong may seem to triumph. Right may seem defeated. But the gravitation of eternal justice is upward toward the throne of God.

JOHN PETER ALTGELD

American Judaism

The sense and hope of survival for us and mankind bespeak and demand on our part an all-enveloping passion for the fundamentals of Judaism; a Judaism adaptable, changeable, interpretable, unshakable; a Judaism alert to life and progress, rich in promise to the faithful, open to all mankind; an American Judaism, strengthening and being strengthened by the aims of the America of Washington and Jefferson and Lincoln and Walt Whitman....

RABBI NELSON GLUECK

Government and Mass Communication

Those who won our independence by revolution were not cowards. They did not fear political change. They did not exalt order at the cost of liberty. To courageous, self-reliant men, with confidence in the power of free and fearless reasoning applied through the processes of popular government, no danger flowing from speech can be deemed clear and present, unless the incidence of the evil apprehended is so imminent that it may befall before there is opportunity for full discussion. If there be time to expose through discussion the falsehood and fallacies, to avert the evil by the processes of education, the remedy to be applied is more speech, not enforced silence. Only an emergency can justify repression. Such must be the rule if authority is to be reconciled with freedom. Such, in my opinion, is the command of the Constitution. It is, therefore, always open to Americans to challenge a law abridging free speech and assembly by showing that there was no emergency justifying it.

LOUIS DEMBITZ BRANDEIS

The Bible and Democracy

Throughout the history of the Western world the Scriptures have been the great instigators of revolt against the worst forms of clerical and political despotism. The Bible has been the Magna Charta of the poor and of the oppressed; down to modern times no State has had a constitution in which the interests of the people are so largely taken into account, in which the duties so much more than the privileges of rulers are insisted upon, as that drawn up for Israel in Deuteronomy and in Leviticus; nowhere is the fundamental truth that the welfare of the State, in the long run, depends on the uprightness of the citizen so strongly laid down.... The Bible is the most democratic book in the world.

T. H. HUXLEY, 1892

SUGGESTED READINGS

Alofsin, Dorothy, *America's Triumph*

Cronbach, Abraham, *The Bible and Our Social Outlook*

Eisenstein, Ira, *Judaism Under Freedom* (Chapters 3 and 5)
Friedman, Lee, *Pilgrims in A New Land*
Golden, Harry L. and Martin, Lewis, *Jews in American History*
Goldstein, Sidney, *The Synagogue and Social Welfare*
Goodman, Abram V., *American Overture*
Kaplan, M., *Faith of America*
Learsi, Rufus, *Jews in America*
Levinger, Elma, *Jewish Adventure in America*
Levinger, Lee, *The History of the Jews in the United States*
Pessin, Deborah, *History of the Jews in America*
Silver, Maxwell, *The Ethics of Judaism from the Aspect of Duty*
Tarshish, Allan, *Not by Power*
Vorspan, A. & Lipman, E., *Justice and Judaism*
The United Synagogue of America, *Justice, Justice Shalt Thou Pursue...*

10

10. THE VOICE OF THE FUTURE

The Ethics of the Messianic Age

The Holy Puzzle

"Now we are ready to discuss a holy puzzle," Rabbi Mayer said. "The third step in the development of the Messiah idea reveals the ethical grandeur of the Jewish faith, and demonstrates the Jewish hope in the future.

"After a succession of false Messiahs, the Jewish people became dissatisfied with the belief in a personal Messiah. 'Why should God send "an anointed one" to redeem mankind by supernatural deeds of wonder?' they asked. Therefore, inspired by the vision of the prophets, the teachings of rabbinic literature and the eternal hope of Israel, the Jewish people matured to the third and the most important part of the Messiah idea–the Messianic Age.

"There evolved the concept of a Messianic era–a future age of universal truth, justice, brotherhood and peace for all mankind. This age will not be brought about miraculously by God. It will come into being when man really listens to the Still, Small Voice, and applies the teachings of God to his society.

"Since this concept developed the Jew has never lost hope, no matter how tragic conditions have been, no matter how Jews were persecuted. He never gave up his belief in the Messianic future, which would be an age, not a man. As he prayed and meditated, the Jew always had the conviction of faith: someday, we will make our world a kingdom of God. Someday, all men will really live by the Ten Commandments. Then the world will be full of the knowledge of God."

"But who was to bring about this Messianic age?" asked Judith. "Was something to happen, and then, presto–the world would change into a perfect society?"

"Your question is important," said Rabbi Mayer. "With the belief in the Messianic age, the Jews realized that the idea of a personal Messiah who was to usher in an age of miracles was not really true to the spirit of Judaism. God will not send a supernatural savior. He is not a Heavenly Magician who will miraculously transform the world into a Garden of Eden. The Jewish people said, 'if we want a better world, then it is not enough to hope and to yearn. We must remember our divine mission; to be a light unto the nations. We must become true servants of God, and through our deeds, and our way of life, work and teach to convert our world into a kingdom of God. Each individual must regard himself as a Messiah to help make this society a reality. God has chosen us as the instruments of His salvation. We have accepted the obligation of building God's Kingdom on earth, and therefore every Jew is charged with the moral responsibility of a sacred mission.' "

"I see it now," said Jonathan. "We are the choosing people because we have chosen to help create this Messianic age of goodness, justice and peace. Now I understand why social action is such an important part of Judaism. It is all bound up with our purpose as Jews."

"That is it exactly," the Rabbi said. "Everything fits together like a jig-saw puzzle, but this is a holy puzzle. Everything we have studied about the Still, Small Voice, is a part of that holy puzzle. Israel as the choosing people accepting a holy covenant, the belief that we are a kingdom of priests and a holy people, Israel as the servant of God destined for a sacred mission and the obligation of creating a Messianic age—all of these parts fit together to form a religious unity. All of these give meaning and purpose to Jewish history and Jewish life today. When we ask: 'What is the meaning of our experience as Jews? What is the purpose of our future?', the answer is to be found by putting together the parts of this holy puzzle.

God's Kingdom

"The Messianic age, the hope for God's Kingdom on earth, is the sublime ideal of the Jewish faith. When Israel suffered for this ideal, the prophet Isaiah comforted the people of Israel in the name of God: 'Keep ye justice, and do righteousness, for My salvation is near to come.' He told them that they were servants of God, and that their suffering was for a divine purpose:"

Yet now hear, O Jacob, My servant
And Israel, whom I have chosen...
Behold, My servant, whom I uphold,
My elect, in whom My soul delighteth;
I have put My spirit upon him,
He shall make the right to go forth to the nations...
I the Lord have called thee in righteousness,
And have taken hold of thy hand,

And kept thee, and set thee for a covenant of the people,
For a light of the nations;
To open the blind eyes,
To bring out the prisoners from the dungeon,
And them that sit in darkness out of the prison-house.

(Isaiah 42.1-7)

"Isaiah dreamed of the Messianic Age and prophesied that 'it shall come to pass in the end of days:

That the mountain of the Lord's house shall be established as the top of the mountains...
And He will teach us of His ways,
And we will walk in His paths...
For out of Zion shall go forth the law,
And the word of the Lord from Jerusalem.
And He shall judge between the nations,
And shall decide for many peoples;
And they shall beat their swords into plowshares,
And their spears into pruning-hooks;
Nation shall not lift up sword against nation,
Neither shall they learn war any more.

(Isaiah 2.2-4)

"The hope for the Messianic age has inspired and sustained the Jew in every age. No matter how difficult his life was, he believed in a better tomorrow. This hope is expressed in the Alenu prayer:

May the time not be distant, O God, when Thy name shall be worshipped in all the earth, when unbelief shall disappear and error be no more. Fervently we pray that the day may come when all men shall invoke Thy name, when corruption and evil shall give way to purity and goodness, when superstition shall no longer enslave the mind, nor idolatry blind the eye, when all who dwell on earth shall know that to Thee alone every knee must bend and every tongue give homage. O may all, created in Thine image, recognize that they are brethren, so that, one in spirit and one in fellowship, they may be forever united before Thee. Then shall Thy kingdom be established on earth and the word of Thine ancient seer be fulfilled: The Lord shall reign forever and ever.

Union Prayer Book

God's Kingdom on Earth

Bernard asked, "When is all this supposed to happen? In this world, or in the next world?"

"Our hope is for this world, Bernard," answered Rabbi Mayer. "Although we believe in the immortality of the soul, Judaism is a religion of this world. We believe that God's kingdom must be created here, and that is why we call it God's kingdom on earth. Judaism believes that we must make *this* world a world of justice, brotherhood and peace—and not postpone the solution of evil and injustice for a world to come.

"That is why Simeon ben Yochai, in *Talmud Sanhedrin*, answered the question, 'when will the Messiah come?' by saying, 'today, if ye hearken to His voice.'

"The importance of meeting the practical obligations of this world is demonstrated by the statement of Rabbi Jochanan ben Zakkai. He taught that 'If you hold a seedling in your hand and you hear the people shout: "The Messiah has come," plant the seedling first, and then go out to welcome the Messiah.'

"Every Jew is challenged to make this world a world of God. Thousands of years ago, God told Abraham, 'thru thy seed shall all the families of the earth be blessed.' This means that you and I must follow the commandments of the Still, Small Voice, to help make the Messianic age a blessed reality."

WHAT DO YOU THINK?

1 How do Judaism and Christianity differ with regard to their belief in the Messianic age? How does Orthodoxy differ from Reform and Conservative Judaism with regard to this belief?

2 Do you think that the belief in a personal Messiah offers more reasonable hope and faith to mankind, than the belief in a Messianic era? Why?

3 How did the belief that Israel is the suffering servant of God serve to strengthen Jewish survival?

4 Would it be safer and more peaceful for Jews if we did not have a divine mission? Suppose we gave up the idea of a divine mission, what would that do to the Jewish faith?

5 We are a people with a mission—but without missionaries. Do you think that Judaism should attempt to convert people to the Jewish faith?

6 Isaiah regarded the people of Israel as the real Messiah. What do you think?

7 How can someone your age help to make the Messianic age a reality?

8 What did Professor Abraham Heschel mean when he said: "... every pious Jew is, partly, the Messiah."?

SOME STATEMENTS TO THINK ABOUT

Children, The Messiahs of Mankind

In little children, it was taught, God gives humanity a chance to make good its mistakes. They are "the Messiahs of mankind"—the perennial regenerative forces in humanity.

RABBI JOSEPH HERTZ

One World At a Time

All men today need the healthy-mindedness of Judaism, the natural piety with which the Jew declares, "One world at a time is enough." For just as we can rely without fear upon the Power greater than ourselves during this earthly journey; just as we can rest and do rest securely upon the bosom of mystery every time we fall asleep at night, so we can trust the universe beyond time also, recognizing that it is the part of wisdom not to seek to remove the veil from before birth or after death, but to live fully, richly, nobly here and now, and make possible a society where other men can so live.

RABBI JOSHUA LOTH LIEBMAN

That Great Day

But, unlike Christians, for whom the Messiah has already come in the person of Jesus, Orthodox Jews believe that the Messiah is still to come, *B'achrees hayomim*, at the time of universal judgment.

Reform Judaism, however, has discarded the belief in a personal Messiah and interpreted the ancient hope as referring to a Messianic age, to a period of peace and human regeneration that will be brought about through human effort and with God's help. When men will be thinking their highest, feeling their deepest and doing their best—in a word, when religion will fill the world and God will be in every heart—then that great day, the Messianic age, will dawn upon the world.

RABBI BARNETT R. BRICKNER

Edifice of Human History

Has Israel any other task than to teach all the races of man to recognize and worship the Only-One as their God? ... The Bible terms Israel, "a peculiar treasure," but this designation does not imply, as some have falsely interpreted, that Israel has a monopoly of the Divine love and favor, but, on the contrary, that God has the sole and exclusive claim to Israel's devotions and service; that Israel may not render Divine homage to any other being. Israel's most cherished ideal is that of the universal brotherhood of mankind. Almost every page of the prayers we utter contains supplication for the hastening of this consummation. We are all helping to rear a great edifice, Divinely ordained for the well-being of man.

All of these efforts and actions are bricks contributed to the edifice of human history; all tend to the carrying out of the plan of the one, same God.

RABBI SAMSON R. HIRSCH
The Nineteen Letters of Ben Uziel

The State of Israel

Michael was trying to make up his mind whether he should ask a question that had perplexed him for months. Finally, he raised his hand and said: "I'm not trying to change the subject, Rabbi, but I wish you would straighten me out on something. It has to do with the State of Israel, and I'm not sure that it fits in with our discussion of the Messianic age."

"Don't hesitate to ask, Michael," said Rabbi Mayer. "The State of Israel should be discussed. It is important for American Jews to understand their relationship to Israel, because historically, national restoration has been part of the Messianic hope."

"I was walking home with a friend," said Michael, "and he asked me whether all Jews planned to live in Israel. I was surprised and asked 'why do you say that?' He said that in Sunday school he learned that the Bible says that all Jews will someday return to Palestine. What do we believe about this?"

Rabbi Mayer said, "To understand American Jews' attitude toward Israel, and the relationship of Palestine to the Messianic hope, we will have to go back thousands of years. When the Jews were exiled to Babylonia, they wept when they remembered Zion. They yearned for the time when they would return home and rebuild their Temple. Later, in 539 Before the Common Era, under Cyrus, they were permitted to return. The Temple was rebuilt and finally destroyed again. As the years went by, the Jews were exiled and dispersed throughout the world. Since they were strangers in foreign lands it was natural that the Bible, the prayerbook and rabbinic literature should reflect the hope of 'the ingathering of the exiles' and the return of the dispersed Jews to Palestine. To this day, traditional Jews pray to return to Zion. On Passover, the traditional Haggadah ends, 'next year in Jerusalem.' "

"But I don't want to leave America and return to Palestine!" exclaimed Judith. "I would like to visit Israel–but not stay. America is my home."

"America is my home, too," said the Rabbi, "and I don't plan to leave and settle in Israel. But you must remember that these prayers were written long before Jews came to America. They were written during periods of persecution when Jews were not given the privilege of citizenship. They were treated as aliens, and were often mistreated and discriminated against, subject to the whims of each king and ruler. They never knew what their fate might be. Fear and terror stalked their hearts.

"During these periods of persecution the Jew dreamed of the time when the Messiah would come and all Jews would be able to return to the holy land to live in security and peace. They believed that the land of the patriarchs and prophets was promised to Abraham and his descendants, that God would fulfil His promise and that they would rebuild their national life in accordance with the commandments of the Torah.

"In Palestine they would create a society of justice and peace. From *Eretz Yisroel,* the historic land of Israel, would radiate a religious light unto the nations. Palestine would become a model nation, an example to all other nations. They believed that is what Isaiah meant when he prophesied: 'from Zion shall go forth the Torah, and the word of the Lord from Jerusalem.' This would take place when the Messiah redeemed the children of Israel and brought them back to their ancient homeland.

"The years went by, and as the persecution of the Jew increased in Russia, Poland, Lithuania, a group came into being named *Chovevei Tzion*—Lovers of Zion. Its purpose was to make plans to migrate to Palestine. Most of the members talked of returning, but did little to make their dreams come true. Some of the most courageous traveled to Palestine to serve as *halutzim*, pioneers. They found a desolate land, with marshes in some places and desert in others. Many of the pioneers remained. Others could not stand the difficult life and returned to Europe.

"Towards the close of the 19th Century an Austrian Jew, a writer, heard the cries of hatred against the Jews. This man, Theodor Herzl, resolved to do something about re-establishing a Jewish nation. Palestine was then under the control of the Turks, and Herzl went to see the Sultan, to try to persuade him to permit the Jews to settle there in great numbers. Although unsuccessful, Herzl kept trying. He was a man of great vision and organizational skill. He organized the World Zionist Organization in Basle, Switzerland, in August, 1897, and built up Zionist Organizations in most of the countries of the world.

"During World War I, a young scientist, Chaim Weizman, who had moved to England from Russia, attracted the attention of the world by his discoveries. A leading Zionist, he drew attention to Jewish claims when England drove the Turks out of Palestine. Lord Balfour, who was the Secretary of State for Foreign Affairs, issued the famous Balfour Declaration on November 2, 1917, declaring 'His Majesty's government view with favor the establishment of a Jewish homeland in Palestine.' The hopes of the Jews of Europe were revived. Thousands of *halutzim* migrated to Palestine to clear the swamps, irrigate the sandy soil and make the desert bloom.

"The Zionist movement grew in strength and in influence. Many Jews in America contributed large sums of money to purchase land for farms and settlements. The great Hebrew University was established. Hadassah, the women's group, built hospitals and schools.

While many European Zionists cherished the hope of living in Palestine, most of the American Zionists never intended to leave America. Their contribution was financial and educational. They wanted to help make Palestine a Jewish State where the oppressed Jews of Europe and Asia might find a haven.

Trouble and dissension flared in Palestine with the Arab riots of 1921, 1929, and 1936-39. Great Britain seemed to be siding with the Arabs, and the dream of establishing a Jewish state seemed hopeless. Many investigating commissions traveled to Palestine, but each report added to the confusion.

The Nazi Nightmare

"In 1933, when Hitler came to power, the Jews of Europe faced the greatest threat of all their history. Hitler and the Nazis determined to destroy the Jews. Those who could escape clamored to go to Palestine, but the doors were closed to them because of the White Paper of March 17, 1939, issued by the British Government. This White Paper, an official statement of foreign policy, declared that after a specific quota had been filled, no more Jews could enter Palestine. What were the Jews of Europe going to do once the door to Palestine slammed shut?

"The Jews of Palestine, resolved to save their brethren in Europe, illegally smuggled as many as they could into the land. The *Haganah*, a Jewish defense army, was organized to assist in this illegal immigration, and to resist the Arab attackers. When Hitler and his armies marched forth to conquer Europe and the world, the Jews of Palestine fought valiantly on the side of the democracies to crush the evil of Nazism, and achieve victory for decency and justice. Hitler failed in his mad effort to destroy Judaism and exterminate the Jews, but first he slaughtered 6½ million of our brothers and sisters. He experienced the same fate as other persecutors—defeat and death. Despite all his efforts to destroy them, the Jews survived.

The Miraculous Fossil

"On November 29, 1947, the world witnessed a modern miracle when the United Nations partitioned Palestine and created the State of Israel. On May 14, 1948, David Ben Gurion, Premier of the Provisional Government, read a declaration of statehood. A dream had come true. Almost 1900 years after the Jewish State had been destroyed, the Temple burned to ashes, and the Jews driven into exile and dispersed throughout the world, a new State was admitted to membership in the United Nations. The new Israeli parliament, called the Knesset, declared that with God's help, the Torah would go forth from Zion, and the word of the Lord from Jerusalem. On January 27, 1949, Chaim Weizman took the oath of office as the first President of Israel, with the hope of making the ideals of the Torah a living reality."

Jonathan said: "It really is miraculous when you think that only a short time before, Hitler had threatened to destroy not only the Jews of Europe, but all Jews wherever they lived. Hitler was dead, and that song we sing was still true: *Am Yisroel Chai*–The people of Israel live."

"Yes, Jonathan," said Rabbi Mayer. "Many dictators have tried to destroy the Jewish people. There were Pharaoh, Haman, Torquemada, and then came Hitler, who said that he wouldn't rest until the world was *Judenrein*–which means free of all Jews. The history of what happened to European Jewry can only be written with a pen dipped in tears. The Jewish people in America and Israel have an even greater responsibility than Jews did before to strengthen Judaism and help make this world a Kingdom of God on earth.

"Some historians in the past predicted that Judaism would be destroyed. To show you that even historians can be wrong, let me tell you about a modern historian who wrote a monumental *Study of History*, and claimed that Jewish culture is a fossil of an earlier Syriac civilization and that Judaism is all but dead. This professor's name is Arnold J. Toynbee. He compares the Jews to other fossil civilizations that are now extinct."

"That shows how wrong a man can be—even a Professor," said Bernard.

"He is wrong," said Rabbi Mayer. "If the Jew is to be described as a fossil, then he is a miraculous fossil, the most astounding fossil of all history. The fossil is very much alive. The fossil has become established in America and has made a significant contribution to the growth and strength of our nation. The fossil has created the modern state of Israel. Look! There is a fossil wearing a cap and gown, graduating from the Hebrew University. Other fossils with pneumatic drills are working at the construction of hospitals and apartment buildings. Look, Professor Toynbee, there is a fossil with a tractor clearing the land; there is a fossil irrigating the soil, building, creating, working, praying. Almost two million fossils in the State of Israel are building a nation that welcomes the persecuted of all lands. It is a nation of self-reliant, dedicated men and women, aflame with the resolve to make of Israel a light unto the nations—a true democracy that is dedicated to the ideals of the prophets and the moral precepts of God."

"Does that mean that Israel is a perfect society?" asked Judith.

"No, I don't believe that Israel is perfect now, or will ever be," said Rabbi Mayer. "The people who live in the State of Israel have many problems to solve. Mistakes have been made, and more mistakes will be made. We may not always agree with everything that is done in Israel, but we are bound to that land by historic and religious ties, and we want to help its people to build their nation, even though it may never achieve perfection."

"Does that mean we have political ties with Israel, and that Israel is 'special' to us?" asked Judith.

"Some people say that Israel is just another nation," answered the Rabbi. "They insist that we should not have any special relationship to the land or the people of Israel. That is not true. The land of Israel has always been sacred to the Jewish people. To us, Israel is special, and we must try to help the people of Israel make their nation strong, not only because we are Jews and have a responsibility to Jews everywhere, but also because we are Americans and we want to strengthen democracies everywhere.

"You and I are citizens of the United States. We have *one* political loyalty–and that is to the United States of America. We pledge allegiance to *one* flag–and that is to the stars and stripes. Our country is America. We do not plan to leave America and emigrate to Israel or any other country–but that does not mean that we cannot help Israel financially, culturally and spiritually. That does not mean that we cannot understand and appreciate the culture of Israel. That does not mean that we cannot hope that Israel will make an important contribution to the strength of the democratic world and together with other nations help to bring a better world into being.

"Wherever Jews live–in America, in Europe, in Israel–we all have the same goal: to build God's Kingdom on earth. This is our sacred mission, and this is our ancient and our modern covenant with God. Far from being a fossil, the Jew is a living, dynamic part of the effort to bring nearer that blessed age when all the peoples, nations and religions of the world will declare: 'one God over all. One brotherhood of all.' "

QUESTIONS FOR DISCUSSION

1 What are the advantages and the disadvantages of an American Jew emigrating to Israel? Do you think that American Jews should be encouraged to live in Israel? Would you like to live in Israel? Should American Jews visit Israel?

2 What are the advantages and dangers that Israel creates or may create for American Jews? Do you think that the State of Israel has increased or decreased the respect of Christians for Jews? What are your reasons?

3 Do you think that Israel is a "Jewish" State? If so, what makes it a Jewish State? If not, why isn't it a Jewish State?

4 There is an organization called the American Council for Judaism that opposes Jewish nationalism. Find out the platform of this organization and discuss why it opposes Jewish nationalism. What is your opinion? (In case you want to write for more information, its address is: 201 E. 57th St., New York, N. Y.)

5 What is the platform and purpose of the Zionist Organization of America? This organization favors Jewish nationalism. Do you think that such an organization will interfere in the affairs of Israel, or will help Israel? (For more information, the address of the Zionist Organization of America is: 145 E. 32nd St., New York, N. Y.)

6 Why do you think that the Jews of Europe survived despite all the efforts of Hitler to destroy them? Why is it that persecutors are doomed to failure and ultimate destruction?

7 What is your opinion of Professor Toynbee's description of the Jew as a fossil? Why do you think he comes to this conclusion?

8 Some of the settlements in Israel are called *Kibbutzim*, collectives. Those who live in them do not have private capital or own anything of their own. They live together as one big family, sharing their possessions, eating together, working together. What is your reaction to this?

9 What is your opinion of the relationship of American Jews to the State of Israel? Does helping Israel mean that we are disloyal to America or more loyal to America? What are your reasons?

10 How do you think that the State of Israel can contribute to the ideal of the Messianic age? Do you think that Israel will help or hinder the effort to make this earth a Kingdom of God? In what way?

SOME STATEMENTS TO THINK ABOUT

The First President of Israel Speaks On Loyalties

It's a clear-cut matter. The citizens of Israel are Israelis; the citizens of the United States are Americans. A parallel is that between an American of Irish descent and Eire. This is a perfectly normal relationship. He has sympathy for Eire, he follows Eire's fortunes with interest, he welcomes visits to Eire, he helps Eire in many ways. It will be the same way with Jews.

DR. CHAIM WEIZMANN

A President of the United States Speaks on Israel

One of the proudest moments of my life occurred at 6:12 p.m. on Friday, May 14th [1948] when I was able to announce recognition of the new State of Israel by the Government of the United States. In view of the long friendship of the American people for the Zionist ideal, it was particularly appropriate that our Government should be the first to recognize the new State.

HARRY S. TRUMAN

Democracy in Israel

The world is watching for the people of Israel to make an increasing contribution to the free world as a model of democracy in action; to set an example of true tolerance and understanding in its relations with its neighbors; to serve as a leader among peace-loving nations; to be a standard bearer of justice and equality for all people.

HERBERT BROWNELL, JR.
Attorney-General of the United States, May 11, 1954

To Foster Our Moral Heritage

The State of Israel is quite different from any other state in its rights and duties, in its authority and its limitations. It was not intended merely for the independence, safety and freedom of its people. It was destined to serve as a safe refuge for every Jew who is oppressed, politically, economically or morally; to insure for him in the historic homeland of our people safety, freedom and equality, in his own right and on the strength and independence of his people, not on the goodwill of others. The State of Israel was also destined to foster and develop in freedom and self-respect the great moral and cultural heritage of our forefathers, our law-givers and our prophets, and enthrone it in modern civilized garb, with the aid of modern science and technology.

DAVID BEN GURION

Can Jews Build God's Kingdom Alone?

"The discussion of the relationship of American Jews to Israel clears up things for me," said Michael. "Now I see that the Jews of America, Europe and Israel must work together to make the Messianic age a reality."

"That is correct in part, Michael," said Rabbi Mayer. "While it is true that Jews of all nations must work together to build God's kingdom on earth, do you think that this great ideal is limited to Jews alone?"

"Yes, I do," Michael said emphatically. "We are the people chosen by God to be a light unto the nations and to bring about a society of justice, brotherhood and peace. That is our mission and purpose as Jews."

"I disagree with Michael," said David. "It's too big a job for the Jews to accomplish alone. God revealed His moral law through Israel and so Judaism may show the way, but I think that other peoples and other religions will have to help, too. There are millions of Moslems, Buddhists, Hindus—and what about the millions of Christians? Don't you think that they have a share in the building of this Messianic Kingdom of God?

"Last summer, when my parents and I visited in New York, we attended sessions of the General Assembly of the United Nations. There we saw representatives of many countries thinking together and working together to bring peace and justice to the world. If we are ever going to have a Messianic age, then all the nations and religions of the world will have to co-operate and work together."

Rabbi Mayer said: "I think that it would be wise for us to think this through before we come to conclusions. There are two extremes that must be avoided. The first is the belief that Judaism has a monopoly on God's love, and that as a result, all the virtues, ideals, and ethical values that are meaningful belong to the Jewish people alone. The other extreme is the tendency to minimize the uniqueness of Judaism and insist that Christianity or some other religion is so like it that we should ignore our identity as Jews and allow Judaism to disappear.

"We cannot accept the belief that God's love is limited to Jews alone, because to us the Fatherhood of God means that all men are brothers, and that all people are His children. Israel entered into a covenant with God to bring His law and His will not only to Jews, but to all mankind. Rabbinic tradition tells us that the Ten Commandments were meant for all nations. 'Love thy neighbor,' means those of every faith. The moral truths revealed by God through the Hebrew prophets were meant for all peoples. Micah asked: 'What doth the Lord require of thee, O man,' not 'O Jew,' 'O Christian,' or 'O Moslem.' Judaism is a universal religion, and teaches the truths, religious ideals and ethical values that apply to all generations and all peoples.

"Let me show you what I mean. Marvin, will you and Jonathan lift up the chart that is on the table? Just set it up so the class may see how different religions may share the same basic religious teachings. The ideals may be expressed differently, but the meaning is the same."

The Chart

Judaism: "What is hateful to you, do not to your fellowman. That is the entire law, all the rest is commentary."

(Talmud Shabbat 31a)

Christianity: "All things whatsoever ye would that men should do to you, do ye even so to them, for this is the Law and the Prophets."

(Matthew 7, 12)

Brahmanism: "This is the sum of duty: Do naught unto others which would cause you pain if done to you."

(Mahabharata, 5, 1517)

Buddhism: "Hurt not others in ways that you yourself would find hurtful."

(Udana-Verga 5, 18)

Taoism: "Regard your neighbor's gain as your own gain, and your neighbor's loss as your own loss."

(T'ai Shang Kan Ying P'ien)

Confucianism: "Is there one maxim which ought to be acted upon throughout one's whole life? Surely, it is the maxim of loving-kindness: Do not unto others what you would not have them do unto you."

(Analects, 15, 23)

Zoroastrianism: "That nature alone is good which refrains from doing unto another whatsoever is not good for itself."

(Dadistan-i-dinik, 94, 5)

Islam: "No one of you is a believer until he desires for his brother that which he desires for himself."

(Sunnah)

"They all say about the same thing!" exclaimed Miriam.

"Yes, Miriam," said Rabbi Mayer. "It is fruitless to argue which came first, or which religion is to receive credit for teaching it. More important is the question: Do we live up to the ideals of our religious faith?

"We believe that there is moral truth in every religious faith. Judaism has never taught that we are the only ones who have the capacity of listening to God's voice. Are not all men created in the image of God? It is true that people call God by different names. However, the name they give to God is not as important as the obedience they give to God's commandments of love, justice, mercy, peace, and brotherhood. In Judaism, God is called *Adonoi*, *Elohim*, *El Shaddai* (God Almighty), *Rebona Shel Olom* (Master of the Universe), *Hakadosh Baruch Hu* (The Holy One Blessed Be His Name), and *Rahamāna* (The Merciful One). Other religions have different names for God. Whatever name we use, we must remember that God is the Creator who has made all men and women in His image. It is because of this belief that Judaism teaches that all people must endeavor to obey the ethical commandments of God, regardless of the name by which they call Him. No one is excluded from God's love. In the words of the psalmist, 'The Lord is near unto all those who call upon Him—who call upon Him in truth.'

"That is why Judaism teaches that the righteous of all the peoples of the world have a share in the future, and are obligated to build God's kingdom. The sages said in the name of God, 'I call heaven and earth to witness that whether it be Gentile or Israelite, man or woman, slave or handmaid, according to the deeds which he does, will the Holy Spirit rest upon him.' (Yalkut). We are also reminded by our tradition of the statement of Maimonides:

> You asked about the gentiles. Keep in mind that "God requires the heart," and that everything depends on the intention of the heart. Therefore our teachers said: "The pious among the Gentiles have a portion in the Future World...."
>
> There is no doubt that he who achieves ethical qualities in the right ways of life and the right wisdom of belief in God merits the Future World.

Judaism and Christianity—Rivals or Partners?

"Do you still think that the sacred task of bringing about the Messianic age should be limited to Jews?" asked the rabbi.

"I'm afraid that I'll have to change my mind," said Michael. "It does seem that Judaism teaches us that we should call in partners to help us achieve God's kingdom on earth. But do you think we will ever be able to get together? There seems to be so many differences between Judaism and Christianity. What's more, there are many other religions who don't think the way we do about the Still, Small Voice."

"Suppose we think about Judaism and Christianity first, Michael," said Rabbi Mayer. "It is true that there are differences that separate the two faiths. There are differences in theology, beliefs, ritual, church and synagogue organization—but surely there must be something that Judaism and Christianity share in common. Where do you think Judaism and Christianity can meet in order to join forces to bring about the Messianic age?"

Joel said, "Maybe it's this. Last week when we had the group from the Methodist Sunday school class as our guests, one of the Christian students asked you to mention some Jewish ideals. You started out by telling about the Fatherhood of God and the brotherhood of man."

"That is right, Joel," said Rabbi Mayer. "And how did the student react?"

"He said that was a Christian ideal, and I remember what you told him. You said, 'That is right, but it is also a Jewish ideal.' And then you spoke about the Jewish belief that man is created in the image of God, and he said again, 'That's Christian.' You agreed with him and said that is Jewish, too. The same thing happened when you mentioned the Jewish quest for truth, justice, righteousness, mercy and peace. The student said 'That's Christian,' and you agreed by saying: 'It is also Jewish.' "

"I remember what happened," said Judith, "when you talked about the Messianic hope and the dream of a just society that would reveal the Kingdom of God on earth."

"And what did the Christian student say, Judith?" asked Rabbi Mayer.

"He said: 'that's Christian,' too, and you agreed that Judaism and Christianity shared not only that ideal, but the same ethical heritage.

That's it!" Judith exclaimed. "That's where Judaism and Christianity meet! What we share is our ethics!"

"Judaism and Christianity do meet ethically," said Rabbi Mayer. "That is why we refer to the Judaeo-Christian ethical heritage. The ritual and the beliefs may differ, but the ethics are essentially the same. Loyal to their own religion, Jews and Christians who follow and practice the ethical teachings of their faith are not rivals. By listening to the Still, Small Voice, Jews and Christians can become partners in the effort to bring about the Messianic age, co-workers in the greatest spiritual building project ever revealed to man—the building of God's Kingdom on earth."

QUESTIONS FOR DISCUSSION

1 Do you believe that the Jews can build God's Kingdom on earth by themselves? What are your reasons?

2 Are there factors that prevent Judaism and Christianity from joining forces to work together to bring about the Messianic age? What should be done to harmonize the differences in order to promote a Jewish-Christian partnership?

3 What are other teachings of Judaism, not mentioned in the above chapter, that show the universalism of Jewish belief?

4 If Judaism is a universal religion and our teachings are religiously beneficial, should we attempt to convert unaffiliated Christians to Judaism? What are your reasons?

5 What are the benefits and the dangers of thinking of Judaism as a universal religion?

6 Do you think it would be practical and wise for Jews to give up Judaism, and Christians to give up Christianity, and create a new religion that would be acceptable to both? What would this new religion be like? What Jewish teachings would be included? What Christian teachings would be included?

7 What do you think Rabbi Joshua Ben Nehemiah meant when he asked: "Have you ever noticed that the rain fell on the field of 'A' who was righteous, and not on the field of 'B' who was wicked? Or that the sun arose and shone upon Israel, who was righteous, and not upon the wicked [nations]? God causes the sun to shine both upon Israel and upon the nations, for the Lord is good to all."

8 In the Greenwich Village section of New York, there is a Jewish congregation and a Presbyterian Church group that occupy the same sanctuary. Do you think this is an example of brotherhood in action? What are the dangers and the advantages of such an arrangement?

9 In Gotthold Lessing's *Nathan der Weise,* written in 1779, we find this quotation:

> "Nathan, sure
> You are a Christian, by Heaven you are,
> None better ever breathed."
> And Nathan answered:
> "That which makes me a Christian in your eyes
> Makes you a Jew in mine."

What does this mean to you? What was Lessing trying to teach?

10 What is the most effective way for Judaism and Christianity to work together to bring about the Messianic age?

SOME STATEMENTS TO THINK ABOUT

From the Jungle to the Stars

Christianity has been the instrument for bringing the ethical treasures of Judaism to mankind. Jesus, who was a child of Israel and the father of Christianity, is thus a perpetual reminder that the two great faiths have a common basis and a common goal. There is no need for either to conquer or absorb the other. In spite of their genuine differences, they have much more in common. Today, the challenge is directed not against Jewish ritual or Christian theology, but against the great body of common religious and ethical ideals that constitute the Judeo-Christian tradition. Men in the past, it is true, have never practiced justice and mercy, but at least they gave lip-service to these aspirations. Thus there was hope that the day would come when men would discover that they were not merely beautiful dreams but the only practical program for an enduring society... Judaism and Christianity must cease to eye each other like jealous rivals and recognize that they are allies in the long and desperate struggle to raise man from the jungle to the stars....

RABBI ROBERT GORDIS

Chain Reaction of Love

For centuries now we've tried everything else; the powers of wealth, of mighty armies and navies, and combinations of nations, machinations of diplomats. All have failed. Before it's too late, and time is running out, let us turn from trust in the chain reactions of exploding atoms to faith in the chain reaction of God's love. Love—love of God and fellowmen, that is God's formula for peace. Peace on earth to men of good will.

ARCHBISHOP RICHARD R. CUSHING

One World or No World

In our day Jews and Christians must unite in the building of the one world—a world of freedom for all under God. There will be one world or no world. There will be co-existence or no existence. This is a great age for humanity. Millions have cast aside chains and gained nationhood and self-determination. At no time have the conditions of the common man been more improved than today in every direction of life. This is the hour where Jew and Christian must battle on all fronts against illiteracy, poverty and racial inequality and, too, we must do all we can toward the abolition of war. The dream of the one world as visioned by the great prophets of Israel is not a fairy-tale. It will come sure as this is day. We however must patiently toil in the building of the one humanity....

RABBI HARRY JOSHUA STERN

The Golden Age of Tomorrow

For Judaism the Golden Age lies not in the past but in the future. Judaism is concerned not with a never-never world in which no one works, but one in which labor is justly recompensed. It wastes no effort in theorizing about a life without death, but devotes much to the building of a life of faith and unselfishness wherein death—a natural phenomenon—has lost its terrors. It speaks not in terms of original sin, but of original virtue which is in God and which man should emulate. Let man but live worthily and the day will yet come when love will triumph over hatred, goodness over evil and men will not only be their brother's keeper, but their brother's brother.

RABBI JULIUS MARK

Rivals or Partners

Diversities, however legitimate, do not transcend the great agreements in principle obtaining among the great faiths. Cathedral and temple, church and synagogue share convictions in a God above, a soul within and a life beyond. They accept as fundamental the belief in the Fatherhood of God and the brotherhood of man. They seek to promote individual righteousness and social justice. They desire to see God's Kingdom established on earth.

They should, therefore, be not rivals nor competitors but partners. They can, with mutual respect and in a spirit of cooperation, wholeheartedly work together towards many common objectives. They can be natural allies in the fight against the forces of evil in the life of the community and the world at large. They can unite in furthering all good causes for man's uplift and the higher life of society. They have a kindred stake in salvaging the ethical and spiritual values of civilization in this time of tragic crisis. Verily, let us have interfaith fellowship!

RABBI H. W. ETTELSON

Into The Future

"We have only a few more sessions," said Rabbi Mayer, "but even though we conclude our formal study of the story of Jewish ethics, it is a story that never ends. Each generation will add new and, we hope, ever more meaningful chapters as Judaism advances into the future."

"I don't want to sound like a pessimist," Joseph said, "but how do we know that there will be a future? With all the talk we hear about atom bombs and H-bombs, maybe the whole world will soon explode into cosmic dust, and there won't be any people on earth to add new chapters to the story of Jewish ethics."

"There are some people who say that, Joseph," replied Rabbi Mayer, "but there have been predictions of the destruction of the world ever since man existed.

"Our concern is not with the destruction of the world, but with its salvation. The ancient psalmist spoke in behalf of every Jew in every age when he said: 'I will not die, but live to declare the glory of God.' It is life, not death that is the concern and the destiny of the Jew. We believe in the future of mankind because we believe in God and in God's divine plan for the building of a good and moral society. God summons us to perfect our world for life, not death. God has given man the freedom of will to conquer war, disease, poverty, ignorance and hatred, and that is why Judaism urges us to use our God-given freedom to work for a better tomorrow. That is why we need the power of a religious faith that inspires us to identify ourselves with a holy cause—the mission of Israel—and to contribute our share to the fulfilment of the Messianic Age.

"Rabbi Abba Hillel Silver expressed a basic teaching of Judaism when he said:

None of us can see beyond the horizon of our own times. What lies ahead, no one knows. But Judaism reminds us that beyond all horizons, there is God. Always God will be there and mankind will be there, and

God's unfolding purpose which embraces in its eternal processes, also our own brief and passing generations, will be there and will prevail.

Burton said: "That's just what our science teacher told us. Not in those words, but the same idea. He said that science will accomplish many amazing things—so amazing that it is difficult for us even to imagine what they will be. Just think: moving highways, travel into outer space, atomic-powered planes, trains and even automobiles!"

"Does your science teacher say that the scientists should stop all their experiments because there won't be a future?" asked Rabbi Mayer.

"Certainly not," said Burton. "Everything that science does is based on the idea that there will be a future. Why, even now, our teacher told us, scientists are measuring the sun's behavior, ocean currents and tides, the earth's magnetic field, gravity and cosmic rays. It's hard to believe, but someday space ships will go whizzing among the stars at unbelievable speed."

"What Burton says is true," said Rabbi Mayer. "Just as the scientists plan for flights into outer space, so scientists in laboratories are working to conquer the diseases that afflict man. Can you imagine a scientist stopping his work because somebody is pessimistic about the future? Should we stop providing funds for cancer and heart research because some people don't believe in the future?"

Eldon said: "It seems to me that what you say about science is also true of religion. We can't just wait for the world to be destroyed and act as though there is nothing we can do about it. We have to do something to try to build a better world, and go ahead with confidence and faith."

"You are right, Eldon," said Rabbi Mayer. "This is the teaching of Judaism and this is the command of the Still, Small Voice. We must put our religious faith to work and seek every means to find a way to achieve peace and international understanding.

"Not only Jews and Christians, but Moslems, Buddhists, those of every faith and every race, must learn to work together and live together in brotherhood. Not only Americans, but those of every nation must join in the effort to solve problems by arbitration and not by guided missiles and cobalt bombs.

The United Nations

"That is why we must place hope in the United Nations. It is true that this organization isn't perfect, but what other organization enables the nations of the world to meet together to even attempt to find a solution of the discord and the conflicts that make for war?"

Rabbi Mayer opened his desk-drawer and took out a pamphlet. He said: "This is the Charter of the United Nations formulated in the year 1945 in San Francisco:

WE THE PEOPLES OF THE UNITED NATIONS, DETERMINED to save succeeding generations from the scourge of war, which twice in our lifetime has brought untold sorrow to mankind, and to reaffirm faith in fundamental human rights, in the dignity and worth of the human person, in the equal rights of men and women and of nations large and small, and

to establish conditions under which justice and respect for the obligations arising from treaties and other sources of international law can be maintained, and

to promote social progress and better standards of life in larger freedom,

AND FOR THESE ENDS to practice tolerance and live together in peace with one another as good neighbors, and

to unite our strength to maintain international peace and security, and

to ensure, by the acceptance of principles and the institution of methods, that armed force shall not be used, save in the common interest, and

to employ international machinery for the promotion of the economic and social advancement of all peoples,

HAVE RESOLVED TO COMBINE OUR EFFORTS TO ACCOMPLISH THESE AIMS.

"Since the time that it was organized," he said, "the United Nations has scored many significant achievements. It has prevented armed conflicts and provided education, economic aid, and medical care for millions of underprivileged people. Whatever its limitations, it is still the most effective way for nations to harmonize their efforts to bring ever nearer an age when the nations of the world will achieve international understanding, brotherhood, justice and peace.

I'll Buy That Dream

"This is Judaism's dream of the Messianic Age. It was the dream of countless teachers and sages of Israel. The prayerbook speaks to us of that cherished hope—the dream of the future, when men will live together as brothers and the world will be as full of the knowledge of God as the waters that cover the sea. Despite opposition, persecution and sorrow, we refused to listen to the pessimists, to the false prophets of doom and destruction. We refused to listen to the spokesmen of darkness. Our hearts and souls were attuned to the Still, Small Voice, that challenged us to drive out the darkness by identifying ourselves with light. It was the Still, Small Voice that reminded us of our sacred destiny: 'Through thy seed shall all the nations of the earth be blessed.' Strengthened in faith, they resolved to fulfil their covenant with God and persist in their mission to be a light unto the nations, and to teach God's moral laws to all the families of the earth."

Rabbi Mayer paused. He looked at the class and smiled. "You may think that I'm preaching a sermon. Frankly, I am. This is the eternal message of our Jewish faith—and whether it is given by a rabbi from the pulpit or a teacher in the classroom, or discussed by a humble shopkeeper, the words may differ, but it is always the same dream—the dream of the future."

"It's a wonderful dream, Rabbi," said Joel, "but how do we make the dream come true?"

"Many years ago, Joel, I heard a song. It impressed me very much.

I'm sorry to say that I can't recall the melody, but I will always remember the title. It was called 'I'll Buy That Dream.' We are all willing to hope, to yearn, to wish, to dream—but how many of us are willing to buy our dreams? Are we willing to work for our dreams in order that they may come true?

"If we really want to bring about the dream of the Messianic age, we can't sit back and expect the United Nations or any other organization to hand it to us. We can't wait for others to earn our dreams for us. Each one of us will have to make a contribution, no matter how small or humble, toward the purchase of the dream.

"We all live in a little society of our own. Our family is a society. We all have our own circle of friends. When we associate with others at school, at club meetings, in sports—that is a little world, too. We have to start with our own little world and apply the ethical teachings of Judaism to it before we can hope to apply the teachings of our faith to the larger world.

"The best place for each individual to start is with himself. Each one of us has to try to live up to the ethical teachings of Judaism every day by our reverence for God and by the way we treat our fellow human beings. This is what Judaism means when it tells us that everyone of the Jewish faith must so live as to be a co-partner with God in the creation of a better world.

"We have traveled a long way since the time we started our search for the answer to the mystery of the Still, Small Voice. We have studied the way Jews in every age have quested for the knowledge of the living God. The search goes on, and will continue through the generations that are yet to be. Even though we will never completely understand the mystery we call God, we know that He is near, and if we listen, we will hear God speaking to us, today, just as He spoke to the prophet Elijah:

> *And behold, the Lord passed by, and a great and strong wind rent the mountains, and broke in pieces the rocks before the*

> *Lord; but the Lord was not in the wind; and after the wind an earthquake; but the Lord was not in the earthquake; and after the earthquake a fire; but the Lord was not in the fire; and after the fire, a Still, Small Voice.*

QUESTIONS FOR DISCUSSION

1 Why does Judaism insist that man must have confidence in the future? In your opinion, why is pessimism regarded as a negation of the Jewish faith?

2 To what extent has the United Nations failed and succeeded in the purpose set forth in its Charter?

3 What did Rabbi Leo Baeck mean when he called Judaism "a religion of ethical optimism"?

4 What did Maurice Samuel mean when he said: "Not in the 'discovery' of God lies the meaning of the Jews, but in what they did with that discovery"?

5 How do you think a person your age can help make real the dream of the Messianic age?

THINGS TO DO

1 Interview an Orthodox, Conservative and Reform rabbi on "Judaism's Concept of the Messianic Age."

2 Write to the United Nations, 45 East 65th Street, New York 21, New York, for material, and then assign students to speak on the organization, the failures, the accomplishments, of the United Nations.

The class should constitute itself as members of the United Nations and discuss a problem in accordance with the procedure of the United Nations.

3 Write to the National Conference of Christians and Jews, 43 West 57th Street, New York 19, New York, and request materials for class study.

4 Discuss in class the theme: "How good is the goodwill movement?" What are the practical results of Brotherhood Week?

5 Write an essay on "How I can make my contribution to the Messianic age."

6 Write an essay on "How the study of the Still, Small Voice has changed my ideas of 'Judaism and Jewish Ethics.'"

SELECTED QUOTATIONS

Your Duty Here on Earth

Judaism is distinguished by its emphasis upon *this world*, in contradiction to all other religions, which emphasize *the other world*. "It is not in heaven" that the Torah or Judaism finds its greatest concern, but in man—in man's thoughts and ways of life, in transforming earth into a veritable heaven. Judaism discouraged the tendency...of spending one's days worrying about heaven and hell—about what is before one's life on earth. Spend your time in learning that which is your duty here on earth: this was Judaism's decree.

ISRAEL LEVENTHAL

Peculiar Sensitivity

Out of centuries of tribulation and suffering and wandering, by virtue of a peculiar sensitivity to revelation, out of a hunger for social solidarity and a passion for righteousness, there came to the early prophets of Israel and of Judah a new conception of God that has ever since spurred men to higher action and has kept before them the haunting realization that apart from His service there is no true hope or happiness for mankind.

DR. NATHAN M. PUSEY
President, Harvard University

The Kind of Judaism We Need Today

A Judaism that is more than an accidental collection of memories....

A Judaism...impelling us to action on behalf of that which is true and right, whatever the cost.

A Judaism that makes us feel uncomfortable in the fact of human need, human stupidity, human greed and human cruelty....

A Judaism that evokes the best of our energy, our intelligence, our devotion, that demands and receives our highest loyalty.

RABBI BERTRAM W. KORN

Science and Religion

I always feel embarrassed when I read of the achievements of the men of science. The men of religion have done so little in comparison. For us there can be no vaccine that will make man love his neighbor, no way of injecting kindness into the veins of school children.

We have the formulae, as thrilling as the ones Einstein evolved, but not the ability to prove them correct. Our formulae are unprovable. "It hath been told thee, O man, what is good...."

But we can't prove it. Our only chance for success is not to prove it, not to say it, but to live it.

RABBI MAURICE DAVIS

The One Common Trait

I look for vast changes in religion. I expect the next fifty years will see a moving away from many of the creeds, the doctrines and the rituals that have come to seem such an essential part of religion, and a moving toward a greater emphasis on man's bond with his fellows and on the good life here on earth. The best faith and the best practice are found in the sympathy of man for man. It is the one trait common to all religions, and the noblest trait of all religions.

CYRUS S. EATON

Looking Into The Future

Looking into the future, I see these things: I see men of good will in every Christian church in the world, Catholic and Protestant, coming to recognize that it is not only un-Christian but indecent to treat Jews as they have been dealt with throughout many centuries. I do know that there is some degree of anti-Semitism and there are some symptoms of anti-Jewish ill-will in America. Yet, on the other hand, I see that all that is finest, that all that is most truly Christian, that all that is most American, is resolved to deal justly by the Jew. I see something more. I see my people putting away the timidity with which they have been too long afflicted. I see them not only free but resolved to put away the attitude of trembling cowardice which may have been inevitable in the ghetto of persecution but is inexcusable under the skies of freedom. Nothing is calculated to end more ingloriously the life of the Jew than if the Jew, for safety's sake, forsakes his ideals, forswears his dreams, and becomes recreant to his faith not only in the divine Fatherhood but in that human brotherhood which at long last can rest only upon the foundations of democracy and human equality.

RABBI STEPHEN S. WISE

The Same Voice

And so, when you see a foreigner who doesn't happen to have the same color skin that you do, or whose eyes are different, or who wears different clothes, or who does not speak English, or who does not pray the same way you do, or whose political beliefs are different, don't think that he is different from you in every way, because that is not so. He is a human being just like you. We have an ancient saying in Asia that "under the roof of heaven, all men are brothers."

CARLOS P. ROMULO

His Kingdom

In a day of deep despair and ever more threatening terror of world devastation, from the pillar of fire by night and the mushroom cloud of death by day, when all of us helplessly cry out, "Whence shall come our help," let us, with our forebears of old, assert, "My help cometh from God—who will not forsake me nor leave me in my need. My help cometh from God who has commanded me to build His Kingdom on earth; yea verily, His kingdom of decency and equity among all the children of men, His kingdom of brotherhood for all."

RABBI MAURICE N. EISENDRATH

SUGGESTED READINGS

Cohon, Beryl D., *Jacob's Well*
Cronbach, Abraham, *Judaism For Today*, Chapters 7, 9, and 10
Fitch, Florence M., *One God*
Hume, Robert E., *The World's Living Religions*
Joseph, Morris, *Judaism As Creed and Life*, pp. 138-172
Klausner, Joseph, *The Messianic Idea In Israel*
Kohler, Kaufman, *Jewish Theology*, Chapters 48 and 53
Learsi, Rufus, *Fulfillment: The Epic Story of Zionism*
Moehlman, C. H., *The Christian-Jewish Tragedy*, pp. 247-257
Pessin, Deborah, *Theodor Herzl*
Schechter, S., *Some Aspects of Rabbinic Theology*, Chapters 5-7
Silverman, William B., *Judaism and Christianity Compare Notes*, Town Hall Series, Union of American Hebrew Congregations